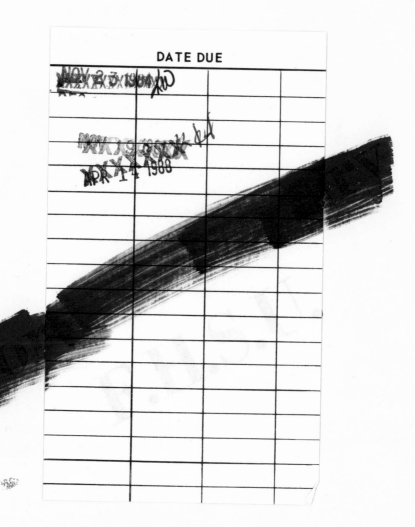

Fundamental
Motor Patterns

Fundamental Motor Patterns

RALPH L. WICKSTROM

Ripon College, Ripon, Wisconsin

Third Edition

Lea & Febiger   1983   Philadelphia

Lea & Febiger
600 South Washington Square
Philadelphia, Pa. 19106
U.S.A.

Library of Congress Cataloging in Publication Data

Wickstrom, Ralph L.
    Fundamental motor patterns.

    Includes bibliographical references and index.
    1. Physical education for children. 2. Motor
ability in children. 3. Child development. I. Title.
[DNLM: 1. Movement—In infancy and childhood.
2. Motor skills—In infancy and childhood. 3. Motor
activity—In infancy and childhood. 4. Physical
education and training—In infancy and childhood.
5. Child development. WE 103 W637f]
GV443.W47 1983   155.4'12   82–21659
ISBN 0–8121–0879–5

FIRST EDITION 1970
SECOND EDITION 1977

PRINTED IN THE UNITED STATES OF AMERICA

Print Number: 5 4 3 2 1

To my wife, JoAnn

Preface

This new edition closely follows the basic approach used in the first two editions. It contains extensive description and discussion of fundamental motor pattern development, and is slanted toward those who are interested in understanding and changing human motor behavior. The original intent has been continued mainly for two reasons. First, the descriptive aspect (the *what*) of motor development is the aspect that is best understood at the present time and it is important as a basis for studying the underlying organization and control processes (the *how*) of motor behavior. Second, there is evidence in the literature that the material in earlier editions has been put to use, and this is an encouraging indication of a growing interest in understanding the specifics of motor pattern development. It is hoped that this revision and the continuation of approach will be of additional value.

The book has been revised extensively to improve its organization and to incorporate new material. Additional information is provided on the motor performances of children and on developmental and mature motor patterns. Some results from recent biomechanics research on high-level skill performance have been included to give a more accurate picture of what is and what is not known about mature form. In each chapter an effort has been made to identify needed research and to illustrate the uncertainty that still characterizes some of the knowledge of motor pattern development.

A section on hopping has been added to the chapter on jumping, and a section on underhand patterns has been inserted into the chapter on throwing. The amount of new information on catching, striking, and kicking is relatively small, so the chapters on those skills have undergone only modest revision.

The interest in studying skill development in terms of developmental patterns has extended recently to motor activities other than basic skills. This new interest has prompted the addition of a new chapter, which includes material on attempts that have been made to understand and describe skill development in dribbling, rope jumping, the forward roll, and horizontal ladder travel according to characteristic motor pattern changes.

Finally, this opportunity is taken to express deep appreciation and to offer sincere thanks to all those whose contributions and cooperation have made this third edition possible.

Ripon, Wisconsin   Ralph L. Wickstrom

Contents

CHAPTER 1

Introduction

Wherever there is life, there is movement. There can be no life without it. Human movement begins before birth and continues until life has ended. It progresses from reflexive, random activity that is subcortically controlled to increasingly more complex patterns that are coordinated in the higher nerve centers. During infancy simple manipulative and locomotor patterns are acquired, and during childhood a multitude of basic skills are added to the movement repertoire. Bruner describes how skill expansion takes place. "Walking, which is a complex serial structuring of component acts, very soon becomes so automatic as to fit easily into a variety of higher-order acts."[6] Children combine the simple skills into patterns of increasingly greater specificity and complexity.

The basic motor patterns that are first learned as general skills are later learned in modified and combined versions as sport skills. This continuing process of motor skill development seems to take place in varying degrees regardless of whether adults do anything to help or to hinder it. The improvement can be explained partly in terms of the increased capability that accompanies growth and development and partly in terms of a natural, untutored process that results from imitation, trial and error, and freedom of movement. That natural process is important, but unless it is supplemented, opportunities for progress of a much higher order can be lost. Specifically, the process can fall far short of producing for each individual what might be considered optimum motor skill development.

The concept of optimum skill development has existed as an ideal for years, but it has lofty possibilities that remain largely unexplored. There is growing evidence that when children are given opportunities to learn motor skills earlier than usual, under conditions that are appropriately encouraging, they tend to respond by developing a higher level of motor skill than is normally expected for their age. The advantage of what might appear to be unusually early introduction to skills is illustrated by the surprising successes sometimes produced when infants are given the opportunity to participate in swimming activities. The early opportunity, more than the so-called swimming reflex, seems to be the really important influence on infant success in swimming. Positive experience with activities such as swimming strongly suggests that the opportunities for enhancing fundamental skill development probably are not offered soon enough in most instances.

The manipulation and control of the circumstances that influence motor development and motor skill acquisition constitute what is commonly called "intervention." It is not a particularly desirable term to use because it carries a strong negative connotation, an implication of interference with a natural process. There certainly is the possibility that intervention can be imprudent, can fail to enhance progress, and can, in fact, produce adverse rather than positive results. However, intervention should be looked at from a positive rather than negative point of view. Its main purpose is to prevent delays in the acquisition of motor skills by encouraging progress at the point when a child becomes developmentally capable of making progress. The aim is to promote optimum skill development. Underlying the aim is the belief that there are critical developmental periods that are ideal for the learning of certain motor skills and that these periods should be exploited. The principal problem associated with intervention and enrichment is determining "what stimuli, in what amounts should be available at what times, in order for optimum motor development to occur."[34]

The appropriate time and type of intervention are critical considerations. There are those who would intervene in the motor development process at birth. The value of large scale intervention during infancy has not been established, even though several infant motor development programs have been suggested and used. There is little research to demonstrate the specific value of either those programs that advocate nonuse of assistive movements and equipment or those that encourage prepractice of future skills with special assistance and equipment.[25] However, one must not conclude that a program lacks value unless it has been systematically evaluated using research procedures. Intervention procedures that are being used with children of all ages are justified mostly on the basis of positive pragmatic, rather than conclusive empirical, evidence. Successful outcomes, as in the case of the infant swimming programs mentioned earlier, serve as pragmatic evidence to help validate the procedures. Eventually the intervention processes that seem to produce the desired results will have to be studied formally in order to gain true credibility.

Enrichment programs must have an increasingly larger research base. Relatively little has been done to study intervention at the preschool level, but progress is being made in the investigation of its use in the primary grades. One example is a study of the effect of instruction on

the overhand throwing of kindergarten children.[30] A total of 120 min-
utes of instruction did not significantly increase throwing velocity, but
it did produce improvements in throwing technique. An analysis of
the motor patterns used indicated an improvement in four of the seven
components that were evaluated.[16] Thus, for a select group of children,
a particular amount and kind of intervention was demonstrated to be
valuable in promoting one motor skill outcome but not another. Much
more research of this type is needed in order to uncover and understand
the procedures that have a positive influence on motor skill development. Intervention procedures are particularly important for the optimum motor development of children, but intervention can be valuable
regardless of the age at which motor skill development takes place.

The concept of optimum skill development is broad and has implications for the approach used by everyone who deals with movement.
Parents, teachers, coaches, therapists, and recreationists have different
roles to play in the total skill development of an individual and they
exert their influence at various levels of development. Their efforts
finally are bonded into a total, a life-span influence. What is done to
promote motor skill development at one level either affects or is affected
by what is done to promote it at other levels. The assurance of a positive
contribution from all those who participate in the promotion of basic
skill development strongly depends upon the common possession of a
broad understanding of motor development and human movement.

MOTOR DEVELOPMENT

Motor development is merely part of the overall process of human
development. It is commonly defined as *changes over time in motor
behavior that reflect the interaction of the human organism with its
environment.* The process encompasses the development of the abilities
that are essential to movement and the subsequent acquisition of motor
skill. Since the 1960s, motor development has been viewed as a lifelong
process, rather than as one that is essentially terminated when adult-
hood is reached. In the interpretation of this expanded concept, it would
seem important to label as development only those changes that are
progressive. If any "change within an individual's life span or during
several years of that life span"[28] is regarded as development, a ques-
tionable dimension is added to the life-span concept. Thus, it is being
suggested with increasing frequency that motor development "also includes changes that occur 'on the other side' of maturity." These changes
are the ones related to "the decline in the level of performance associated with the aging end of the continuum."[37] The decline and the
prevention of the decline in motor performance due to aging are important areas of study, but decline is a negative change that is inconsistent with the context of development as a progressive process.
Changes in motor performance that are irreversible are not really de-

velopmental, regardless of the age period in which they occur. Changes, that are *progressive*, such as learning a new motor skill or improving an old one, should be regarded as part of motor development regardless of whether the change takes place during an early-life, mid-life or, late-life period.

The motor development that ordinarily occurs in infancy and childhood is the foundation for what could be virtually an open-ended process. A familiarity with what happens during these early periods is essential background for understanding the life-span concept of motor development. There is a vast amount of literature describing growth and development during the early years of life. The accumulated evidence indicates that the sequence of development is predictable and approximately the same for all children, but the rate at which specific changes take place varies from one child to another. The evidence also shows that neuromuscular development follows a cephalocaudal pattern and a proximodistal direction and proceeds from gross to specific refinement. These generalities concerning physical growth and neuromuscular development are not age-related, but they give a valuable preview of what will be happening during the early years of motor skill acquisition.

Motor development has a profound influence on the overall development of the child, especially in the earliest period of life. As Schilling has pointed out, "Movement is the first and basic form of human environment communication."[32] The idiom is made possible by the rapid physical growth that takes place during the first two years of life. The child gradually gains control over gross movements and develops the ability to perform simple motor acts. The scope of his movement increases rapidly as he progresses from crawling and creeping to a basic upright pattern of locomotion. Learning to walk is a signal event because it offers the infant a wider exposure to those aspects of his environment that encourage the expansion of motor behavior.

The early motor achievements of children have been observed and chronicled by Gesell,[13] Bayley,[4] Wellman,[40] Shirley,[36] and other pioneers in the field of motor development. The information accumulated from their research has made it possible to gain some insight into the natural progress that takes place as children journey toward the achievement of mature motor patterns. The value of the information is limited because it is based upon what children do under ordinary circumstances and not what they can do if given the most favorable opportunity. This is a significant qualification that applies to the bulk of the data on motor performances of children. The gap between what children do and what they can do must be determined, understood, and bridged as the quest for widespread optimum motor development continues.

MOVEMENT TERMINOLOGY

This section contains a brief consideration of some of the terms that will be used in the subsequent discussion of motor skill development.

An effort has been made to clarify intended meanings and avoid some of the confusion and misunderstanding that inevitably is connected with terminology.

Movement. Movement, generally, refers to action and change. A *single movement* is a specific change in position by a body segment. The normal anatomic parts of the human body are segments that move. Because of the structure of the body, the size of the segments can vary. When an arm is involved, the hand might move independently, or the hand and the forearm might move together as a segment, or the entire arm might move as a unit. Single movements gain significance as they become interrelated, merge into patterns, and become recognizable acts.

Movement Pattern. A combination of movements organized according to a particular time-space arrangement is called a pattern. Movement patterns range from simple two-segment combinations to highly structured and complex gross body sequences. The meaning of the term *movement pattern* has been the subject of many interpretations. It is used here primarily in reference to the patterns of the basic motor skills and a few narrowly defined sport skills. Other equally useful interpretations give the term broader meaning. It is often used to refer to an enlarged pattern formed by joining two or more basic skills into a continuous sequence. The fundamental skills of running or jumping can be combined into a simple run and jump pattern or into a complex type of running high jump such as the straddle style. A myriad of combined skill patterns eventually are included in the normal motor activities of children and adults.

The term *movement pattern* is also used to refer to the common elements that appear in many skills performed in the same plane. This interpretation stresses the interrelationships of basic skills and encourages an understanding of the global aspect of movement. Batting in baseball, the forehand stroke in tennis, and the sidearm throw in softball are performed at different velocities according to unique timing patterns, but in essentially the same horizontal plane with enough common elements to suggest a general movement pattern. The similarities in skills performed with an overarm pattern can be seen in Atwater's excellent illustration (Fig. 1–1). It is important to remember that the observed similarities in movement patterns performed in the same plane are similarities in configuration and not necessarily similarities in kinematic or kinetic factors, which tend to be quite specific.

Form. Form is the process entailed in movement. "Form is a way of performing, a work method, a design of performance."[22] It includes movements, the time-space arrangements of movements, and the total visual effect produced. The relative quality of the process is indicated by the use of qualifying terms that provide a range in quality between good and bad, mature and immature, skilled and unskilled, effective and ineffective, or satisfactory and unsatisfactory. Positive qualifying terms imply economy of movement and conformance to effective me-

Fig. 1–1. A variety of unilateral throwing and striking skills shown at point of release or contact. The different skills share common pattern elements in leg action, trunk action, arm position, and trunk-arm relationship. (From Atwater, A.: Biomechanics of Overarm Throwing. In Exercise and Sport Sciences Reviews. Vol. 7. Philadelphia, The Franklin Institute Press, 1980.)

chanics; negative qualifying terms indicate major departure from the compound of similarities in the form used by highly skilled performers.

Performance. While the term *form* is used to describe the process of movement, the term *performance* is used to indicate the product of movement. Performance can be used to refer to the act (the child threw a ball) or to signify the outcome (a distance of 150 feet). A measured performance is not good, bad, satisfactory, or unsatisfactory in absolute terms. It is relatively good or bad depending upon the extent to which an expected outcome is achieved. A running high jump of 42 inches could be an exceptionally good performance for a child, but it would ordinarily be a mediocre jump for a normal adult male because of the differences in the usual standards of expectation.

There is a positive but not direct causal relationship between form and performance. Mature form tends to enhance performance, but high-level performance is not totally dependent upon mature form. This side of the process-product relationship needs to be understood, especially as it applies to children and to optimum skill development. If a child and an adult both use mature form when throwing for distance, the throw by the adult undoubtedly would be much farther. If two children of the same age and sex use identical form to throw for distance, it is possible that one might throw much farther than the other. In instances in which the quality of form is constant and the outcome of performance is different, the difference usually can be traced to a group of factors called human abilities. Strength, speed of movement, reaction time, and eye-hand coordination are among the physical traits that are directly related to quality of performance. Some of the abilities such as speed of movement, strength, and neuromuscular integration are particularly important factors influencing performance in tasks in which the outcome is measured in terms of height, distance, or frequency. Other traits have an important bearing on performance when outcomes are affected by accuracy.

Another facet of the relationships between form and performance is also based upon ability factors and should be mentioned in passing. It is illustrated by a situation in which two performers have the same high level of performance even though one uses good form and the other has a minor but detectable defect in form. Equal performance in this case is possible because of differences in ability factors. The performer with the flaw in form probably has an abundance of some or all of the ability factors required for the particular skill and is able to compensate for the problem by putting some of the abundance to use. Strength could well be the important ability factor that allowed the performer to make up for the simple departure from good form. Although compensation of the sort mentioned can be successful, temporary success is not a compelling reason to continue using less than fully effective motor skill patterns. For optimum performance, all ability should be applied directly to the task rather than used in part to overcome minor deviations in form. It is especially important to emphasize the basic aspects of good form when fundamental skills are being learned because, ultimately, good form is more productive of good performance than poor form.

Fundamental (Basic) Motor Skill. Basic skills are common motor activities with specific patterns. They are the general skills that form the bases for the more advanced and more specific motor activities, such as sport skills. Running, jumping, throwing, catching, galloping, skipping, kicking, and climbing are typical of the identifiable general motor activities included in the category of fundamental skills. Each fundamental skill has a broadly defined minimal standard, a standard that gives the skill its uniqueness. The minimal standard for running, for example, requires that the feet move forward alternately and that the push-off from the support foot be followed by a brief period of nonsupport. When this standard is met, the skill of running has been achieved at its barest level of proficiency. The form used in achieving the minimal standard can be regarded as minimal form. Improvement in form beyond the minimal standard is a gradual process leading toward the acquisition of mature form.

Mature Motor Pattern. The mature motor pattern for a fundamental skill is the composite of the common elements in the form used by skilled performers. There have been objections to the use of the term *mature* because of the implication that it refers exclusively to adults. In the context of motor pattern development, however, mature merely means fully developed. Mature motor patterns are skill-related rather than age-related; they are models of form that represent levels of skill that can be reached during childhood but might not be reached then or during any later period of life. One mature motor pattern that eludes many adults is the normally slow-developing overhand throwing pattern. If it is not acquired by the end of adolescence, it may never be acquired because of the gradual disappearance of encouraging opportunities for making additional progress.

Other terms are used frequently to convey the idea of a mature motor pattern. Some of these terms are fundamental motor pattern, mature form, good form, and skilled form. These terms are not identical in meaning, but they all successfully set forth the idea of a movement pattern that is basic yet highly effective.

Developmental Motor Pattern. A developmental motor pattern is any movement pattern used in the performance of a fundamental skill that meets the minimal requirement for the skill but does not measure up to the mature pattern. By this definition, all developmental patterns are relatively immature and involve less than skilled form. The features typically present in the developmental patterns of most basic skills have been identified. Changes in the effectiveness of movements and timing in successive developmental patterns symbolize progress toward the achievement of mature patterns. Several special terms—unitary pattern, arm-dominated pattern, block rotation, and opening up—have been devised to help describe some of the unique aspects of developmental patterns.

Unitary Pattern. A unitary pattern is one in which the movements are performed simultaneously rather than sequentially. Many of the developmental patterns in throwing, striking, and jumping tend to be unitary. A unitary pattern becomes a *dissociated pattern* as the movements are performed according to sequential or serial timing.

Arm-Dominated Patterns. In an arm-dominated pattern, the arm(s) is the only major segment moving or is the segment initiating and leading the movement. If the primary movement is confined to the arm(s) and upper spine, the pattern is more accurately termed *top-dominated*. Throwing and striking patterns often fall into either of these two categories.

Block Rotation. Block rotation is unitary movement of the entire trunk: pelvis, spine, and shoulders rotate simultaneously. It occurs regularly in developmental throwing and striking patterns.

Opening Up. A movement pattern is "opened up" when body parts move simultaneously in opposite directions. This important process increases range of motion, unlocks unitary action, and contributes significantly to the development of velocity in various forms of throwing and striking.

Sport Skill. Many of the skills used in sports are advanced versions of basic skills that are used in particular ways. The golf swing is an advanced form of striking, the running high jump is an advanced form of jumping combined with running, and the football pass is a special form of throwing. The presence of all or part of a fundamental motor pattern can be detected in the patterns used in these sport skills.

THE STUDY OF MOTOR SKILL DEVELOPMENT

It has become increasingly more obvious that motor skill development is a complicated and prolonged process. At birth, a child has the structural and functional capacity for only rudimentary movement and possesses no demonstrable gross movement patterns. Single movements must be put together to form simple combinations. When these primitive patterns (subroutines) are performed with sufficient consistency, they are enlarged into more distinct patterns. The rate of progress in motor development is determined by the combined effects of maturation processes, learning processes, and exogenous influences.[32] These processes and influences must all be studied to explain *how* the observable changes in motor behavior occur. Much more attention must be given to research on the underlying mechanisms of motor behavior. Unless concern with the description of *what* happens during skill development is coupled with a discovery of *how* it happens, the study of the process will continue to be a lopsided and incomplete endeavor, as it has been for several decades.

Keogh suggested three interrelated avenues of research that need to be pursued in a total effort to identify and understand developmental changes in the organization of movement patterns:[21]

1. Identification of the organization of observable movement sequences of skills (careful and precise analysis of the movement components that are organized to make up the specific motor skills).
2. Identification or inference of the systems or mechanisms underlying the organization of movement planning and movement execution (conceptualize and test appropriate models and theories).
3. Determination of the ways these mechanisms function in the development of movement skill.

The second and third avenues of research offer an opportunity to deal with what has been referred to as a "seemingly large discrepancy between description and explanation."[39] Both avenues entail the use of complicated research techniques, and both have yielded results that have more theoretic than practical value. Nonetheless, they are fruitful avenues and of major importance in the study of motor skill development.

A descriptive type of research has been used with overwhelming frequency in the study of motor development and it has improved in quality over the years through the use of more precise techniques. A continuation of descriptive studies is essential to provide more accurate information on skills previously studied and new information on motor activites not yet researched. The additional knowledge about *what* happens during the execution of a motor pattern will be an invaluable asset when the other aspects of the behavior involved are studied; it will serve to make a difficult task somewhat easier.

THE STUDY OF FUNDAMENTAL MOTOR PATTERNS

The first five years of life generally are regarded as a period during which fundamental motor patterns emerge as the child deals with problems of locomotion and as he learns to manipulate some of the available objects in his environment. The elementary school years that follow are more a period of skill refinement than a period of new skill acquisition. During the early school years a child usually has the opportunity to acquire motor patterns that are more mature, and he is broadly exposed to sports skills. Progression to higher standards of performance can and should occur at various times in subsequent years. This plan of motor skill development is not always achieved according to the general schedule just outlined. Achievement may be accelerated if the child attains optimum motor development or it may be greatly delayed if opportunities for skill development are unavailable. These extremely different possibilities for rate of achievement clearly reflect the life-span concept of motor development and suggest a need for understanding the entire range of skill development. A comprehensive study of fundamental motor patterns is central to that goal.

LONGITUDINAL AND CROSS-SECTIONAL DATA

The only method of studying the changes involved in motor pattern development that is consistent with the notion of development is the longitudinal approach. This approach provides for data to be collected repeatedly on the same individual over an extended period of time. Despite the obvious value of the longitudinal design, there are notable difficulties in the collection and interpretation of longitudinal data.[2,31] One important limitation—data continuity—rarely receives sufficient consideration. Ideally, there should be no gap in the information about the development of a particular motor skill by a given individual. Unfortunately, there are always gaps even when the longitudinal design is used. Information concerning the changes in behavior that occur during the intervals between data collection is always missing. Clearly, the length of the interval between times of data collection can be a major limitation. Studies in which data are collected annually are not as revealing as those in which observations are made every three or every six months. In those instances in which change can take place rapidly, a one month interval might even be too long. The only way to minimize the problem of gaps in data continuity is to determine the length of the interval between collections carefully, taking into consideration both the nature of the skill and the age of the subjects being investigated.

Because of the many difficulties inherent in the collection of longitudinal data, a cross-sectional approach has been employed in much of the research on motor pattern development. By collecting data on groups of subjects at different age levels, it has been possible to piece together an acceptably accurate and reliable picture of the development of specific motor patterns, insofar as the development is reflected in successive age group behavior. The picture of pattern changes presented in cross-sectional studies is reasonably well supported by the data on changes found in a limited number of longitudinal investigations. The vital difference between the two approaches is that only the longitudinal design can deal with the nature of skill development as it occurs in a given individual. The special kinds of information about individual development that can be gleaned from longitudinal studies are available only in small amounts because most studies have involved few subjects. There is an understandable temptation to overstate their significance, but this must be assiduously avoided. Judgments on the significance of the limited longitudinal data should be reserved until a sufficient amount has been accumulated in future studies.

DATA COLLECTION

In order to determine the nature of the changes that occur during motor pattern development, it is necessary to analyze and compare motor patterns. The specific information generally sought in motor pattern analysis includes a description of (1) the movements in a pattern, (2) the range of motion at each active joint, (3) the angular velocities accompanying segmental movement, (4) the timing of movement sequences, (5) the amount of time devoted to each phase of a pattern, and (6) projection angles and velocities. Additional information is sought when kinetic as well as kinematic comparisons are made, and this is being done with increasing frequency.

The type of data that can be collected depends on the sophistication of the equipment available. The equipment currently used allows cinematographic, electrogoniometric, electromyographic, and force plate data to be collected independently or in combination.[7] The accuracy of the data gathered in movement studies has improved gradually and is impressively high due to procedures such as those using the digitizer and computer-programmed analysis. Unfortunately, some factors in the collection of data cannot be controlled by the use of accurate and reliable equipment. These are the human factors.

Preschool children, especially infants, tend to be less than ideal subjects, mainly because testing situations are unnatural for them. They often respond by being somewhat apprehensive, overly inquisitive, inattentive, sporadic, or uncooperative. Negative responses are usually heightened when equipment must be attached to the child and when highly restrictive protocols are used. Children need ample time to adjust to the new and often bewildering aspects of a testing situation. The low-keyed familiarization procedures used by some investigators have been found to contribute significantly to the vitally important adjustment process. Unless an atmosphere is created in which children can move in ways that are natural for them, the information collected will be spurious and a false indication of their movement patterns.

The velocity factor is another variable that is difficult to control when performance data are being collected. Because maximum *controlled* velocity is required to produce skilled motor patterns in running, jumping, throwing, striking, and kicking, these skills must be performed with appropriate effort. The patterns used in most of the basic skills vary according to the amount of velocity generated. Consequently, data can be distorted if either too little or too much force is used in the execution of a skill. Precollection rehearsal usually helps control the velocity variable and it does not contaminate the data in most motor pattern studies unless a learning variable in involved.

The collection of data on the model selected to represent skilled form ordinarily is not a problem, but the selection of the model can be a major one. The literature on motor pattern development contains examples of egregious misjudgments in the selection of the models used to represent mature form. In most of these cases, *adult* form was confused with and substituted for *mature/skilled* form, and the result was inappropriate selection of a model. The mature pattern for a fundamental skill should be based upon the performances of those who have had the opportunity to develop the skill to a high level of competence. There are minor differences in the forms used by highly skilled performers, but these are mostly stylistic variations and not important differences in the basic pattern of movements. After the minor individual variations in form have been winnowed out, the common elements that remain are the ingredients of the model for the mature motor pattern. It would be an overstatement to imply that there is unanimous agreement concerning which movements to include in a skilled motor pattern. However, the degree of concurrence seems to be fairly high among those who have had the most experience in the study of human movement and know the technical and biomechanical essentials of good form. When selecting models for mature motor patterns, they would avoid a pitfall such as using the exaggerated form of a baseball pitcher as the model for the basic overhand throw[14] and they would not assume that a person who is skilled in several motor tasks is automatically skilled enough to be used as a model in another.

INTERPRETATION OF DEVELOPMENTAL CHANGES

Since the 1930s, the changes that take place during intra-skill motor development have been described primarily in terms of stage progress. The term *stage* ordinarily is used in a practical, nontheoretic context to describe motor patterns as steps in the developmental process. Accordingly, each stage for a given skill is defined as a distinct movement pattern that is present at one of the progressive levels of skill development. When the developmental changes in a particular skill are interpreted in terms of stages, decisions regarding when the process of skill acquisition begins and when it ends must be made, and the number of stages and movement characteristics of each must be determined. The number of stages inevitably varies from skill to skill and from one investigator to another according to available data and intended use. There is an arbitrary factor in the process, part of which can be illustrated by differences in stage determination regarding the study of the overarm throw. Wild (1938) observed six types of throws in the development of the mature pattern and later converted them to four stages.[41] The lack of differentiation in trunk movement in Wild's stages was noted by Hanson (1961) who suggested refinement to clarify this aspect of the pattern.[17] Leme (1973) expanded Wild's six original types to a total of ten and gave more attention in the stages to changes in the length of stride.[23] Roberton (1975) hypothesized 25 stages of throwing, using only the pelvic-spinal and arm movements in the pattern.[26] Gallahue (1982) reduced the number of stages in throwing development to three for the purpose of simplicity in evaluation.[12] Stage description changes in accordance with the number of stages used.

Investigators at Michigan State University have used stages in the interpretation of developmental changes in several studies, starting in 1966. As longitudinal and cross-sectional data accumulated, the stages for basic skill development were modified and refined. In the current system, at Michigan State University, whole-pattern stages are the basic units with sub-stages included for more precise identification. "Advancement from one stage to the next is characterized by (1) biomechanically more efficient and effective movement and (2) the incorporation of more patterns or sub-routines into the total movement."[35]

A different approach to the study and use of stages is being taken by

Roberton, who has begun an investigation into the theoretical validity of stages in motor development.[29] She began by testing the validity of two of the main concepts of stage theory: universality (stage sequence is the same for all individuals) and intransivity (order of the stage sequence cannot be changed). In a two-phase study of the overarm throw, she collected within-time and across-time data on a group of first graders. There was evidence of a universal, intransitive stage sequence for the arm action stages that had been hypothesized but not for the hypothesized trunk movement stages. The across-time data revealed that change occurred within movement components but that it did not take place uniformly for all components in the motor pattern. The evidence for this finding became the underpinning for a proposed component model for intra-task motor development. According to Roberton's model, since change occurs in different pattern components at different rates, developmental stages can exist only in pattern components. The whole motor patterns can be evaluated only according to the effectiveness of component action. The extent to which the component model and the component stage concept have wide application needs to be determined in the future by applying them to data from motor skills other than the overarm throw and the forward roll, skills in which pattern component development seems less variable.

Attempts have been made recently to avoid the controversy and the problems that are connected with the use of the stage concept. Terms such as *level* and *phase* have been substituted for the word stage. The replacement of the debatable term with one that is benign temporarily circumvents controversy, but it does not obviate the need to deal straightforwardly with underlying questions regarding stage validity, whole-pattern stages, and pattern component stages. The concepts are more important than the words chosen to describe them and they are not altered by changing labels.

Developmental changes can be explained in a different and broader way by describing them in terms of trends. Trends are changes in components or whole patterns that indicate the general course of skill development. They can appear as broad changes in timing, range of motion, joint angles, segmental relationships, segmental velocities, angular velocities, and other parameters. Interpretation by trend seems particularly appropriate when development is more continuous than step-like and when change is registered more in amount than in type of movement. The trend can also give an overview of the developmental direction for an entire skill, as when there is "change from movements in the anteroposterior plane to movements largely in the horizontal plane,"[41] or when there is change in kinetic variables—"a developmental trend in the direction of greater magnitude of force with age."[11]

Stages and trends differ in the degree of preciseness with which they describe the course of change. Whereas a stage has many specifics and it aptly describes individual status at a particular point in development, a trend refers more to general, class change over time. Still, they are not mutually exclusive ways of interpreting changes in motor skill development nor are they contradictory.

MOTOR PATTERN DEVELOPMENT OF HANDICAPPED CHILDREN

Optimal motor development is a goal that should apply to all children. However, until recently it has not been a realistic developmental goal for those classified as being "exceptional," the physically and mentally handicapped. The quality of the motor development opportunities available to these groups of children was abysmally low until the last quarter of a century when heightened concern for them began to bring about gradual improvement. Nothing has had an impact on the rate and quality of improvement in opportunities for the handicapped to equal that of the passage of Public Law 94-142, the Education For All Handicapped Children Act of 1975. The law provides for the education of every child in the least restrictive environment and a special provision states that every child who is receiving a public education must participate in an appropriate physical education program. Fulfillment of the special provision starts with an assessment of the status and capability of each handicapped child to determine whether he can profitably be "mainstreamed" into a regular class or must receive special instruction. What is known about normal motor behavior and development becomes important in this connection because the information is used in making comparisons and judgments that determine assignment to regular or special education.

Assessment and evaluation are less difficult for children with some types of handicaps than for children with other types because more has been learned about the motor behavior and development that is typical for them. Most research on the motor skill development of exceptional populations has been directed toward those whose major handicap involves some degree of mental retardation. Collectively more is known about the educable mentally retarded (EMR), the trainable mentally retarded (TMR), and the profoundly mentally retarded (PMR) than any other general class of handicapped children. The findings indicate that children with less-than-average intelligence generally lag behind their intellectually normal counterparts both in level of gross motor proficiency and in level of motor pattern development. The findings also show that the more severe the mental retardation, the greater the negative effect will be on all aspects of motor development. EMR children, the least retarded group, lag only about 2 years behind normal children of the same age in motor achievement, and many are capable of achieving mature motor pattern status if given the opportunity and enough time.[24] In a study by Hemmert,[19] it was found that about half of the EMR children in each age group from 9 to 15 years had already achieved mature motor patterns for 8 of 11 skills, according to standards in the Ohio State University SIGMA. The proportion of children at that level of motor pattern development might seem a bit unusual; however, it must be considered in light of what is known about the physical capabilities of those with moderate retardation. Studies such as the one by Dobbins and Rarick indicate that in the physical realm EMR children are more like than they are unlike their intellectually normal peers.[10]

Mentally retarded children at all levels of severity usually suffer from lack of opportunity for normal motor development. The deprivation has a complicated and cyclic effect on their status and progress. It leads to chronic inactivity, and this contributes to the incidence of obesity, which is a common problem for the group. Obesity, in turn, encourages more inactivity. Because of the decline in activity, strength and skill do not develop normally and handicapped children become less acceptable as companions in childhood play. They suffer from social isolation. As the influence of obesity, lack of strength, and low motor ability continues, handicapped children are increasingly separated from their normal peers, and the opportunities usually available for motor development are increasingly diminished. This insidious cycle has a more profound effect on severely retarded children. In some instances they actually regress in the quality of the motor patterns they use. This has been found to be the case with Down's syndrome (mongoloid)[20] and TMR[42] children. Both groups tend to become less active as they grow older and as a result show a decrease in the maturity of their gait patterns.

Implementation of the Education For All Handicapped Children Act will greatly improve the handicapped child's opportunity for motor skill development. It will also encourage additional study of the problems handicapped children have with the development of fundamental motor patterns. One reason why additional research on skill development is necessary is because P.L. 94-142 contains the provision that an "individualized education plan" (IEP) be made out for any child who requires special education. Specific short-term and general long-range goals must be established for each IEP. Before specific goals can be determined, the special problems that limit progress for those with various handicapping conditions must be identified. There is some research in which those problems have been identified. For example, in a recent study, DiRocco and Roberton found that lack of force production in the overarm throw was a major problem for mentally retarded children.[9] After analyzing the children's motor patterns for sources of difficulty, they were able to make specific suggestions for intervention procedures to deal with the problem.

Many children who are mentally retarded also suffer from one or more physical handicaps. Those who are multiply-handicapped can be so severely afflicted that practically no motor pattern development is possible for them. The motor development of these children becomes the responsibility of special therapists. There are also children of normal intelligence whose handicaps are primarily physical in nature. Children in this group who are profoundly handicapped also need help from specially trained therapists. Fortunately, many children with physical handicaps are only mildly disadvantaged and they are being mainstreamed. Optimum motor development for them is more easily achieved because the limitations characteristic of most physical handicaps are reasonably well understood and the resulting motor behavior is predictable. Motor pattern development for those with mild physical handicaps is guided along the lines of expected normal development, but within the limitations imposed by the handicapping condition. Incidentally, anyone who is familiar with the effects of various types of cerebral palsy on motor performance should be able to identify the mildly spastic child in Figure 8–13. The exaggerated activity of muscle flexors, which is typical of the spastic condition, can be seen to affect the kicking pattern in a predictable and recognizable way.

MOVEMENT AND MECHANICS

Mechanics is the branch of physics that deals with motion and the effect of forces on bodies. It includes *kinematics,* which describes motion, and *kinetics,* which describes the effect of forces in the production of motion. When mechanics is applied to the study of human motion it is called *biomechanics*—"the science that examines the internal and external forces acting on a human body and the effects produced by these forces."[18]

It is understandable that biomechanic analysis has become indispensible in the study of motor development. The general laws of mechanics offer a sound, logical basis for analyzing and evaluating movement. They serve as a standard by which the validity of human motion can be measured[38] and make it possible to understand motor development beyond the descriptive level. A biomechanics approach is used in the determination of skilled form for basic motor patterns as well as in the interpretation of developmental patterns, developmental trends, and individual performance. Movement patterns routinely are evaluated on the basis of "biomechanical quality," advancement from one developmental skill stage to the next is thought to be characterized by movement that is "biomechanically more efficient," and intertask relationships have been described in terms of mechanics rather than just in terms of movements.

While the biomechanical approach has been useful in many ways, it has been particularly helpful in clarifying the relative importance of muscular strength in motor pattern development. Force must be applied to produce movement and the source of force in the human body is muscular strength. In order to use mature form in a basic skill, muscular contraction must produce enough force to start, accelerate, stop, or change the direction of movement effectively according to a prescribed pattern. Ordinarily adults have sufficient strength for mature motor patterns so that available strength is not so much a limitation on form for them as it is a restriction on maximum performance. With children the situation can be quite different; lack of strength often dictates form and limits performance. This is quite noticeable during the first few years of life when the child's movement patterns, especially in velocity-oriented skills, are closely related to the level of his neuromuscular development and to the amount of force he has available.

Velocity production is an essential consideration in most fundamental motor skills. Velocity results from the application of force over a given period of time. The forces in a motor pattern can be applied (1) at essentially the same time, as is done in a unitary pattern, with the result that the velocity produced is limited by the time factor as well as by the magnitude of the forces; or (2) successively, as is done in sequential patterns, in which speed is built up increasingly as the forces are added in conformance with the principle of summation of forces. According to that principle, the force that produces the first movement is added to the force that produces the next movement and the summation continues until the pattern is complete. The most favorable timing for the addition of forces in all motor patterns is not fully understood, but it is thought that each new movement in a sequence should begin when the previous one has reached its maximum velocity. This provides for a maximum contribution from each force and the greatest possible final velocity. Thus, when velocity production is the goal of a motor pattern, it is biomechanically more effective to apply the available forces successively rather than simultaneously. If this point is employed in the evaluation of developmental motor patterns, the superiority of the sequential over the unitary type of pattern becomes clear and the developmental phenomenon, "opening up," is put in proper perspective. The appearance of "opening" marks the transition from unitary to sequential motor pattern development in certain skills.

The importance and value of biomechanics in the study of motor development could be illustrated in many additional ways; however, it seems unnecessary to pursue so obvious a point. A rudimentary knowledge of biomechanics is absolutely indispensable, because movement cannot be understood at more than a superficial level without that scientific background.

APPLICATIONS AND OTHER CONSIDERATIONS

In a sense, the *raison d'être* for the study of motor development is the optimization of development for everyone. The nature of the development process and its results can be discovered but the enterprise is futile if it ends without turning discovery into practice. The transformation of theory and knowledge into applications that are both effective and practical is a precarious process at best. The process requires accurate interpretations, reasoned procedures, thoughtful judgments, adaptable mentality, and a sure sense of practicality. Of all these factors, none is more important or has received more consideration than that concerning the practicality of applications.

MOTOR PATTERN EVALUATION

The developmental sequences resulting from the study of fundamental motor patterns are useful in the evaluation of motor pattern status and developmental progress. The way in which evaluation is performed in a particular situation depends upon how much and what kind of information is needed and will be used. Evaluation procedures are time-consuming and complex, so evaluation should be performed not for its own sake but for its use in promoting motor skill development. For teachers who have contact with 350 to 500 different children each week, extensive individual evaluation of specific motor skills is impractical if not impossible. Since they have little time available for giving individual attention or for evaluation, gross information usually is all that is needed. For teachers who have ample time to guide students individually in the improvement of their motor behavior, extensive and detailed information is of great practical value.

Developmental motor pattern sequences are available and can be adapted for use in detailed or gross analysis. If sequences with designated whole-pattern stages or levels are used in evaluation, the result of the evaluation of each individual is recorded as a number corresponding to the level observed. Such would be the case when using the following stages in running proposed by Seefeldt, Reuschlein, and Vogel.[33]

Stage 1. The arms are extended sideward at shoulder height (high-guard position). The stride is short, and of shoulder width. The surface contact is made with the entire foot, simultaneously. Little knee flexion is seen. The feet remain near the surface at all times.

Stage 2. Arms are carried at 'middle guard' (waist height), the stride is longer and approaches the mid-saggital line. The surface contact is usually with the entire foot, striking simultaneously. Greater knee flexion is noted in the restraining phase. The swing leg is flexed and the movement of the legs becomes anterior-posterior.

Stage 3. The arms are no longer used primarily for balance. Arms are carried below waist level and may flex and assume a counter-rotary action. The foot contact is heel-toe. Stride length increases and both feet move along a mid-saggital line. The swing leg flexion may be as great as 90 degrees.

Stage 4. Foot contact is heel-toe at slow or modest velocities but may be entirely on the metatarsal arch while sprinting. Arm action is in direct opposition to leg action. Knee flexion is used to maintain the momentum during the support phase. The swing leg may flex until it is nearly in contact with the buttocks during its recovery phase.

Descriptions of these stages are detailed, but with the use of such relative terms as short, little, near, and longer, they are only moderately precise. Looseness in the preciseness of stage descriptions is justifiable on a practical basis because of the difficulties inherent in the visual, non-aided type of observation routinely used in motor pattern evaluation. Fine distinctions measured in inches or degrees cannot be made unless film-aided or other special observation procedures are used.

If developmental sequences are broken into component stages or levels, the results of evaluation are usually recorded on a check list that provides a profile of detailed information regarding the status of motor pattern development. A model for such a check list has been suggested by Roberton and Halverson for use in connection with their component approach to motor skill analysis.[28] All pattern components and the stages in each are listed. The stage into which a child's movement most closely fits is checked for each component and the accumulation of checks forms the profile of the total pattern.

Effective motor pattern evaluation requires special preparation on the part of the person who performs it, regardless of whether whole-pattern or pattern component analysis is employed. Total familiarity with the stage sequences to be used is the first requirement. The characteristics of each stage or level must be memorized so as to know exactly what to look for. The second requirement is the ability to observe effectively and see what is actually happening during live movement. Observation skill is difficult to acquire and it has been pinpointed as the weak link in the process used in motor pattern evaluation. Identification of the *"knowing but not seeing"* phenomenon has led to the realization that more attention must be paid to the development of observation skills.[3] Halverson has suggested and worked with a progression that is both logical and productive.[15] It proceeds cautiously from film-assisted to live-action observation, building on success. The transition to live-action observation is difficult, but progress is still possible with a generous amount of concentrated practice. Eventually the limits to what can be seen in live observation are reached.

Naked-eye, live-action *observation techniques* are used in conjunction with the development of "seeing" skill.[5,8] These techniques help make "seeing" possible. Included are techniques that deal with where to look from, what to look for, and how to look for what. While many decisions about observation and techniques are made during pre-observation planning, none is more important than the decision of what to look for. The key points and critical features of the skill to be observed must be identified. The specified characteristics of set patterns and components are helpful, but only as a starting point. Since it is difficult to see more than one action at a time when evaluating motor patterns, the more critical actions should be identified for each evaluation. Often one component will be especially revealing and will assist in the evaluation of others. For example, it would be possible to learn much about many of the features in a running pattern by first observing the action of either the heel or the knee of the recovery leg. In some of the component and developmental stages of a skill, there are critical features that cannot be evaluated discretely by naked-eye observation. One of those features is the action of the forearm in the overarm throw.[15] A clue to what happens in forearm action can sometimes be found in the actions of other pattern components. For instance, a high level of maturity in forearm lag can be expected if a forceful pattern shows both a step with the contra-lateral leg and lateral trunk flexion at release. The particular expectation could help make it possible to *see* more clearly what happens during subsequent observation of forearm component action.

A test of practicality for the use of set developmental sequences in motor skill evaluation is whether the stages are "too difficult to see without the use of motion pictures or extensive periods of training."[27] Some of those who have developed the sequences have applied an informal version of the test with success and others are just beginning to apply it. Another criterion of practicality, which is of particular concern to the teacher, is whether the information that the developmental sequences yield is worth the time required to use them. Teachers legitimately question the value of knowing the precise component level of each child for all the basic skills they are expected to learn, especially when the price of the information is an inordinate amount of valuable class time. If the set developmental sequences are impractical because of the time factor, other evaluation procedures involving "critical factors" have to be devised. Suggestions in this direction are offered at the end of some of the chapters that follow.

MISAPPLICATION OF KNOWLEDGE

When efforts are being made to find practical applications for new information, inadvertent misapplication of knowledge can occur despite honest and serious intent. Almost anyone who tries to be innovative is vulnerable and could be guilty of misinterpreting the implications of new knowledge. Those working in the area of motor development need to be especially cautious about misapplying the developmental sequence concept. A new developmental sequence should be *determined* on the basis of data collected on the actual performances of age group subjects. It is a misapplication of an important concept if a proposed developmental sequence is based only upon extrapolated personal experience and is otherwise unsupported. One way to guard against any sort of misapplication is to approach new proposals with a touch of skepticism rather than with blind faith. New applications of knowledge should be evaluated for probable validity and effectiveness *before* as well as *after* use.

REFERENCES

1. Atwater, A.: Biomechanics of overarm throwing movements and of throwing injuries. *In* Exercise and Sport Sciences Reviews. Vol. 7. Edited by R.S. Hutton and D.I. Miller. Philadelphia, The Franklin Institute Press, 1980.
2. Baltes, P.B.: Longitudinal and cross-sectional sequences in the study of age and generation effects. Hum. Dev., 11:145, 1968.
3. Barrett, K.: Observation for teaching and coaching. J. Health Phys. Educ. Rec., 50(1):23, 1970.
4. Bayley, N.: The development of motor abilities during the first three years. Monogr. Soc. Res. Child Dev., 1:1, 1935.
5. Brown, E.W.: Visual evaluation techniques for skill analysis. J. Health Phys. Educ. Rec. and Dance, 53(1):21, 1982.
6. Bruner, J.: Organization of early skilled action. Child Dev., 44:1, 1973.
7. Cavanagh, P.: Instrumentation and methodology of applied and pure research in biomechanics. *In* Biomechanics of Sports and Kinanthropometry. Edited by F. Landry and W. Orban. Quebec, Editeur Officiel, 1978.
8. Cooper, J., Adrian, M., and Glassow, R.: Kinesiology. St. Louis, C.V. Mosby, 1982.
9. DiRocco, P., and Roberton, M.: Implications of motor development research: the overarm throw in the mentally retarded. Phys. Educ., 38(1):27, 1981.
10. Dobbins, D.A., and Rarick, G.L.: Structural similarity of the motor domain of normal and educable retarded boys. Res. Q. Am. Assoc. Health Phys. Educ., 46(4):447, 1975.
11. Fortney, V.: The kinematics and kinetics of the running pattern of two-, four-, and six-year-old children. Unpublished dissertation. Lafayette, IN, Purdue University, 1980.
12. Gallahue, D.: Understanding Motor Development in Children. New York, John Wiley and Sons, 1982.
13. Gesell, A.: The First Five Years of Life. New York, Harper and Brothers, 1940.
14. Halverson, L.E.: Development of motor patterns in young children. Quest, 6:44, 1966.
15. Halverson, L.E.: Learning to observe children's motor development, part II. Developing skill in "seeing" movement. Report to the National Convention of AAHPER, New Orleans, 1979.
16. Halverson, L.E., and Roberton, M.A.: The effects of instruction on overhand throwing development in children. *In* Psychology of Motor Behavior and Sport. Edited by G.C. Roberts and K.M. Newell. Champaign, IL, Human Kinetics, 1979.
17. Hanson, S.: A comparison of the overhand throw performance of instructed and non-instructed kindergarten boys and girls. Unpublished master's thesis. Madison, University of Wisconsin, 1961.
18. Hay, J.: The Biomechanics of Sports Techniques. 2nd Ed. Englewood Cliffs, N.J., Prentice-Hall, 1978.
19. Hemmert, T.J.: An investigation of basic gross motor skill development of moderately retarded children and youth. Unpublished doctoral dissertation. Columbus, Ohio State University, 1978.
20. James, R.J.: Multivariate analysis of the walking behavior in institutional Down's syndrome males. Unpublished doctoral dissertation. Madison, University of Wisconsin, 1974.
21. Keogh, J.: The study of movement skill development. Quest, 28:76, 1977.
22. Lawther, J.: Directing motor skill learning. Quest, 6:68, 1966.
23. Leme, S.: Developmental throwing patterns in adult female performers within a selected velocity range. Unpublished master's thesis. Madison, University of Wisconsin, 1973.
24. Rarick, G.L., and Dobbins, D.A.: Basic components in the motor performance of educable mentally retarded children: implications for curriculum development. Department of Physical Education, University of California, Berkeley, 1972.

25. Ridenour, M.V.: Programs to optimize infant motor development. *In* Motor Development: Issues and Applications. Edited by M.V. Ridenour. Princeton, N.J., Princeton Book Co., 1978.
26. Roberton, M.A.: Stability of stage categorizations across trials: implications for the 'Stage Theory' of overarm throw development. Unpublished doctoral dissertation. Madison, University of Wisconsin, 1975.
27. Roberton, M.A.: Motor stages: heuristic model for research and teaching. *In* Proceedings of the NCPEAM/NAPECW National Conference. Edited by L.I. Geduilas and M.E. Kneer. Orlando, FL, 1977.
28. Roberton, M., and Halverson, L.: The developing child—his changing movement. *In* Physical Education for Children: A Focus on the Teaching Process. Edited by B. Logsdon, et al. Philadelphia, Lea & Febiger, 1977.
29. Roberton, M.: Stages in motor development. *In* Motor Development: Issues and Applications. Edited by M.V. Ridenour. Princeton, N.J., Princeton Book Co., 1978.
30. Roberton, M., Halverson, L., and Langendorfer, S.: Longitudinal changes in children's overarm throw ball velocities. Res. Q. Am. Assoc. Health Phys. Educ., *50*:2, 1979.
31. Schaie, K.W.: A general model for the study of developmental problems. Psychol. Bull., 64:92, 1965.
32. Schilling, F.: Motor development as a process of adaptation. *In* Motor Behavior of Pre-school Children. Edited by H. Muller, R. Decker, and F. Schilling. Schorndorf. Germany, Verlag Karl Hofmann, 1975.
33. Seefeldt, V., Reuschlein, S., and Vogel, P.: Sequencing motor skills within the physical education curriculum. Paper presented at the AAHPER National Convention, Houston, 1972.
34. Seefeldt, V.: Critical learning periods and programs of early intervention. Paper presented at the AAHPER National Convention. Atlantic City, 1975.
35. Seefeldt, V., and Haubenstricker, J.: Patterns, phases or stages: an analytical model for the study of developmental movement. Paper presented at the Symposium on Motor Skill Development. Iowa City, 1979.
36. Shirley, M.M.: The First Two Years: A Study of Twenty-Five Babies. Vol. 1. Minneapolis, University of Minnesota Press, 1931.
37. Smoll, F.: Developmental kinesiology: toward a subdiscipline focusing on motor development. Paper presented at the Symposium on Motor Skill Development, Iowa City, 1979.
38. Steindler, A.: Mechanics of Normal and Pathological Locomotion in Man. Baltimore, Charles C Thomas, 1935.
39. Wade, M.: Developmental motor learning. *In* Exercise and Sport Sciences Reviews. Vol. 4. Edited by J. Keogh and R.S. Hutton. Santa Barbara, CA, Journal Publishing Affiliates, 1976.
40. Wellman, B.: Motor achievements of preschool children. Childhood Educ., *13*:311, 1937.
41. Wild, M.: The behavior pattern of throwing and some observations concerning its course of development in children. Res. Q. Am. Assoc. Health Phys. Educ., 9(3):20, 1938.
42. Windell, E.J.: Evaluation of gait patterns of trainable mentally retarded children. Unpublished doctor of physical education dissertation. Bloomington, IN, Indiana University, 1971.

CHAPTER 2

Walking

Walking is a natural form of upright locomotion. Its motor pattern is distinguished by progressive alternate leg action and continuous contact with the supporting surface. A full cycle in the motor pattern—one stride—consists of a swing phase and a stance or support phase for each leg. The swing leg moves forward to regain contact with a heel-strike before the toes of the support foot break contact with the supporting surface. The momentary double support that occurs is important because normal walking is done at a slow to moderately fast pace and there is a risk of losing control of equilibrum in each stride.[15] When locomotor velocity is increased to a critical point, heel-toe continuity is broken by periods of nonsupport and the form of locomotion is changed from walking to running.

Many of the parameters of gait are directly affected by the velocity of a particular form of locomotion.[16] The specific ways in which they are affected will be discussed later in this chapter and in Chapter 3.

PREWALKING-WALKING PROGRESSION

More than half a century ago Shirley referred to walking as the most spectacular and probably the most important single phase of motor development.[27] Her evaluation of the relative importance of walking might seem a bit overdrawn today, but it helps establish the acquisition of upright bipedal locomotion as a prime developmental event. Until a child can walk independently, his environment with its potential for motor experience and overall development is severely limited.

The rate at which a child develops the ability to walk is controlled to a great extent by his own rate of maturation. He cannot move independently in the upright position until he has developed sufficient muscular strength, adequate antigravity reflexes, and minimally effective balance mechanisms. He cannot walk efficiently and effectively until his nervous system is capable of controlling and coordinating his muscular activity. The presence of cephalocaudal direction in the maturation of nervous control is apparent as the developmental process proceeds. The child progresses from crawling, to creeping, to cruising or hitching, and finally to walking. The process is orderly but typically involves minor regressions, as noted in Gesell's system of reciprocal interweaving.[8] Some infants seem to retain immature locomotor patterns that can be performed effectively while advancing to new and more mature ones. One example is an infant who does not give up creeping entirely as a form of locomotion even two months after being able to do unsupported walking.[13] Another example is a child who has the mature characteristics of normal gait during walking but reverts to an immature pattern when attempting to run.[4]

Individual differences in the age at which each of the prewalking milestones might be achieved are shown in data published by Burnett and Johnson.[4] The averages and ranges are as follows: crawling, 7.0 months (4.5 to 9.5); creeping, 8.5 months (5.0 to 14.5); cruising, 10.0 months (7.0 to 11.5); and independent walking, 12.5 months (9.0 to 17.0).

The prewalking-walking progressions of 20 infants were studied in detail for a period of 2 years by Shirley.[27] She found that nearly every baby passed through four distinct stages of development in the walking process.

Stage I. The infant makes dancing and patting steps against the floor from a supported position. He neither stiffens his knees nor supports his weight.

Stage II. The infant stands with support. He uses his feet for weight bearing and his outstretched arms (which are held) for balance.

Stage III. The infant walks when led by both hands.

Stage IV. The infant walks alone.

Shirley obviously confined her stages to progress as measured by changes in the upright position and did not include sequential changes in the total development of locomotion. If locomotor developments in the horizontal position had been included, it could be seen that most infants reach Stages I and II in the walking process described by Shirley before they are able to creep. Thus the interpretation of these four stages must include an awareness of the limitations imposed by excluding horizontal locomotor patterns.

MOTOR PATTERNS IN THE DEVELOPMENT OF WALKING

Initial attempts at independent walking are precarious adventures. Balance is lost easily and falls are common, but progress is rapid. Once the child is able to take a few controlled steps, his progress in walking proceeds at an exponential rate, at least in terms of the number of continuous steps taken.[26] Rapid progress is manifested, too, by the many improvements in his movement pattern.

The initial patterns used in independent walking clearly demonstrate that all neophytes experience difficulty in maintaining dynamic balance, especially lateral dynamic stability, during the swing phase of the pattern. The rigid, halting initial pattern is characterized by short steps, flat-footed contact, outtoeing foot angle (heel-toe angle from line of progression), wide dynamic base (distance of each heel from center line during double stance), flexed knee at contact with quick knee extension, little purposeful ankle movement, excessive hip flexion and limited hip extension, slight pelvic tilt (drop of pelvis away from support side), no pelvic rotation (forward-backward movement around the vertical axis), forward trunk inclination, and arms fixed in sideward elevation with half-flexed elbows (Fig. 2–1).

Improvement in each feature of the pattern is more gradual than abrupt. The rate of improvement varies to some extent from one feature to another but the interrelatedness of the pattern provides for common progress. The changes are notably consistent with the cephalocaudal course of nervous system development. To illustrate, the average ages at which various gait characteristics appeared in the patterns of the 28

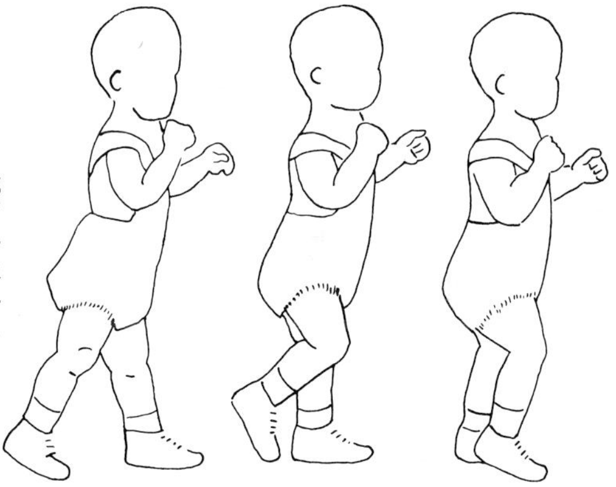

Fig. 2–1. The unsteady walking pattern of a $14^1/_2$-month-old girl 7 days after taking her first unsupported steps. She shows "high guard" arm position, flat-footed contact, and single-knee-lock leg action.

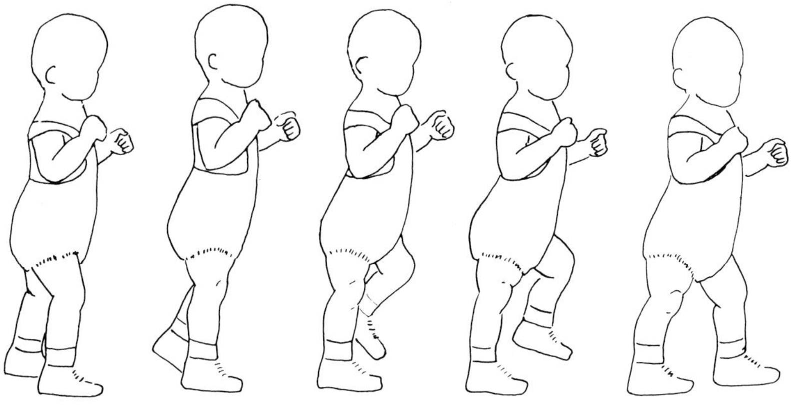

children studied by Burnett and Johnson were as follows: pelvic tilt, 13.4 months; pelvic rotation, 13.8 months; flexion at midstance, 16.3 months; feet-within-trunk-width base, 17.0 months; synchronous arm movement, 18.0 months; heel-strike, 18.5 months; mature foot and knee mechanism, 19.5 months.[4]

Development toward a mature pattern of walking can best be described in terms of the gradual changes that take place in the parameters of gait. These changes can be regarded as general trends, most of which are distinctly interrelated.

DEVELOPMENTAL TRENDS IN GAIT PARAMETERS

STEP LENGTH

The length of the stride is extended by small annual increments. The magnitude of the changes is suggested by Scrutton's data based on heel-to-heel step measurements of 97 children.[24] Average length of step increased from 10 inches at age 1 year, to 11.5 inches at age 2 years, to 13.0 inches at age 3 years, to 15.0 inches at age 4 years. The consistency of step length for each leg also improved and the length of step for right and left legs became increasingly more similar.

When Beck examined the gait patterns of 52 children between the ages of 11 months and 14 years, he found that the average stride length was 38% of the child's height regardless of age.[2] The positive relationship between step length and anthropometric features was supported by a subsequent study involving 186 children between the ages of 1 and 7 years in which step length was found to increase linearly with increasing limb length.[29] The investigators proposed that the "linear relationship provides a valuable test for neuromuscular maturation." Another indication of the influence of stature on a gait parameter came from a slightly different approach in which a step factor—ratio of step length to leg length—was utilized. Little difference was found in the mean step factor for two different groups of children ranging in age from 1 to 7 years.[24,29]

FOOT CONTACT

Flat-footed contact is the norm for beginning unsupported walkers, with a few infants starting as "toe steppers." Significant progress in this feature of the pattern takes place in just a few months. Early changes in the ankle-knee-hip mechanism result in less plantar flexion of the foot and lead to heel-strike at contact (Fig. 2–3). A recent study showed that heel-strike is present in most children by the age of 18 months.[29] This report basically agrees with an earlier report that showed heel-strike is acquired about 22 weeks after the beginning of unsupported walking.[4]

Fig. 2-2. Lateral stability in the initial phase of independent walking is provided by a dynamic base greater than the trunk width.

DYNAMIC BASE

Foot placement is relatively wide for most infants when they take their first independent steps. The dynamic base narrows rather promptly and soon falls within the lateral dimensions of the trunk, thereafter continuing medialward toward the line of progression (Figures 2-2 and 2-4). After the initial rapid improvement, there is only a slight tendency for dynamic base to narrow during childhood. When Scrutton and Robson measured the dynamic base of a group of children ranging in age from 1 to 11 years, they found only a 1-inch difference between the average for 1-year-olds and 9- to 11-year-olds.[25] Yet, when they converted the data to a base factor—dynamic base divided by leg length—the base factor diminished greatly with age due to the increase in leg length.

FOOT ANGLE

The average degree of outtoeing decreases during the first year of walking and then remains relatively constant with advancing age.[6] Methods used to measure foot angle vary significantly enough to prevent meaningful comparisons of published data. However, one must

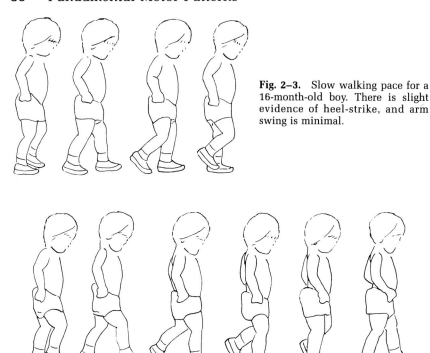

Fig. 2–3. Slow walking pace for a 16-month-old boy. There is slight evidence of heel-strike, and arm swing is minimal.

remember that foot angle varies widely in any given age group. When included angle (right plus left) was used as the measure of foot angle, one group of children under the age of 5 years showed ranges of 36°, 41°, 39°, and 41° on consecutive years.[24] The wide range reveals the presence of more intoeing than might be expected. Furthermore, the incidence of intoeing foot angles increases with age as the amount of outtoeing decreases. This point is important because intoeing gaits are considered abnormal.

HIP FLEXION-EXTENSION

The infantile pattern of walking stresses flexion and minimizes extension at the hip. The large amount of hip flexion at the end of the forward leg swing sometimes gives the appearance of "high stepping" even though foot clearance is minimal. Gradually there is a decrease in maximum hip flexion at the end of the swing phase and an increase in maximum hip extension at the end of stance. The latter change was cited by Statham and Murray as the main mechanism involved at the developmental level when increased skill produced longer strides.[28] By about age 2 years, the total flexion-extension angle at the hip is nearly the same as that of 7-year-old children and adults.[29]

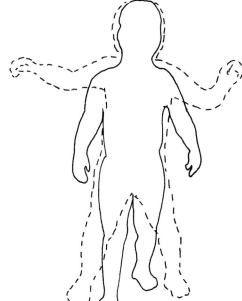

Fig. 2–4. Dynamic base narrows quickly, high-guard arm position is abandoned, and heel-strike is usually present in walking form by age two years. (Adapted from Burnett and Johnson.[4])

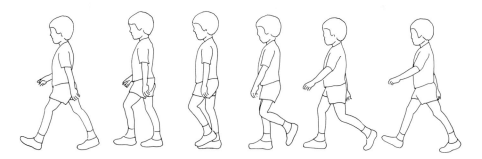

Fig. 2–5. A 5-year-old boy uses heel-strike and "double knee lock" when walking and shows mature arm swing.

KNEE-ANKLE MECHANISM

Changes in the function of this aspect of the walking pattern strongly influence progress toward mature gait. The stance phase in beginning walking form starts with flat-footed contact, the knee in flexion and the foot slightly plantarflexed. In 1-year-olds the knee remains flexed during the stance phase, but in 1½-year-olds there is progressive flexion after foot strike followed by extension to the starting knee angle.[29] The lack of knee extension at the earlier age was attributed to inadequate strength in the plantarflexor muscles of the ankle. Burnett and Johnson observed a slightly different early knee pattern without evidence of a knee-flexion wave following contact.[4] The beginning walkers in their study quickly extended the forward knee after making foot contact. Despite the noted minor difference, children in both groups progressed to extension-flexion-extension movements at the knee. This is a definite trend toward the mature "double knee lock" pattern (Fig. 2–5), which involves heel-strike with knee in extension, immediate plantarflexion of the foot and knee flexion until near midstance, and knee extension and heel raise prior to the swing phase. While the knee goes from extension to flexion to extension, the ankle goes from plantarflexion to dorsiflexion to plantarflexion. The extension-flexion-extension change is smooth and allows the weight of the body to move forward fluidly over the supporting limb.

PELVIC TILT

There usually is a trace of lateral pelvic tilt at the onset of independent walking. The amount of tilt increases slightly as walking improves, but little change occurs in this parameter with age. Forward pelvic tilt initially is greater for infants but at two years of age is about the same as for adults.

PELVIC ROTATION

Ordinarily pelvic rotation appears after unsupported walking begins and slowly becomes part of the pattern. Progress in this parameter depends on the degree of maturation of overall leg action in the pattern. It is also velocity-dependent.

TRUNK INCLINATION

The slight forward inclination of the trunk and accompanying downward tilt of the pelvis in the initial pattern of walking is probably a carry-over from cruising and other types of supported walking. The flexion posture, of which forward inclination of the trunk is a part, becomes less pronounced as balance improves and as walking becomes more controlled. Evidence for this change in trunk erectness was found in the decrease in the EMG discharge pattern of the rectus abdominis muscle. The amount of action from the abdominal muscle began to lessen about a month after independent walking was achieved.[3]

ARM ACTION

The arms begin to unlock from an abducted, elbow-flexed position and are gradually lowered and held at the sides of the body (Fig. 2–4). This change in arm position frequently accompanies the narrowing of the dynamic base. Once lowered, the arms begin to swing. The swing might be confined initially to flexion at the elbow during contralateral leg swing.[4] Within a few months of the start of independent walking, reciprocal arm swing is present. The arms are swung in opposition to leg action by most children by the age of 18 months.[29]

EVALUATION OF PROGRESS IN WALKING

Walking is an extremely complex skill despite the surface simplicity. Adult form for the skill may not be achieved until as late as mid-adolescence, depending upon the stringency and nature of the criteria used in the evaluation of progress.[3,14] The most elementary and utilitarian method is careful observation of the configuration of the pattern that the child uses in walking. A feature-by-feature comparison of that pattern with the model of adult form shows that a child typically progresses to the point at which his pattern of walking barely demonstrates the presence of the obvious elements in mature gait, most especially proper knee-foot action and arm swing. A majority of children have reached this level by two years of age, and detectable improvement in the segmental pattern as well as in rhythm and coordination continues to occur for another 2 to 3 years (Fig. 2–5). When the child is 4 or 5 years old, the utility of the observation method is lost as a means of discerning subtle refinements in the configuration of walking patterns. There does not seem to be any difference in gait between the child and the adult at that point.[7] However, it has been demonstrated in a number of ways that improvement in walking actually does continue for several years.

Okamoto used electromyography to study progress in walking skill.[22] He measured progress in terms of changes in the functional mechanisms of the muscles used. Infants, without exception, used their muscles inefficiently. They timed contractions improperly and used muscles that did not contribute directly to the movement pattern as they began to walk without support. Characteristics of the infantile pattern were disappearing at the end of the second year, and the adult form of leg action was being acquired. From that time on, the discharge patterns of the muscles involved in many of the movement characteristics began to show similarities to the adult pattern. Based on his electromyographic data, Okamoto concluded that the period around the third year is the most important for the transition to the adult pattern. He found partial contractions of unnecessary muscles until the sixth year, but by the seventh year most had disappeared and the discharge patterns were almost identical to those of the adult.

Additional information regarding developmental changes in EMG patterns during walking is becoming accessible. The new information has broadened the base for comparisons that help assess specific neuromuscular progress. The following are findings from one such study:

There is no change with age in gluteus medius activity. With increasing age, the gluteus maximus shows a slight trend toward shortening of the time that it is active during stance phase. The vastus medialis also shows a reduction in the time that it is active during both stance phase and swing phase as age increases, while the tibialis anterior shows a gradual reduction in the time it is active during stance phase as age advances. The gastrocnemius-soleus complex has normal adult phasic activity from two through seven years old, but the children who were one year and one and one-half years old showed late swing-phase and premature stance-phase activity of this muscle. Both the medial and lateral hamstrings of the children show prolonged stance-phase activity compared with adults, but the activity gradually decreases with increasing age.[29]

Thus, the muscles that are primarily responsible for some of the developmental changes have been identified and, when proper equipment is available, can be monitored for progress toward the mature neuromuscular pattern.

Progress in walking can also be evaluated by measuring changes in the magnitude and the timing of movements in the pattern. Grieve and Gear verified that the very young child shows no consistency of timing in his walking pattern and is unpredictable in the way in which he changes speed.[9] One consistent aspect found in the young child's immature walking behavior was a predictable relationship between the time of swing and length of stride. Progress can be measured in terms of this feature. Grieve and Gear traced the progression of change from a positive relationship between the time of swing and the relative speed of walking, through a reversal to a negative regression between the time of swing and relative speed. Gradual changes of this sort cannot be observed directly but must be the result of careful measurement and calculation. Another change that must be measured rather than observed visually is the decrease in the proportion of time spent in stance. Because of the characteristic period of double support, the percentage of time in the whole walking cycle spent in stance remains larger than in swing, but the relative amount becomes progressively less.

It has been mentioned that mature patterns of joint angles and basic coordination of arms and legs can be observed in most children who have reached the age of 3 years. Unless these features can be determined precisely, they have diminished value in assessing progress in walking as age increases. An alternative is available from Sutherland et al. who suggested five important variables that are determinants of mature gait.[29] Each variable is influenced dramatically by the normal increase in limb length and by improvement in neuromuscular control, and each is a useful measure of progress. The variables are the following: (1) cadence, which decreases with age; (2) walking velocity, which increases with age; (3) step length, which increases with age; (4) duration of single limb stance, which increases in percentage with age; and (5) ratio of pelvic span to ankle spread, which increases with age at a diminishing rate.[29] Cadence, walking velocity, and step length are the easiest of the five variables on which to collect data.

MATURE PATTERN OF WALKING

To appreciate the special features that characterize the development of gait during childhood, one must have the characteristics of adult gait clearly in mind.[1]

In the adult pattern of walking (Figs. 2–6 and 2–7), the weight of the body is supported alternately by right and left legs with both legs contributing support during the transitional phases. There is a smooth cycle of alternating single and double leg supports during forward translation

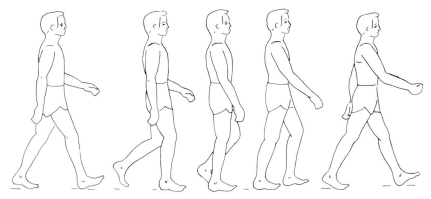

Fig. 2–6. Mature pattern of walking—lateral view. Key features are heel-strike, "double knee lock," and coordinated arm swing.

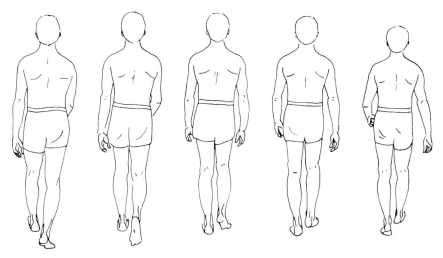

Fig. 2–7. Mature pattern of walking—posterior view. Dynamic base is narrow and arm opposition is reflex-controlled.

of the body. The rhythmic shifting of support from right leg, to both legs, to left leg, and back to both legs produces three-dimensional movement of the walker's center of gravity. While his center of gravity is moving forward, it is simultaneously moving upward or downward and toward one side or the other, depending upon which is the primary support side. If the gait is normal and the pace is moderate, the total vertical displacement for a full cycle in the average adult pattern is less than 2 inches, and the total lateral displacement is approximately the same.[23] The displacement of the center of gravity of the body during walking can be effectively controlled only if all elements of the pattern are properly coordinated.

LEG ACTION DURING STANCE PHASE

A leg is in the stance phase of the walking cycle from the instant of heel-strike until the moment of toe lift. While in stance it proceeds through the "double knee lock" sequence, which helps control the peak of the arc of the movement of the center of gravity and also helps maintain continuity of forward motion. At heel-strike, the hip is moderately flexed, the knee is straight, and the ankle is in a neutral position. Immediately after heel-strike, the foot begins to plantarflex, and the knee begins to flex. This action is continued for the brief time it takes for the foot to come into full contact with the supporting surface. Then reversal begins with dorsiflexion of the foot and extension at the knee. There is extension at the hip throughout most of the stance phase. About halfway through the support phase, the heel begins to rise from the contacting surface, and shortly thereafter the swing leg enters stance with heel-strike. The back support leg then makes its final contribution to forward motion with foot extension as the leg begins to flex first at the knee and then at the hip.

LEG ACTION DURING SWING PHASE

In the transition from the stance to the swing phase, all adult lower limb patterns are characterized by a stereotyped sequence of reversal in the direction of rotation, with the knee flexing first, the hip second, and the ankle last. This particular sequence of movements, along with a small amount of toe elevation in the early part of the swing phase, contributes to the ease of clearance. When the walking surface has been cleared by the foot of the swing leg, flexion at the ankle ceases, and action at the knee which already had abruptly been reversed from flexion to extension continues. The early beginning of extension at the knee during forward swing allows the foot to be brought into the heel-strike position with a minimum of flexion at the hip.

For normal adults, flexion-extension reversals in one leg "occur no less than 10 times within the brief span of a walking cycle." Furthermore, the hip, knee, and ankle of a leg rarely flex or extend in the same direction at the same time. "Thus the complex movement patterns of walking entail the ability to flex one joint as adjacent joints are extending, and vice versa. One cannot help being impressed with the sensory-motor control required to produce such coordinated movement.[17] One also cannot fail to see the relationship between this complex coordination and the delay in fully acquiring all aspects of mature gait.

PELVIC AND THORACIC ROTATION

Measurable amounts of pelvic rotation are not always present in normal gait, but some rotation usually occurs and the action becomes important as walking velocity is increased. The pelvis rotates backward on the side of the support leg and forward on the side of the swing leg. At the same time that the pelvis is rotating, it is shifting laterally toward the support leg and is tilting downward on the side of the swing leg. Both lateral shift and lateral tilt increase in amount until midstance and then the process is smoothly reversed. These two adjustments in pelvic motion minimize displacement of the center of gravity in the frontal plane during walking.

Thoracic rotation normally accompanies pelvic rotation and occurs in the counter direction. Although its function is to counterbalance pelvic rotation, thoracic rotation usually is less in total amount.

ACTION OF ARMS

Arms swing reflexly in opposition to leg action. The direction of arm swing is slightly medialward, but it continues to be basically in the anteroposterior plane. Movement occurs at both the shoulder and elbow of each arm. There is more than twice as much flexion as there is extension at the shoulder during a normal walking pace. Approximately the same total amount of flexion-extension takes place at the elbow, and it occurs in the same pattern. There is flexion during the forward swing and extension during the backward swing.

The configuration of the adult pattern of walking shows smoothness, rhythm, and uniformity, but despite the external appearance, the adult pattern lacks perfection, as is the case with all mature motor skill patterns. Ismail used a force platform to analyze the walking patterns of a group of adult males who had normal gaits.[10] He discovered that the force traces for the right and the left foot for a given individual are not identical and concluded that in adult normal gait one foot is favored over the other. Apparently this minor deviation from uniform force production does not adversely affect the normality or effectiveness of adult gait. There are many other minor deviations in the parameters of normal gait that are similarly benign.[15,18,19,30]

EFFECT OF VELOCITY ON GAIT

Adult gait is most certainly a highly integrated pattern of movement. This is true to the extent that changes in one parameter, such as walking speed, produce changes in the overall pattern of movement.[1] Since people normally walk at a variety of speeds, it is reasonable to expect changes in most aspects of the walking pattern when speed is either increased or decreased.

Some insight into the specific effects of increasing the speed of walking can be gained by examining the results of a major study involving 60 normal males, representing five age categories between 20 and 65 years.[19] Forward walking speed for 30 persons in the group was increased from an average velocity of 115 cm/sec to 218 cm/sec. This 44% increase was accomplished by taking 22% more steps per minute and by taking strides that were 19% longer. These changes resulted in alterations in nearly every aspect of gait (Fig. 2–8). In summary, the changes were the following: a decrease in the time spent in all phases of the walking cycle, with the time in a swing phase decreasing less than the time in either stance or double support phase; an 18% increase in stride width with less uniformity in this feature; a slight decrease

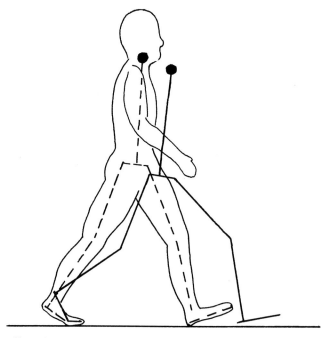

Fig. 2–8. Effect of increased speed on the movement pattern used in walking. The solid lines represent fast speed and the broken lines normal speed. (Redrawn from American Journal of Physical Medicine 45:8–24, 1966. © 1966, The Williams and Wilkins Co., Baltimore.)

in the amount of outtoeing; an increase in the amount of hip flexion, so that the total thigh excursion was greater; greater knee flexion at heel-strike and in early stance; a slight decrease in ankle flexion during stance and a slight increase during swing; a considerable increase in ankle extension and heel rise for the support foot at the moment of opposite leg heel-strike; a higher toe kick at the end of the swing phase but a lower toe point at heel-strike; an increase in forward pelvic tilt; a 43% increase in pelvic rotation and a 31% increase in counter-direction thoracic rotation; and an increase in total vertical excursion and a decrease in total lateral excursion. These changes would not seem so significant if they were expressed merely in terms of centimeters or degrees, so some have been highlighted by expressing them in terms of percentage of change.

Similar relationships between speed of walking and various gait parameters have been reported elsewhere.[1,5,9,12] One additional change, foot-ground reaction force, has not yet been mentioned in this discussion but it is receiving increasingly more attention. In normal walking, an adult exerts a maximum foot-ground force by each foot that is more than total body weight.[11] That maximum peak appears twice in the force wave, once at heel-strike and again at toe-off. The maximum amount of force varies, being less in unenergetic walking and more in vigorous, fast-speed walking. Vertical force amplitudes have been found to vary linearly with velocity[1] and the same has been reported for some of the lateral and fore-aft force amplitudes.[1,12]

The extensiveness of the observed alterations in adult gait parameters due to increase in the speed of walking leaves little doubt about either the effect of speed on gait or the interrelatedness of the features of the movement pattern. Nevertheless, it should be remembered that the adult pattern can be used effectively as a basic model for making observational judgments concerning rudimentary developmental changes in gait.

SEX AND AGE FACTORS IN GAIT

Normal adult men and women have gait patterns that are similar in configuration but quite different in dimension.[15,20,21] For example, in the groups studied by Murray et al.,[21] the men had fast-speed stride lengths 106% of their height while the women has stride lengths only 93% of their height. Because of the interrelatedness of gait parameters, the shorter strides produced less excursion in all measurements for the women. Two particularly telling differences were the smaller total excursion in hip flexion-extension and the lesser amount of transverse pelvic rotation.

In the upper range of age, 65 years and older, the dimensional differences in gait between men and women remain.[20,21] In addition, both sexes show what has been identified as a possible senile or presenile pattern. Characteristic of this pattern are decreases in speed of walking, length of stride, ankle-knee-hip saggital rotations, shoulder flexion, elbow extension, and swing to stance ratio. It also includes increases in stride width and outtoeing. Some of these changes suggest a reversion to the gait pattern used by infants when they are just beginning to deal with the problems of unsupported walking.

REFERENCES

1. Andriacchi, T.P., Ogle, J.A., and Galante, J.O.: Walking speed as a basis for normal and abnormal gait measurements. J. Biomech., 10:261, 1977.
2. Beck, R.D.: The influence of stature and age on the walking patterns of normal young children. Unpublished doctoral dissertation. Urbana, University of Illinois, 1979.
3. Bernstein, N.A.: The Coordination and Regulation of Movements. Oxford, Pergamon Press, 1967.
4. Burnett, C.N., and Johnson, E.W.: Development of gait in childhood. Part II. Dev. Med. Child Neurol., 13:207, 1971.
5. Cavanagh, P.R., and Gregor, R.J.: Knee joint torque during the swing phase of normal treadmill walking. J. Biomech., 8:327, 1975.
6. Engel, G.M., and Staheli, L.T.: The natural history of torsion and other factors influencing gait in childhood. Clin. Orthop., 99:12, 1974.
7. Foley, C.D., Quanbury, A.O., and Steinke, T.: Kinematics of normal childhood locomotion—a statistical study based on TV data. J. Biomech., 12:1, 1979.
8. Gesell, A.: The ontogenesis of infant behavior. In Manual of Child Psychology. Edited by L. Carmichael, New York, John Wiley, and Sons, 1954.
9. Grieve, D.W., and Gear, R.J.: The relationship between length of stride, step frequency, time of swing and speed of walking for children and adults. Ergonomics, 9:379, 1966.
10. Ismail, A.H.: Analysis of normal gaits utilizing a special force platform. In Medicine and Sport. Vol. 2: Biomechanics. Edited by J. Wartenweiler, E. Jokl, and M. Hebbelinck. Baltimore, University Park Press, 1968.
11. Jacobs, N.A., Skorecki, J., and Charnley, J.: Analysis of the vertical component of force in normal and pathological gait. J. Biomech., 5:11, 1972.
12. Jansen, E.C., and Jansen, K.F.: Vis-velocitas-via: alteration of foot-to-ground forces during increasing speed of gait. In Biomechanics VI-A. Edited by E. Asmussen. Baltimore, University Park Press, 1978.
13. Kazai, N., Okamoto, T., and Kumamoto, M.: Electromyographic study of supported walking of infants in the initial period of learning to walk. In Biomechanics V-A. Edited by P.V. Komi. Baltimore, University Park Press, 1976.
14. Kurochkin, Y.V., Alyakin, L.N., and Sinitzky, Y.F.: Characterization of walking of children by data of podography and electrogoniometry. Ortop. Travmatol. Protez., 35:44, 1974.
15. Larsson, L., et al.: The phases of the stride and their interaction in human gait. Scand. J. Rehabil. Med., 12:107, 1980.
16. Mann, R.A., and Hagy, J.: Biomechanics of walking, running, and sprinting. J. Sports Med., 8:5, 1980.
17. Murray, M.P.: Gait as a total movement pattern. Am. J. Phys. Med., 46:1, 1967.
18. Murray, M.P., Drought, A.B., and Kory, R.C.: Walking patterns of normal men. J. Bone Joint Surg., 46-A:2, 1964.
19. Murray, M.P., Kory, R.C., Clarkson, B.H., and Sepic, S.B.: Comparison of free and fast speed walking patterns of normal men. Am. J. Phys. Med., 45:1, 1966.
20. Murray, M.P., Kory, R., and Clarkson, B.: Walking patterns in healthy old men. J. Gerontol., 24:169, 1969.
21. Murray, M.P., Kory, R., and Sepic, S.: Walking patterns of normal women. Arch. Phys. Med., 51:637, 1970.
22. Okamoto, T.: Electromyographic study of the learning process of walking in 1- and 2-year-old infants. In Medicine and Sport. Vol. 8: Biomechanics III. Edited by E. Jokl. Basel, Karger, 1973.

23. Saunders, J.B., Inman, V.T., and Eberhart, H.D.: The major determinants in normal and pathological gait. J. Bone Joint Surg., 35-A:543, 1953.
24. Scrutton, D.S.: Footprint sequences of normal children under five years old. Dev. Med. Child Neurol., 11:44, 1969.
25. Scrutton, D.S., and Robson, P.: The gait of 50 normal children. Physiotherapy, 54:363, 1968.
26. Shapiro, H.: The development of walking in a child. J. Genet. Psychol., 100:221, 1962.
27. Shirley, M.M.: The First Two Years: A Study of Twenty-Five Babies. Vol. 1: Postural and Locomotor Development. Minneapolis, University of Minnesota Press, 1931.
28. Statham, L., and Murray, M.P.: Early walking patterns of normal children. Clin. Orthop., 79:8, 1971.
29. Sutherland, D.H., Olshen, R., Cooper, L., and Woo, S.L.: The development of mature gait. J. Bone Joint Surg., 62-A:3, 1980.
30. Zuniga, E.N., and Leavitt, L.A.: Analysis of gait: a method of measurement. *In* Biomechanics IV. Edited by R. Nelson and C. Morehouse. Baltimore, University Park Press, 1974.

CHAPTER 3

Running

Running is a vigorous form of locomotion and a natural extension of the basic skill of walking. In the previous chapter, walking was described as a pattern in which one foot moves ahead of the other and the heel of the forward foot touches the ground before the toe of the opposite foot pushes off. The distinguishing factor in running is a phase in which the body is propelled through space with no support from either leg. According to Slocum and James, "Running is really a series of smoothly coordinated jumps during which the body weight is borne on one foot, becomes airborne, is then carried on the opposite foot and again becomes airborne."[51] Bare satisfaction of the nonsupport requirement for running produces a version commonly known to adults as jogging. This simple form is characterized by a slow pace, a short stride, and a bouncing motion. Running at increasingly greater velocities leads progressively to the ultimate version, sprinting.

PERFORMANCE TRENDS IN RUNNING

Few investigators have been concerned with the objective measurement of the running speed of preschool children. The performances of children in this age group tend to be erratic, and there is reason to believe that some of the younger ones do not fully grasp the concept of sprint effort. Nevertheless, it is generally accepted that during the preschool age period they undergo a progressive increase in their speed of running. By the age of 5, most children have developed reasonably acceptable running form and understand what it means to run as fast as they can.

Procedures for testing the running speed of school children have not been consistent from one study to another. They have included sprinting for distances ranging from 30 to 50 yards and have provided for standing as well as running starts. The results obviously are not directly comparable, but when considered in toto they are informative and give shape to the total picture of running performance. A summary of studies regarding the motor performances of elementary school children shows a consistent year-to-year improvement in running speed for both boys and girls from age 5 to age 11. Boys tend to have the edge over girls, but at ages 5, 6, and 7 their performances are quite similar.[19,32] This basic performance pattern is supported by the AAHPER Fitness Test norms, which show year-to-year improvement in the 50 yard dash and a slight advantage for males ages 9 through 14.

Data from some of the more recent research on running, especially from the investigations of preschool and primary grade children, show either no difference in performance between boys and girls or a minor advantage for boys.[23,31,42,47] Racial difference in running speed has also been a factor under investigation. Although there is some indication that black children perform at a higher level than white children on short sprint events,[35,42,45] findings on this point are not unanimous.[13,23,33]

DEVELOPMENT OF RUNNING SKILL

Running is a natural part of the development of human locomotion, and it is a skill that appears at an early age. Before a child can run, he learns to walk independently and acquires the additional abilities necessary to deal with the demands of the new skill. The child must have sufficient strength to propel himself upward and forward into the non-support phase with one leg. He must also possess the ability to coordinate the faster movements required in the running stride and retain his balance in the process. According to Gesell, these abilities or capacities are not generally present before 18 months of age, but by the age of 2 years most children can run well enough to satisfy the minimum standard.[24]

The transition from one upright locomotor skill to another is not necessarily a smooth one. It has been observed by Burnett and Johnson that "the first attempts to run take on all the characteristics of the immature walk even though walking is observed to be mature."[6] Characteristic aspects of the reversion are widening of the base, abduction of the arms to the high guard position, landing with a flat foot, and having knee extension at midsupport. Their explanation for the turnabout involved Gesell's concept of *reciprocal interweaving* during development in which there is alternation from mature to immature stages.[25] Adjustments by most children are made soon after the skill is acquired in its most rudimentary form (Fig. 3–1), and a continuous process of refinement ensues, resulting from the combined influences of maturation and learning (Fig. 3–2). The process may extend well into puberty,[3] but such a protracted delay is usually associated with children who are not normal rather than with those who are.

The child begins by running in a straight line, which is the easiest use of the new skill. During play in the preschool years there is an increasing demand for the ability to change direction quickly, to dodge,

Fig. 3–1. Running form of an 18-month-old boy.

and to stop abruptly. Gradually the skill of running improves, not only in terms of the speed of body movement, but also in terms of the ability to run in variable patterns and on different surfaces and terrains. Harper studied several variables in the technique used by 5-year-old boys and girls to change direction 180° from a full speed run.[27] She found differences in the technique used in the performances, yet 78% of the reversals were to the left, all were accomplished in 4 to 8 steps, and boys and girls did not differ significantly in either running velocity or reversal time.

KINETICS AND KINEMATICS OF DEVELOPMENTAL PATTERNS

The kinds of problems that arise in connection with the development of throwing, jumping, striking, and other basic skills seem to be missing

Fig. 3–2.   Running pattern of a 3-year-old boy using effective leg action.

in the development of running. Unless the child is handicapped, he begins to run without fanfare, and ordinarily displays a form that draws little attention. For many years the systematic study of the development of running was neglected, but that situation has changed. A growing concern to know more about normal and effective movement has stimulated research in the mechanics of most fundamental skills, including running. Research over the past quarter century has made a significant contribution to the understanding of the developmental changes in the patterns of running that parallel the yearly improvements in speed.

Nine studies have been particularly helpful in defining the developmental changes in running patterns. The studies contain cross-sectional and longitudinal data, cover a reasonably wide age range, and focus on most of the important features of running. Clouse (1959) analyzed the running patterns of 6 carefully selected preschool boys, ages $1\frac{1}{2}$ to $5\frac{1}{2}$ years.[8] Dittmer (1962) selected 2 good and 2 poor female runners on the basis of time and studied the girls yearly from age 6 to age 10.[14] Fortney (1964) selected 4 second-grade boys who were above average, 4 who were average, and 4 who were below average in running speed and studied the changes in the action of the swing leg over a 5-year period.[21] Glassow, Rarick, and Halverson (1965) did a cinematographic analysis of the running form of 15 boys and 15 girls randomly selected from the first-, third-, and fifth-grade children in their motor development study.[26] Beck (1966) focused on the path of the center of gravity of 12 good runners—4 boys from grades 1, 3, and 5—and analyzed the changes that had occurred after they passed on to grades 2, 4, and 6.[2] Mersereau (1974) noted the changes in the running patterns of 4 infant girls from age 22 to age 25 months.[40] Smith (1977) studied the running patterns of 3 girls and 2 boys whose performances had been filmed annually for periods varying from 5½ to 11 years.[52] Brown (1978) analyzed the patterns of 3 preschool, 4 kindergarten, 6 second-grade, and 6 fourth-grade girls whose performances were well above average for age.[5] Fortney (1980) included a kinetic analysis in her study of the running patterns of 6 2-year-olds, 12 4-year-olds, and 10 6-year-olds.[22] All the studies did not analyze the same aspects of running form but collectively they covered all the important features. Most of the findings were substantially in agreement and most of the developmental trends were remarkably similar. In summary, the major trends showed the following:

1. An increase in the length of the running stride.
2. A decrease in the relative amount of vertical movement in each stride.
3. An increase in hip, knee, and ankle extension at takeoff.
4. An increase in the proportion of time in the nonsupport phase of the stride.
5. An increase in the closeness of the heel to the buttock on the forward swing.
6. An increase in the height of the forward knee at takeoff.
7. A decrease in the relative distance that the support foot is ahead of the center of gravity of the body at contact.

The better runners in an age group show greater progress in the variables identified in the developmental trends (Figs. 3–3 and 3–4). However, all children seem to follow these developmental trends regardless of how they are classified in terms of running speed within an age group.

A few findings in the studies previously cited touch on developmental features that are less obvious but nevertheless merit attention. The 4 female infants studied by Mersereau when they were 22-months-old and later when they were 25-months-old were airborne longer following takeoff from the left foot than from the right foot at first test but the inconsistency in support time had diminished 4 months later.[40] The uneven leg action typical of early walking patterns seems to be present in early running patterns as well. It is not unusual for an infant to get into flight after push-off from one foot but not the other or to have erratic into-flight excursions. Mersereau also found a slight increase in the distance the swing foot contacted the ground ahead of the body. This finding was modest verification that the trend toward bringing the foot closer under the body's center of gravity is preceded briefly by a change in the opposite direction. Progress in running performance is

Fig. 3–3.   A 5-year-old girl with well-coordinated arm and leg action but typically limited range of motion.

Fig. 3–4.   A 5-year-old boy demonstrating arm and leg movements more advanced than those used by the girl in Figure 3–3.

rapid and these features are rarely, if ever, actually noticed, but it is well to note their existence.

Fortney found developmental trends in many of the parameters of the running patterns of the 2-, 4-, and 6-year-old children she studied and at the same time found significant differences in several of the parameters between the 2-year-olds and the other two groups.[22] Her findings suggest that changes are proportionately greater before the age of four than in successive years. They also give support to the notion that running is one of the fundamental motor patterns reasonably well established by the preschool period. In connection with the kinematic analysis, Fortney found significant differences between boys and girls in five aspects of swing leg action, yet the groups did not differ in running velocity. Unfortunately, the reason for the sex differences in leg swing was unexplained by the data. Fortney's kinetic data produced vertical force curves for the three groups that showed the same basic shape with an impact peak and a thrust peak. Her data also revealed a surprising amount of impact force by the foot at landing. The peak was 2.2 times body weight for the 2-year-olds, 3.9 times body weight for the 4-year-olds, and 3.4 times body weight for the 6-year-olds. The amounts for the four- and six-year-old groups were unexpectedly large and exceeded the relative impact force reported for adult runners. The peak vertical force at thrust, however, was less for the three groups than for adults and the 2.0, 2.4, and 2.6 times body weight figures showed a developmental trend. The horizontal forces during the braking and propulsive phases were much smaller than the vertical forces for all groups, and the forces in both phases were significantly larger for the 4- and 6-year-olds than for the 2-year-olds. The similarities in the force curves for children at a given age seemed to support Mersereau's conclusion that they form "bands" of temporal organization that describe the general movement characteristics of the age group.[41]

Smith's longitudinal study of 3 girls and 2 boys indicated that stride rate did not increase with velocity or age as was expected according to the results of other reports.[52] Her data did show that as age and velocity increased, the relative contribution of stride length and stride rate to running speed changed. Before the age of 9, stride rate was the greater contributor. The long range change in stride rate, or in any other parameter for which there is contradictory or scant evidence, must be clarified by studying the performances of larger numbers of children. Until that is done, the parameters are of little value in the assessment of developmental progress.

Until now, developmental running form has been studied almost exclusively from the side view and analysis has been limited mostly to the movements of the legs. Important rotatory movements occurring around the vertical axis of the body can be observed effectively only when the perspective is changed by moving the vantage point 90° for a frontal or dorsal view of the runner. From this angle, twisting and turning movements involving the arms, trunk, and legs appear to be natural and essential to the movement pattern of running. Unfortunately, the literature on motor pattern development contains no precise information on the nature of these rotatory movements and their influence on developmental form. The observations that follow, therefore, must be considered tentative and open to modification following further study.

During the earliest stages of running, the movement pattern seems to be characterized by extensive movements around the long axis of the body. The extent to which some of the exaggerated movements can be observed depends on the willingness of the child to run with full effort. The 24-month-old boy in Figure 3–5 was running with unusual

Fig. 3–5. Posterior view of a 24-month-old boy running with unusual effort. His speed produces precarious balance, which he counters by arm movements in the horizontal plane. The outward swing of the knee of his recovery leg is also apparent.

Fig. 3–6. Exaggerated rotation during the beginning of the swing phase causes the foot of the recovery leg to cross the midline before passing under the trunk.

abandon and had difficulty maintaining balance at the rapid pace. Some aspects of his leg action illustrate movements that appear commonly in the running patterns of young children and with progressively less frequency in the patterns of older children. The movements of the recovery leg are particularly interesting when viewed from the back. The knee of the recovery leg swings outward and then around and forward in preparation for the support phase. In children who have just learned to run, this knee action is accompanied by a toeing-out of the foot of the recovery leg. Aside from the natural tendency for the child to abduct his foot, the toeing-out appears to be a possible adjustment that allows the foot to be swung forward without being raised more than a few inches. Later, when the outward rotatory movement of the knee is more vigorous, the recovery foot first crosses the midline of the body before moving around and forward (Fig. 3–6). These exaggerated leg and foot movements are lessened progressively as skill improves. A regular increase in the length of the running stride contributes significantly to the elimination of some of the less productive rotatory leg movements. The decrease in amount of outward knee swing and the corresponding decrease in medial foot swing could be added tentatively to the developmental trends observed from the side view.

Arm movements in the running pattern have been classified predominantly as automatic reactions. For every action by the legs in a developmental running pattern there seems to be an accompanying and predictable reaction by the arms. For example, in the earliest stage of running when pace is slow and the legs are relatively straight (Fig. 3–1), the arms bend very little. During the same period when the stride is short, the arcs through which the arms swing are also short. When the knee of the recovery leg swings out to the side and then forward, the opposite arm makes an exaggerated forward hooking motion toward the midline of the body. If the support leg is straight and thrusting

Fig. 3–7. Children of various ages demonstrating similar arm patterns. From left, one-and one-half-year old, 2-year-old, 2-year-old, 5-year old, 4-year-old, 3-year-old, and 6-year-old. The arm on the forward swing crosses the midline of the body, and the opposite arm swings outward and then loops inward at the end of the backswing.

vigorously, the opposite arm remains relatively straight and swings obliquely outward to balance the heavier lever and to balance the outwardly swinging knee. The persistence of these basic adjustive arm actions at different ages is emphasized in Figure 3–7. The arm moves outward and backward while remaining nearly straight and loops inward at the back end of the arc. On the forward swing, the arm moves closer to the trunk, bends more at the elbow, and swings quickly toward the midline of the body. Minor differences in the amount and type of arm movement can be observed, but the similarities are more apparent. They suggest several trends in the developmental form of arm action in running:

1. The hand hooks less toward the midline of the trunk at the end of the forward swing, and the arm loops outward less on the backswing.
2. The arms swing through a longer arc in the anteroposterior plane.
3. The arms are bent more toward a right angle at the elbow.

These trends represent development toward what is regarded generally as a mature pattern of arm action in running. They do not include the immature high and middle guard arm positions in which the arms are used chiefly to help maintain balance.

MATURE PATTERN OF RUNNING

The study of developmental running patterns has been based upon the performances of children attempting to run at maximum velocity because it is the sprint pace that has been used as a basis for determining mature running form. A compelling reason for using the sprint is the relatively constant type of performance that it yields.[10,12] The high degree of effort required[17] produces maximum movement and a reasonably stable pattern both in kinematic and in kinetic parameters.[38]

In a complete cycle of the running pattern, each leg goes through a support phase and a recovery phase, and the full sequence produces two periods of nonsupport. The essentials of the mature pattern (Fig. 3–8) can be summarized as follows:

1. The knee and ankle of the support leg bend slightly after the foot has made contact with the ground.
2. Action of the support leg at the hip, knee, and ankle propels the body forward and upward into the nonsupport phase.
3. As the recovery leg swings forward to a high knee raise, the lower part of the leg is flexed, bringing the heel close to the buttock.
4. Extension at the hip and knee of the recovery leg causes the foot to move backward rapidly and contact the ground approximately flat and under the body's center of gravity.

Fig. 3–8. *Upper.* Mature pattern used in running at the sprint pace. *Lower.* College track men running at different paces during competition—880 pace at left, 2 mile pace at right.

5. The trunk maintains a slight forward lean throughout the stride pattern.
6. Both arms swing through a large arc in an oblique vertical plane and in synchronized opposition to the leg action.

The outlined pattern agrees fundamentally with the findings of many studies in which various aspects of sprinting form were examined in depth. The evidence that has been provided by these studies is particularly applicable in a more detailed examination of the various parts of the basic pattern.

THE FORWARD TRUNK LEAN

The forward trunk lean is slightly greater in sprinting than in running at any lesser pace, but the trunk should still be nearly erect. The sprinter must adjust for the additional amount of air resistance he encounters when running at top speed and he must position his pelvis during propulsion to allow for the full, effective flexion and extension of his legs. Altfillisch in an early study reported a forward lean of 20 to 25° from the vertical but did not indicate the means for measuring the angle.[1] More recent measurements of trunk lean indicate that it is less than 10°, depending to some extent on pace.[28] Some of the confusion regarding this aspect of form can be attributed to a misunderstanding of the difference between forward trunk lean and total body angle at takeoff. Dyson suggested that there is an illusion of exaggerated forward lean in sprinting due to the extreme body position at the moment the propulsive leg is thrusting the body into flight.[15] The angle of the total body, including the propulsive leg, measured at the push-off is quite different from the angle of forward trunk lean. James and Brubaker explain that "excessive forward lean reduces mobility of the lumbar spine-pelvic unit, reduces hip flexion relative to the running surface, prevents maximum forward placement of the recovery foot, places excessive stress on the foot at foot strike, and requires additional effort from the postural muscles to maintain balance."[30]

THE ARM ACTION

Arm action in running is compensatory and synchronous with the action of the legs. Because the leg action in sprinting is forceful and extensive, the arms must move in like manner. The hand swings nearly to shoulder level and slightly toward the midline of the body on the forward swing, and the elbow reaches almost as high on the back swing, bringing the hand back beyond the hip. Both shoulders might be raised slightly at the ends of the swing because of the forceful and extreme arm movement but this elevation should be achieved without producing unnecessary tension.

During the forward-backward excursion of the arms, the angle of the elbow changes somewhat in many expert sprinters. The angle increases on the downward movement of the backward swing and decreases to about a right angle on the upward swing of the backward movement. This position is retained on the forward swing until just before the end when the angle tends to decrease slightly. Altfillisch found a difference of approximately 6 inches in the height of the path of the hand during forward and backward swings.[1] According to his findings, the path of the wrist was below the hip line on the backward swing and above it on the forward swing. It is reasonable to expect the arm to straighten a bit on the downward part of the backswing because the leg with which it is in opposition has its greatest vertical leverage during that phase of the stride, and the slightly extended arm is a better compensating lever.

Less is known about arm action than almost any other aspect of sprinting. The lack of interest in learning more about it could be traced to its secondary role in the running pattern (to maintain balance),[36] or to the difficulty of studying a three-dimensional movement. Current evidence suggests that arm action is probably the most individualized and variable feature of the running pattern regardless of velocity.

CONTACT BY THE SUPPORT FOOT

The support foot contacts the ground approximately under the body's center of gravity. If contact is ahead of or behind this point during the full sprint stride, the effectiveness of leg propulsion is diminished. Contact ahead of the optimum point produces a braking effect, and contact behind it reduces the range of propulsive effort. If the runner's foot contacts the ground at an effective point relative to his center of gravity, his foot is virtually flat when it lands.

The evidence on precisely how the foot lands is not in full agreement. Practically all of the 33 sprinters studied by Fenn came down flat-footed or slightly on the heel when running at full speed.[20] A few runners touched down on the side of the foot, presumably because of the tendency for the foot to supinate in the nonsupport position and to land on or near the midline of the body. Nett's analysis of film showing Olympic-class sprinters revealed that the ball of the foot touches fractionally before the rest of the sole and confirmed that the heel subsequently contacts the ground.[44] Less uniformity in footfall was shown by the 24 runners filmed at sprint pace by Mason.[39] The footfall distribution for the group was 8 heel-toe, 11 toe-heel-toe, and 5 toe only. Two other sprinters filmed running on a treadmill showed only toe contact.[37] Apparently the exact contact position of the support foot can vary slightly without either creating a braking effect or reducing the propulsion range at the ankle.

ACTION OF THE SUPPORT LEG

Immediately after the foot contacts the ground, the knee of the support leg bends slightly to stop the downward movement of the center of gravity and to allow the body weight to move forward smoothly with a minimum of wasteful upward and downward movement.[20] Bending at the knee after the foot has been planted has the additional effect of creating a favorable change at the ankle joint. The amount of dorsi-flexion at the ankle is increased before the beginning of extension, thereby increasing the effective distance over which the foot can thrust.

The actual propulsive force of the support leg is a backward, down-ward thrust produced by extension at the hip, the knee, and the ankle. This force raises the center of gravity slightly and pushes the body upward and forward into the nonsupport phase. The emphasis in sprinting is on the forward component of propulsive force, and this results in a long stride with a minimum of body rise.

ACTION OF THE LEG DURING RECOVERY

The vigorousness of the support leg thrust causes a slight contin-uation in extension at the hip after takeoff. Almost immediately after takeoff, the support leg goes into the important recovery, or swing, phase. The knee begins to swing forward quickly as the lower leg flexes, bringing the heel of the recovery leg close to the buttock. In effect, this bending action reduces the resistance leverage against the swinging leg, permitting it to move forward quickly, and at the same time "the vigorous forward swing of the recovery extremity increases ground reaction of the support extremity and enhances forward thrust."[30] The flexion of the knee is thought to be more passive than active, considering the muscular activity recorded at the hip and knee during the swing phase.[36]

The thigh of the recovery leg reaches the height of its forward swing at approximately the same time that the toe of the support leg leaves the ground. At that instant, the thigh of the swing leg begins to rotate backward, and the lower leg begins to extend. Just before the foot of the recovery leg contacts the ground, it is moving backward at a rate roughly equal to the forward speed of the body.[51] These adjustments, according to Dillman,[11] are essential in the effort to minimize the retarding effect at contact.

EFFECT OF SPEED ON RUNNING PATTERNS

The pattern of running obviously changes when the speed at which it is done is increased or decreased. Some of the changes in the adult pattern associated with increased speed are similar to the developmental trends already cited in the running patterns of children. The similarities should be apparent in the following discussion and the important differences will be mentioned.

STRIDE RATE AND STRIDE LENGTH

Because speed of running is a product of step rate and step length, an increase in either or both will produce an increase in velocity. However, the relationship with speed is not a direct one in the case of either parameter.[34] For adults, step length increases linearly up to a speed of about 7 m/sec and then levels off.[48] For a given individual, step length increases only to a maximum effective point and then goes no further in contributing toward increased speed. Step rate is the factor primarily responsible for greater velocity at higher running speeds. The relationship of stride rate to running speed is curvilinear and the curve continues upward after stride length has leveled off and stabilized at the higher speeds.[11]

The developmental trend that shows stride length increasing as running speed increases is in agreement with the relationship between the two parameters found at the adult level. A similar consistency does not exist for the relationship between stride rate and velocity. A clear-cut developmental trend has not been found, so a comparison with the adult relationship is not yet possible. The small amount of evidence on the stride rate of children indicates that it might increase, might remain essentially unchanged, or even decrease as running velocity increases. It is important to note that the children were studied only while sprinting and not while running at different speeds as the adults in the other studies have been.

TEMPORAL ELEMENTS

As stride rate increases, time of stride decreases in an inverse relationship for adult runners. A decrease in stride time is accompanied by changes in the relative amount of time spent in support and in nonsupport. Support time in a stride decreases and in-flight time increases. In one recent study contact time decreased from .38 seconds when running velocity was only 40% of maximum speed to .24 seconds when running was done at maximum speed.[34] The contact time variable is put in a broader velocity context by results from another study that showed the length of stance phase was 61% when walking at a 3-mph pace, 31% when running at a 12-mph pace, and 22% when sprinting at a 17.2-mph pace.[37]

Time in contact is another variable that seems to change as running velocity is increased during the developmental period. Beck[2] and Dittmer[14] found a small increase in stride time over a 1-year period even though there was an increase in running velocity. A conflicting observation was made by Smith who found a slight decrease in support time with increasing velocity for the five children she studied.[52] The small groups of children in these three longitudinal studies were tested only at maximum speed and changes were based on year-to-year comparisons. Certainly there is need for further investigation of the contradictory findings regarding the temporal components in developmental trends. This investigation should be performed using both cross-sectional and longitudinal data, variable speed protocols, and much larger groups of subjects.

VERTICAL MOVEMENT

After determining the amount of body rise of 18 college athletes running at various velocities, Rapp concluded that body rise and running speed are inversely related.[46] The same finding has been reported elsewhere. Top level sprinters in one study had a vertical oscillation of 10.9 cm when running at a speed of 3.9 m/sec and 6.7 cm when running at the faster pace of 9.3 m/sec.[34] The reduction in vertical oscillation of the body's center of gravity as running speed increases indicates the change to greater emphasis on forces that promote horizontal motion and relatively less on those that produce vertical motion.

LOWER LIMB ANGULAR DISPLACEMENT

There is some confusion over the changes in angular displacement that occur at the hip, knee, and ankle as running speed is increased.

The confusion can be traced primarily to differences resulting from the use of over-ground and treadmill protocols in research on running. Significant differences between the two methods have been found for both males and females when running speed reaches or exceeds 6 m/sec.[16,43] There are differences in stride length, stride rate, vertical displacement, and time in-flight, and these differences seem to have a bearing on the question of how much angular displacement actually occurs at lower limb joints as running speed increases. Investigators agree that total hip and total knee excursion increases as velocity is changed from a slow to a moderate pace.[29] Hip extension at takeoff increases slightly and hip flexion on the forward swing also increases. Knee extension during propulsion is greater[18] and knee flexion in the forward swing is larger.

A critical issue is what happens to knee extension during propulsion at higher speeds. Studies of adult runners show that in over-ground running, the knee goes nearly into complete extension just prior to takeoff at a fast but submaximal speed and does not extend further as pace is increased. Brandell reported a 175° knee angle at takeoff for a 6.2 m/sec runner and a 171° angle for a 8.9 m/sec runner.[4] When comparing the form of two international level sprinters, Dapnea noted incomplete knee extension at takeoff for the faster of the two and essentially complete extension for the other.[9] The few degrees of grace from full extension might be explained by Mann's observation of the runners in his study.[36] "As toe-off was approached, the knee extensors decreased in activity to protect the rapidly extending joint from forceful hyperextension."

The almost complete knee extension that is seen in rapid over-ground running is not found in fast treadmill running. The male subjects studied by Sinning and Forsyth *decreased* the maximum amount of knee extension at takeoff as treadmill speed was increased from 183 to 396 m/min.[50] The amount of knee extension at the higher velocity was approximately the same as the 160° maximum reported by Mann and Hagy for treadmill running at a 17.2-mph pace.[37]

The accumulation of research using the two protocols goes far beyond what has been presented here. It leads increasingly toward the conclusion that they are task-specific and not of equal value for dealing with the kinematics of sprinting.

SUPPORT FOOT

At lower speeds the support foot lands ahead of the body's center of gravity[7] and tends to contact the ground first with the heel. This part of the pattern changes as speed of translation is increased. When the body is moving forward at top speed, the recovery leg moves backward at a corresponding pace to provide contact at a point under the body's center of gravity and the resulting foot contact is flatter. The change in

Fig. 3–9.   Running form of a 9-year-old girl.

Fig. 3–10.   Running form of a 9-year-old boy.

Fig. 3–11.   Running form of a 3-year-old girl.

Fig. 3–12.   Running form of a 15-month-old child.

footfall from slow to sprint speed is significant, but the change at higher speeds has been found to be less variable. Sixteen of Mason's 24 skilled male runners kept the same footfall for fast distance and for sprint pace while 7 changed from heel-toe to toe-heel-toe and one changed to toe only for the increased pace.[39]

One additional change in foot support might appear if pace is increased to a great extent. The amount of outtoeing that helps in lateral stability during long-distance running sometimes changes and decreases as the demand for forward thrust is increased in sprinting.[51]

ANALYSIS OF FORM IN RUNNING

Key aspects of the movement pattern used in running can be observed quite easily because the pattern is repeated and the observer has successive opportunities to appraise each feature. When analyzing a runner's form (Figs. 3–9, 3–10, 3–11, and 3–12), one might ask the following specific questions:

1. Is the support leg practically straight at takeoff?
2. Does the heel of the swing leg come close to the buttock during recovery?
3. Does the knee rise well at the front of swing?
4. Does the foot land relatively flat and under the body?
5. Is the trunk basically upright with the head in proper alignment?
6. Do the arms swing slightly toward the midline with elbows bent?

The answers to these questions can disclose the more immature aspects of form but will not quantify the developmental level. Any of the first three questions will help with a general evaluation because all three deal with closely interrelated features of form.

In an effort to make motor pattern identification relatively uncomplicated for teachers, Seefeldt, Reuschlein, and Vogel presented developmental changes in running in the form of stages rather than as trends.[49] The stages, which can be found on page 19 in Chapter 1, were based upon mixed longitudinal data on approximately 150 children ranging in age from $1^1/_2$ to 8 years. If those stage descriptions are perused, it will be seen that they do not include all of the trends outlined earlier in this chapter. Rather, they highlight some movement characteristics that represent changes to more advanced levels of skill and are reasonably easy to observe.

REFERENCES

1. Altfillisch, J.: A mechanical analysis of starting and running. Unpublished master's thesis. Iowa City, University of Iowa, 1947.
2. Beck, M.: The path of the center of gravity during running in boys grades one to six. Unpublished doctoral dissertation. Madison, University of Wisconsin, 1966.
3. Bernstein, N.A.: The Coordination and Regulation of Movements. Oxford, Pergamon Press, 1967.
4. Brandell, B.: An analysis of muscle coordination in walking and running gaits. In Medicine and Sport. Biomechanics III. Edited by E. Jokl. Basel, Karger, 1973.
5. Brown, E.W.: Biomechanical analysis of the running patterns of girls three to ten years of age. Unpublished doctoral dissertation. Eugene, University of Oregon, 1978.
6. Burnett, C.N., and Johnson, E.W.: Development of gait in childhood. Part II. Dev. Med. Child Neurol., 13:207, 1971.
7. Cavanagh, P., Pollock, M., and Landa, J.: A biomechanical comparison of elite and good distance runners. Ann. N.Y. Acad. Sci., 301:328, 1977.
8. Clouse, F.: A kinematic analysis of the development of the running pattern of preschool boys. Unpublished doctoral dissertation. Madison, University of Wisconsin, 1959.
9. Dapnea, J.: Changes of speed in a sprint. Ath. J., 61:32, 1981.
10. Deshon, D.C., and Nelson, R.C.: A cinematographical analysis of sprint running. Res. Q. Am. Assoc. Health Phys. Educ., 35:451, 1964.
11. Dillman, C.J.: Effect of leg segmental movements on foot velocity during the recovery phase of running. In Biomechanics IV. Edited by R. Nelson and C. Morehouse. Baltimore, University Park Press, 1974.
12. Dillman, C.J.: Kinematic analyses of running. In Exercise and Sport Sciences Reviews. Vol. III. Edited by J.H. Wilmore and J. Keogh. New York, Academic Press, 1975.
13. DiLucci, J.M., and Shows, D.A.: A comparison of the motor performances of Black and Caucasian girls age 6–8. Res. Q. Am. Assoc. Health Phys. Educ., 48:4, 1977.
14. Dittmer, J.: A kinematic analysis of the development of the running pattern of grade school girls and certain factors which distinguish good from poor performance at the observed ages. Unpublished master's thesis. Madison, University of Wisconsin, 1962.
15. Dyson, G.: The Mechanics of Athletics. London, University of London Press, 1970.
16. Elliott, B.C., and Blanksby, B.A.: A cinematographic analysis of overground and treadmill running by males and females. Med. Sci. Sports, 8:2, 1976.
17. Elliott, B.C., and Blanksby, B.A.: The synchronization of muscle activity and body segment movements during a running cycle. Med. Sci. Sports, 11:4, 1979.
18. Elliott, B.C., and Blanksby, B.A.: A biomechanical analysis of the male jogging action. J. Hum. Mov. Studies, 5:42, 1979.

19. Espenschade, A.: Motor development. In Science and Medicine of Exercise and Sports. Edited by W. Johnson. New York, Harper and Brothers, 1960.
20. Fenn, W.O.: Work against gravity and work due to velocity changes in running. Am. J. Physiol., 93:433, 1930.
21. Fortney, V.: The swinging limb in running of boys ages seven through eleven. Unpublished master's thesis. Madison, University of Wisconsin, 1964.
22. Fortney, V.: The kinematics and kinetics of the running pattern of two- , four- , and six-year-old children. Unpublished doctoral dissertation. Lafayette, IN, Purdue University, 1980.
23. Frederick, S.D.: Performance of selected motor tasks by three- , four- , and five-year-old children. Unpublished doctor of physical education dissertation. Bloomington, Indiana University, 1977.
24. Gesell, A.: The First Five Years of Life. New York, Harper and Brothers, 1940.
25. Gesell, A.: The ontogenesis of infant behavior. In Manual of Child Psychology. Edited by L. Carmichael. New York, John Wiley and Sons, 1954.
26. Glassow, R.B., Halverson, L.E., and Rarick, G.L.: Improvement of motor development and physical fitness in elementary school children. Cooperative research project no. 696. Madison, University of Wisonsin, 1965.
27. Harper, C.: Movement responses of kindergarten children to a change of direction task—an analysis of selected measures. Unpublished master's thesis. Madison, University of Wisconsin, 1975.
28. Haven, B.H.: Changes in the running patterns of highly skilled women runners during competitive races. Unpublished doctor of physical education dissertation. Bloomington, Indiana University, 1977.
29. Hoshikawa, T., Matsui, H., and Miyashita, M.: Analysis of running pattern in relation to speed. In Medicine and Sport: Biomechanics III. Edited by E. Jokl. Basel, Karger, 1973.
30. James, S., and Brubaker, C.E.: Biomechanical and neuromuscular aspects of running. In Exercise and Sport Sciences Reviews. Vol. I. Edited by J.H. Wilmore. New York, Academic Press, 1973.
31. Johnson, W.: A comparison of motor creativity and motor performances of young children. Unpublished doctor of physical education dissertation. Bloomington, Indiana University, 1977.
32. Keogh, J.: Motor performance of elementary school children. Department of Physical Education, University of California, Los Angeles, 1965.
33. Lipe, L.M.: An investigation of aspiration and motor performance levels of negro and white sixth grade students. Unpublished doctor of education dissertation. Tallahassee, Florida State University, 1970.
34. Luhtanen, P., and Komi, P.: Mechanical factors influencing running speed. In Biomechanics VI-B. Edited by E. Asmussen. Baltimore, University Park Press, 1978.
35. Malina, R.N.: Growth, maturation and performance of Philadelphia negro and white elementary school children. Unpublished doctoral dissertation. Philadelphia, University of Pennsylvania, 1968.
36. Mann, R.: A kinetic analysis of sprinting. Med. Sci. Sports and Exerc., 13:5, 1981.
37. Mann, R., and Hagy, J.: Biomechanics of walking, running, and sprinting. Am. J. Sports Med., 8:5, 1980.
38. Mann, R., and Sprague, P.: A kinetic analysis of the ground leg during sprint running. Res. Q. Am. Assoc. Health Phys. Educ., 51:2, 1980.
39. Mason, B.: Kinematic and kinetic analysis of selected parameters during the support phase of running. Unpublished doctoral dissertation. Eugene, University of Oregon, 1980.
40. Mersereau, M.: A cinematographic analysis of the development of the running pattern of female infants at 22- and 25-months of age. Unpublished master's thesis. Lafayette, IN, Purdue University, 1974.
41. Mersereau, M.: The relationship between measures of dynamic process, output, and dynamic stability in the development of running and jumping patterns of preschool age females. Unpublished doctoral dissertation. Lafayette, IN, Purdue University, 1977.
42. Milne, C., Seefeldt, V., and Reuschlein, S.: Relationship between grade, sex, race,

and motor performance in young children. Res. Q. Am. Assoc. Health Phys. Educ., 47:4, 1976.

43. Nelson, R.C., Dillman, C.J., Lagasse, P., and Bickett, P.: Biomechanics of overground versus treadmill running. Med. Sci. Sports, 4:4, 1972.

44. Nett, T.: Foot Plant in Running. Track Technique No. 15, March 1964, pp. 462–463.

45. Ponthieux, N.A., and Barker, D.G.: Relationships between race and physical fitness. Res. Q. Am. Assoc. Health Phys. Educ., 36:4, 1965.

46. Rapp, K.: Running velocity: body-rise and stride length. Unpublished master's thesis. Iowa City, University of Iowa, 1963.

47. Ryan, T.M.: A comparison of selected basic gross motor skills of moderately retarded and normal children of middle childhood age utilzing the Ohio State University scale of intra gross motor assessment. Unpublished doctoral dissertation. Columbus, Ohio State University, 1977.

48. Saito, M., Kobayashi, K., Miyashita, M., and Hoshikawa, T.: Temporal patterns in running. In Biomechanics IV. Edited by R. Nelson and C. Morehouse. Baltimore, University Park Press, 1974.

49. Seefeldt, V., Reuschlein, S., and Vogel, P.: Sequencing motor skills within the physical education curriculum. Paper presented at the AAHPER meeting, Houston, 1972.

50. Sinning, W.E., and Forsyth, H.L.: Lower limb actions while running at different velocities. Med. Sci. Sports, 2:28, 1970.

51. Slocum, D.B., and James, S.L.: Biomechanics of running. J.A.M.A., 205:97, 1968.

52. Smith, S.: Longitudinal changes in stride length and stride rate of children running. Unpublished master's thesis. Madison, University of Wisconsin, 1977.

CHAPTER **4**

Jumping

A jump is a motor skill in which the body is propelled into the air by a thrust from one or both legs and then lands on one or both feet. This broad definition encompasses all motor acts commonly called hops, jumps, leaps, and bounds. Jumping can be done in an upward, downward, forward, backward, or sideward direction and in a variety of ways. Both direction and type of jump are important considerations in the development of basic jumping skill and each will receive due attention in this chapter.

JUMPING ACHIEVEMENTS OF PRESCHOOL CHILDREN

By the time a child has developed the ability to run he has also acquired the physical abilities necessary to jump. When he propels himself forward and upward into flight with one foot and lands on the other while running, technically he has satisfied the minimal requirement for a successful jump. However, jumping should be regarded as a more difficult skill than simple running because it ordinarily entails more vigorous and extensive nonsupport movements. Adequate preparation for a successful assault on the awaiting array of jumping skills requires a child to have more than just enough strength to thrust his body into the air. He must also be capable of coordinating more elaborate movements while maintaining balance if he is to be effective in accommodating the complexities of the new skills. In addition to physical prerequisites, there are the nebulous qualities of courage and confidence that can have a major impact on the development of jumping skill. Gutteridge and others have observed that children are apt to revert to an earlier mode of jumping when the height of the jump is increased or when a new type of jump is introduced.[12] The child's perception of the difficulty of each new jump is one of the critical factors influencing the rate at which he acquires jumping skill.

A child foregoes independence and opts for the security of a helping hand when performing the step-down that usually precedes the first

Fig. 4–1.   Upper: 37-month-old boy showing a vigorous jump down from a two-footed takeoff to a two-footed landing. Note the compensatory "winging" of the arms and the slight unevenness of the feet. Lower: 33-month-old girl using the step-down form that leads toward her first downward jump.

Fig. 4–1 *continued.*

effort at jumping. He grasps someone's hand for balance and from a support on one foot steps down, contacting a lower level with the opposite foot (Fig. 4–1). The child is just degrees away from performing a first true jump after being able to walk down a step holding the hand of an adult. With an increase in the length of the step, a quick lift-off by the support foot, and a brief nonsupport period followed by a balanced landing on the foot of the forward leg, a real jump has been achieved. The jump is done rather rigidly at first, with the support and lead legs remaining relatively straight and with the arms in opposition but also elevated sideward for balance. As the step-down jump is done less gingerly and more confidently, the outward lunge caused by a straight support leg is reduced and the step is shortened. Changes in form accompanying the shortened step are a quicker and higher lift of the support leg to enhance the flight phase and a greater lift from the arms with a slight retraction of the shoulders for balance.

The child moves from the step-down jump through a general sequence of achievements marked by increased heights and new types of jumps. It is during the third and fourth years of life that rapid progress is made in the development of jumping skill as measured by specific achievements. Bayley[3] and McCaskill and Wellman[30] have chronicled some of the skills demonstrated by children of preschool age and have assigned a tentative motor age to each (Table 4–1). The range in motor performance of children is wide enough to make the task of assigning a precise age expectation to a particular achievement a risky business. Thus, it is wise to regard the age assignments for the achievement of jumping skills as tentative.

Another and perhaps more useful way to view the jumping achievements of young children is in terms of jumping technique or type of jump. This approach is concerned with whether the child can jump down from 1 foot before he can do it from 2 feet more than with whether

TABLE 4–1. JUMPING ACHIEVEMENTS OF PRESCHOOL CHILDREN*

Achievement	Motor Age (months)	Source
Jump from 12-inch height; 1 foot ahead	24	M&W
Jump off floor; both feet	28	B
Jump from 18-inch height; 1 foot ahead	31	M&W
Jump from chair 26 cm high; both feet	32	B
Jump from 8-inch height; both feet	33	M&W
Jump from 12-inch height; both feet	34	M&W
Jump from 18-inch height; both feet	37	M&W
Jump from 30-cm height; both feet	37.1	B
Jump forward 10–35 cm from 30-cm height; both feet	37.3	B
Hop on 2 feet 1–3 times	38	M&W
Jump over rope 5–20 cm high; both feet	41.5	B
Hop on 1 foot 1–3 times	43	M&W

*Adapted from information in studies by Bayley[3] and McCaskill and Wellman.[30]

TABLE 4–2. TYPES OF JUMPS ACHIEVED BY CHILDREN IN TERMS OF PROGRESSIVE DIFFICULTY

Jump down from one foot, land on the other foot
Jump up from two feet, land on two feet
Jump down from one foot, land on two feet
Jump down from two feet, land on two feet
Run and jump forward from one foot, land on the other
Jump forward from two feet, land on two feet
Run and jump forward from one foot, land on two feet
Jump over object from two feet, land on two feet
Jump from one foot to same foot rhythmically

he can jump down with 1 foot from a height of 18 inches before he can jump down with 2 feet from a height of 12 inches. A technique-related approach is speculative to some extent because the data needed to support a particular progression of types of jumps are incomplete. Many of the jumping skills have been studied in isolation rather than in relation to one another, so that the relative difficulty of each must be based partly upon suggestive rather than fully substantive data. A list of types of jumps arranged tentatively in progressive order appears in Table 4–2. The time interval between the achievement of the different types of jumps is quite variable insofar as it ranges from a considerable time lag to almost simultaneous achievement. Improvement in the performance of a jump that has been learned, normally is shown by the ability to increase the height or the distance factor of the jump.

PERFORMANCE TRENDS IN JUMPING SKILL

Data published by Bayley,[3] Gutteridge,[12] and McCaskill and Wellman[30] stand as evidence that there is regular progress in the development of jumping skill by preschool children. The children who were subjects in these studies were tested on a wide variety of discrete jumping tasks. Their performances showed that they were able to perform jumping tasks of greater difficulty at each successive preschool year.

Jumping performance is more frequently measured by the vertical jump or the standing long jump than it is by a series of diverse tasks. These two types of tests ordinarily are used on school-age children but have also been used on preschool children in a few recent studies. Frederick measured the vertical jumping ability of 3- to 5-year-old children who were attending day care centers.[10] He found an age increase in performance, a superiority of boys over girls, and an advantage of black over white children. Performance in the jump and reach test is better each year starting at the age of 5 years according to Jenkins[20] and Wilson.[43] Boys were better vertical jumpers than girls in this age range. Dinucci compared 6-, 7-, and 8-year-old black and white girls on the jump and reach and on the standing long jump.[8] He found no racial difference in performance, but did find an age increase. The group of

6- to 9-year-old normal children studied by Rarick and Dobbins showed male superiority in the vertical jump at ages 6, 8, and 9.[35] The study also revealed a superiority of normal over EMR children in the same age range. Boys in the intellectually retarded group were superior to EMR girls from age 6 to age 12, and then at age 13 the girls were better.

The standing long jump currently is a more popular standard measure of the comparative jumping ability of school children than the vertical jump. Keogh summarized the results of 11 studies done over a 35-year period that contained data on the performances of school children in the standing long jump.[23] He found variations in the mean performances reported, but concluded that there was a consistent linear improvement at successive ages and grade levels. He found no important differences in performance between boys and girls in the standing long jump until age 8, when boys were the better performers. At ages 9 and 10 the boys were about 1 year, or 3 to 5 inches, in distance ahead of the girls. Contrary results on the sex differences in standing long jump performance were reported in a study in which the school children had participated in a special program that was designed to improve strength, develop skill, and stimulate organic function.[11] Girls did not fall behind when given the benefit of a physically stimulating physical activity program. Standing long jump performances for boys and girls were essentially the same at ages 7 through 12 years.

Some recent studies support the developmental trend of improved performance at succeeding ages and/or succeeding grades, but show conflicting results when comparisons are made on the basis of race or sex. Milne et al. found no significant racial differences but did find male superiority in the performances of 553 kindergarten, first-, and second-grade children.[31] No sex differences were found in the performances of the small group of $3^1/_2$- to $6^1/_2$-year-old children tested by Johnson,[22] but in another study of young children, Frederick found $3^1/_2$- to $5^1/_2$-year-old boys were superior to girls and black children were superior to white children in the standing long jump.[10] No racial difference appeared in the performances of a group of 6- to 8-year-old girls in the Dinucci study.[8] Ryan added another dimension to the comparison of performance in the standing long jump with the use of the Ohio State SIGMA.[39] He found no difference in the maturity of jumping form used by 6- to 8-year-old boys and girls.

Hopping is a difficult and complex form of jumping for young children. Although it does not require maximum effort, it does call upon the ability to perform controlled, rhythmic movement. Repeated vertical jumps from two feet can be done before true hopping can (Table 4–1), but neither version of jumping is acquired at an early age. The ability to perform 2 or 3 consecutive forward hops was achieved at the average age of 49.3 months by the children in Bayley's[3] longitudinal study and at 43 months in the data reported by McCaskill and Wellman.[30] Jenkins used a 10-point rating scale rather than a precise test of hopping skill with the result that 33% were rated as being proficient at age 4, 79% at age $5^1/_2$, and 90% at age $6^1/_2$.[20] Keogh collected quantitative data on the hopping ability of 5- to 9-year-old children and found that by age five 31% of the boys and 10% of the girls still could not hop 5 consecutive times on the right foot and 5 consecutive times on the left foot.[25] Keogh also found that 31% of 5-year-old, 13% of 6-year old, and 6% of 7-year-old boys could not hop for a distance of 50 feet in a timed test.[26] Girls in comparable age groups had 19%, 1%, and 7% failures respectively. On another hopping test consisting of two hops on one foot followed in rhythm by two hops on the other, the percentage of girls passing was much greater than the percentage of boys at each age, 6 through 9 years. English boys performed at the same general level as American boys.[24] The superiority of girls over boys on hopping tests appears consistently in the literature. Ryan verified the advantage when the Ohio State University SIGMA was used to rate the hopping *form* of 6- to 8-year old normal and severely retarded children.[39] The girls used more mature form than the boys at each age, and the normal children used more advanced form than the TMR children. The two intellectually disparate groups demonstrated a large gap in level of skill.

DEVELOPMENTAL FORM IN THE VERTICAL JUMP

A child can perform a minimal vertical jump at an early age, but only with a technique that is variable and unpredictable. When the movements finally congeal into a detectable pattern, it is identified by (1) minimal preliminary crouch, (2) sideward elevation of arms and shoulders, (3) small forward lean at takeoff, and (4) quick flexion at hips and knees following takeoff. Halverson et al. discovered two of these features when studying the development of hopping with very young children.[14] Arms were raised to middle or high guard position and instead of providing an upward thrust, the hopping leg was quickly raised to cause the body to become airborne.

Some aspects of form depend upon whether the jump involves reaching for an object or is simply general upward movement. In an informal film study on vertical jumping, a small group of 4-year-old children were asked to jump as high as they could. The responses were highly individualistic, but did display two common elements in the form: the shoulders were hunched upward followed by outbalancing motions with the arms, and the legs were drawn up well under the body immediately after lift-off (Fig. 4–4). An interesting transition in form occurred when the set task was changed and the children were asked to jump up and try to touch the tester's hand. The arms were lifted well and the whole body was thrust into full extension (Fig. 4–2). Poe verified the importance of using an overhead target to elicit an effective

Fig. 4–2. Position of 4-year-old children at the height of a vertical jump in which they reach for an object. Their bodies are fully extended with a slight forward lean. The two boys use effective arm opposition.

vertical jump from young children.[33] Sixteen of 22 children between the ages of 23 and 35 months were able to complete the task of jumping vertically to touch a target. These successes suggest that the observation by Hellebrandt et al. that young children cannot catapult the body into the air by the sudden extension of both legs simultaneously applies more to infants than those who have reached the age of two years and beyond.[18]

Poe described the movement characteristics of a group of 2-year-old children in the performance of a vertical jump.[33] She studied both the overt configurations and the kinematics of the performances and then compared the findings to a model provided by a skilled adult performer. Six patterns were identified, but they could not be ranked confidently because three contained adultlike as well as immature traits. Despite this problem, the range of displacement at ankles, knees, hips, and arms increased steadily from Pattern I to Pattern VI, suggesting trendlike motor pattern improvement. One third of the 2-year-old children employed the most adultlike pattern (VI), which included a moderate to deep preparatory crouch, forceful upward flexion of both arms in conjunction with lower extremity extension, and nearly complete body extension in flight. Pattern V was slightly closer to the adult pattern when patterns were compared on the basis of key aspects of body configuration, but Pattern VI more closely paralleled the adult pattern in a comparison of displacement and velocity measurements.

Wilson studied the changes in form in the jump and reach version

Fig. 4–3. Lateral and posterior views of a 4-year-old boy performing a vertical jump. Upper: He crouches, lifts his arms, and thrusts his body upward and slightly forward into full extension. Lower: He uses more effective arm opposition, but also more forward reach.

of the vertical jump at successive ages from 4 to 11 years.[43] Improvement in form for this age group was noted in terms of:

1. A small progressive increase in crouch.
2. More effective arm lift.
3. Improved extension at takeoff and in flight.
4. Greater extension of the trunk at the crest of the reach.

Similar results came to light from longitudinal data on two girls who were studied over a 2-year period starting at age 3 years.[34] The subjects showed increased flexion at the knees during the preparatory crouch, increased extension throughout the body at takeoff, and more effective arm action during the upward thrust.

Effective form during an early stage of the developmental period is demonstrated by the 4-year-old boy in Figure 4–3 as he jumps and reaches. His crouch causes his legs to bend at the knee slightly in excess of 90°. Upward movement is initiated with both arms followed immediately by extension at the hips, knees, and ankles. His body is fully extended after the takeoff and at the crest of the jump. The side view shows the typical tendency to jump forward slightly at the takeoff. One aspect of his form that is not particularly effective is the action of his nonreaching arm in the upper sequence of the illustration. In the lower sequence showing a back view, his form improves when his nonreaching arm is swung downward in reaction as the other arm stretches upward. Similar body extension, forward jump, and arm opposition can be observed in two of the children in Figure 4–2. If the vertical jump does not require purposeful reaching by the arms, less mature

Fig. 4–4. Immature form in the vertical jump showing "winging" arm action, incomplete extension, quick flexion of the legs, and slight forward jump.

arm and leg action is seen in the jumping pattern (Fig. 4–4). When the arms have a particular task, the head extends as the eyes focus upon the objective of the impending arm action. The slightly backward head position is conducive to effective body extension during the jump. By contrast, the forward head position in Figure 4–4 is consistent with the ineffective tucking and flexing that pervade the jumping pattern.

MATURE PATTERN IN THE VERTICAL JUMP

The sequence of movements in the mature pattern of the vertical jump is comparatively uncomplicated. When the special arm actions that occur after the takeoff are disregarded temporarily, the fundamental pattern consists of four movements in the following sequence:

1. There is flexion at the hips, knees, and ankles during the preparatory crouch.
2. The jump begins with a vigorous forward and upward lift by the arms.
3. The thrust is continued by forceful extension at the hips, knees, and ankles.
4. The body remains in extension until the feet are ready to retouch, and then the ankles, knees, and hips flex to absorb the shock of landing.

The concept of an effective basic pattern in the vertical jump was verified in a study by Haldeman.[13] He selected the 5 best vertical jumpers from 806 junior and senior high school boys and studied the techniques they used in jumping. His analysis showed a similar pattern of movements for all 5 jumpers. Although they used a common pattern of movements, the jumpers varied in such details as the degree of flexion at the hip and the trunk in the preparatory crouch and the movement of the nonreaching arm.

Some of the details of the basic pattern have been isolated for study.[16] The effect of foot spacing on the performance in the vertical jump was the detail that Willson studied.[42] He tested a group of 160 male subjects between the ages of 13 and 15 on 16 different foot spacings. According to his findings, the vertical jump scores decreased progressively as the anteroposterior foot spacing increased, and scores also decreased when lateral spacing exceeded 10 inches. Martin and Stull used college-age males as their subjects and also determined that lateral foot spacing between 5 and 10 inches was better than 0- or 15-inch spacing.[29] However, their results on anteroposterior foot spacing were in slight disagreement with those of Willson. Vertical jump performance was better in their study when anteroposterior spread was 5 to 10 inches, with a slight preference for the closer spacing.

The effectiveness of various angles of the knee at the end of the preparatory crouch was studied by Heess.[17] He used 108 eighth-grade boys as subjects, and each boy performed vertical jumps with prelim-inary knee angles at 45, 65, 90, 115, and 135°. The angles of 65 and 90° produced the best jumps, and the extreme angle of 135° produced the poorest. The college men tested by Martin and Stull, by contrast, per-formed best with a knee angle of 115° and better at 90 than at 65°. The authors suggest that practice or learning effect might be the cause for the different results. It seems clear than an effective crouch is possible for individuals within a rather wide range, but the shallow and deep positions should be avoided. From the standpoint of mechanics, the deeper position provides a greater distance over which to apply force but it also creates greater resistance to be overcome. Thus, most effective jumpers utilize a mid-position.

Another aspect of the preparatory crouch that has been looked into by several researchers is the effect of a preparatory counter-move-ment.[1,4,40] Tveit used a force plate when he tested over 300 fourteen-year-old children on the vertical jump.[40] Each child jumped starting in a stationary crouch with a 90° angle at the knee and also jumped starting with a downward counter-movement. The counter-movement was pro-vided by going into the crouch and without hestitation launching into the jump. Force plate data showed less forward and backward impulses and more vertical force when a jump was immediately preceded by a preparatory counter-movement. Tveit concluded that these force changes represented better coordination in the execution of the jump.

ARM ACTION

The girls who were studied by Lewis demonstrated that arms have a favorable influence on performance in the vertical jump.[28] When their arms were used, the girls jumped higher than when their arms were restricted. An explanation for the improved performance was provided in a study of the use of the force platform in athletics activities. Proper arm action raised the center of gravity to the highest possible point prior to takeoff, and the vigorous upward arm swing evoked extra force for the propulsion of the body.[32]

The movement pattern of the arms depends upon the purpose of the jump. When there is no special task for the arms and no demand for maximum height, arm action could be mostly a shoulder shrug with the arms not rising above shoulder level during the jump. If the task is to grasp a rebounding basketball or to grasp a horizontal bar, both arms move directly upward at the same time and reach for their common goal. In the jump ball in basketball and in the jump and reach test, the nonreaching arm is pushed downward just prior to the peak of the jump. This final downward arm movement tilts the shoulder girdle laterally and raises the hand of the reaching arm higher in reaction (Fig. 4–5).

Fig. 4–5. Mature form in the vertical jump and reach. There is a preparatory crouch. Then the arms begin the upward movement, followed quickly by extension at the hips, knees, and ankles. As one arm reaches upward, the other swings downward sharply in opposition.

LEG ACTION

Following the initial movement by the arms, powerful forces from the hips and the legs are applied to thrust the body upward. In close and overlapping succession, extension occurs at the hips, knees, and ankles, with the forces that provide the movement at the hips and the knees being the most powerful.[2] The sequence of movements in the mature pattern remains constant, but the range of motion at the involved joints varies from one individual to another. The optimal crouch for the vertical jump is an individual matter but includes an effective angle at the hip as well as at the knee. Couper found that good jumpers had more erect trunks at the low point of the prejump crouch than poor jumpers.[7] The athlete in Figure 4–5 demonstrates well how the trunk remains in a relatively upright position during the crouch and the jump. He also shows the mature pattern of hip, knee, and ankle extension in the leg thrust.

DEVELOPMENTAL FORM IN THE STANDING LONG JUMP

The vertical jump represents one of the two major directions in which jumps are oriented, and the standing long jump represents the other. The two forms of jumps share many common pattern elements, despite the basic difference in the intended direction of each.

Fig. 4–6. Form used in the standing long jump by a 5-year-old girl. It is a unitary pattern with semistepping leg action. Her arms move sideward for balance and downward and backward to compensate for in-flight forward leg action. (Drawn from film loaned by Ruth Glassow.)

The vertical jump and the standing long jump seem to rise from a common origin. They first appear as an upward jump from two feet with a slightly forward takeoff angle. Hellebrandt et al. recognized the basic similarity when they reported that the early form in the standing long jump is more like a bipedal hop than a forward jump for distance.[18] From the common forward-upward direction at the beginning, the take-off vector of one jump moves increasingly toward the vertical and the takeoff vector of the other toward the horizontal. As the direction of the thrust in the standing long jump progresses from the vertical toward the horizontal, changes in overt form occur. The changes are interrelated and follow a common course leading to the mature pattern. Some of the more significant changes are the following:

1. An increase in the preliminary crouch.
2. An increase in the forward swing of the arms in the anteroposterior plane.
3. A decrease in the takeoff angle.
4. An increase in total body extension at takeoff.

Fig. 4–6 *continued.*

5. An increase in thigh flexion during flight.
6. A decrease in the angle of the leg at the instant of landing.

Most of the changes begin to occur fairly promptly, but progress is variable and complicated by the problem of precarious balance as well as the tendency to use a one-footed takeoff (Fig. 4–6). The coordination of arm and leg movements required merely to launch the body forward into the air from two feet is awkward and unnatural for a child, and coordination is even more difficult if the attempt to jump is a vigorous one. Thus it is quite common to see a one-footed takeoff or landing, a "winging" arm movement, or a high-guard arm position in the pattern of an immature jumper.

Synchronization of the action of both legs at takeoff, in flight, and at landing is difficult because it is a significant departure from the natural stepping action the child acquires when learning to walk and run. Children revert to stepping at various times during the developmental period, particularly when the body is in a forward off-balance position. Gradually they become able to synchronize the action of both legs in all phases of the jump and repress the stepping tendency.

The earliest pattern of arm movement in long jumping from a two-footed takeoff is the counterproductive "winging" motion. As the body is thrust forward and upward into flight, the shoulders are retracted

Fig. 4–7. Form used in the standing long jump by a 4-year-old boy. His preliminary arm swing moves his body forward, but his forward arm action is not well-coordinated with his leg and hip extension. His arm action is slow and incomplete, but it is performed mostly in the proper plane.

and the arms are swung backward and upward in the opposite direction. Fortunately, extreme "winging" does not persist but gives way to a sideward lift into a high-guard arm position. The high-guard position with arms raised sideward to more or less shoulder level helps immensely in the maintenance of balance, but has little other value in the standing long jump. This equilibratory arm action in the frontal plane typically appears as a part of a unitary pattern in which most movements in the jump occur simultaneously. Little by little the arms move forward into an anteroposterior plane swing and begin to contribute directly to the development of propulsive force (Fig. 4–7). Spontaneous adjustments in dorsiflexion and ventroflexion of the head occur during the long jump to keep the head in the proper position in relation to gravity. The precise adjustments are related to the levels of effort and

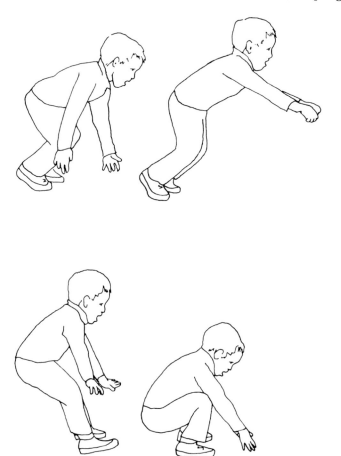

Fig. 4–7 *continued.*

skill development and are thought to be important in the facilitation of performance in vigorous jumping.[18,41]

Some of the features of the jump that change during the developmental period have been shown to differentiate quality of performance within a group. Halverson found that the inclination of the leg at takeoff and at landing distinguished the good jumpers among a group of kindergarten children.[14] The good performers had a more horizontal takeoff angle and a more horizontal thigh position at landing. Range and speed of movement at the hip and the knee joints were also identified as distinguishing factors in her study.

Zimmerman's study of college women who were skilled and unskilled broad jumpers revealed the persistence of elements of immature form at the adult level.[44] The nonskilled jumpers had limited arm movements and continued to swing their arms sideward as their legs came forward for landing. They did not achieve full extension at takeoff, and they hurried flexion at the hips and knees in the forward swing of the legs during flight. Further, the nonskilled jumpers consistently had larger leg angles at takeoff and at landing. It is apparent from these findings by Halverson and Zimmerman that even in widely separated age groups the poor performers show similar features and degrees of immature form.

Average rather than skilled or unskilled male jumpers were studied by Roy.[37] Standing long jump performances of 15 seven-year-olds, 15 ten-year-olds, and 20 thirteen-year-olds were recorded on a force platform and kinematographic records were collected on five boys from each group plus five randomly selected sixteen-year-olds. One major finding was that horizontal velocity at takeoff tended to increase with age but vertical velocity remained relatively constant. When Roy combined his findings with other published data, he concluded that many kinematics of jumping "were well established at school age and remained essentially constant through midadolescence for average performers." The movement sequence remained the same but there were individual differences in timing.

MATURE FORM IN THE STANDING LONG JUMP

The standing long jump is an explosive flash of closely integrated movements with a distinct underlying pattern (Figs. 4–8 and 4–9). In a skillful performance, the following pattern of movements occurs:

1. Joints are cocked by crouching and swinging the arms backward and upward.
2. Arms swing forward and upward and body extension begins in quick succession at the hips, knees, and ankles. (The movements continue until the body is fully extended and off the ground.)
3. Lower legs flex.
4. Hips flex, bringing knees forward, and arms and trunk move forward and downward.
5. Lower legs extend just prior to landing.
6. Knees bend at impact and body weight continues forward and downward in the line of flight.

THE CROUCH

Because the entire body weight does not have to be lifted directly upward in the standing long jump as it does in the vertical jump, the preparatory crouch can be deeper. The benefit of the deeper crouch is the increased distance provided over which to apply force prior to the takeoff. The 16 male college students studied by Henry were able to crouch an average of 6 inches more in the standing broad jump than in the vertical jump without sacrificing maximum performance.[19] Fel-

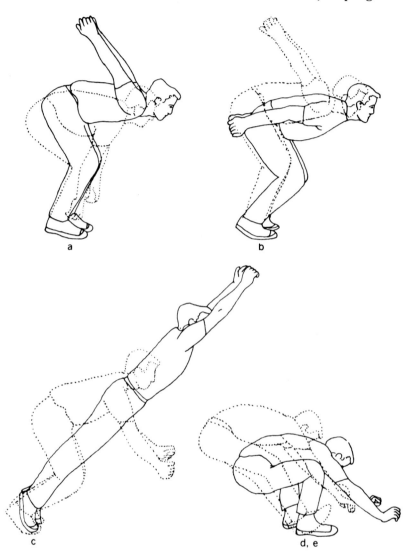

Fig. 4–8. Mature form in the standing long jump prior to takeoff and at landing. Before takeoff: (a) Weight moves forward as arms perform preliminary swing; (b) weight continues to move forward as the arms start a downward and forward swing; and (c) heels are lifted, arms swing forward and upward, and a series of propulsive forces thrust the body into full extension. Landing: (d) Legs are extended and well forward, and trunk and arms are forward in reaction; and (e) knees flex when heels contact the ground, and arms and trunk reach forward to prevent a backward fall.

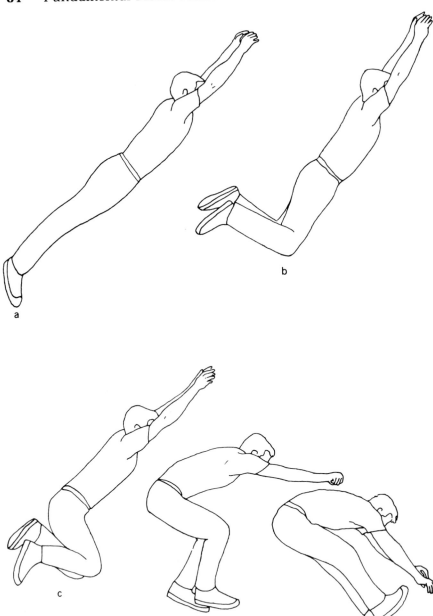

Fig. 4–9. Mature form in the standing long jump during flight: (a) Body is fully extended at takeoff; (b) lower legs flex while trunk and arms offer a long lever for reaction; (c) knees come forward as the hips flex and lower legs continue to flex; (d) legs swing forward and begin to extend in preparation for landing, and trunk and arms continue forward and downward in reaction to the leg movement; and (e) legs are approximately straight at the knees and reach forward for maximum distance at landing.

ton found that the good jumpers among the college women she studied obtained deeper flexion in all the joints involved in the preliminary crouch than the poor jumpers.[9] Skilled jumpers automatically seem to assume the amount of crouch that is the most effective for them, considering the strength they have available for propulsion in the jump. Extremes of either depth or shallowness in the crouch do not produce effective propulsion.

THE ARM SWING

One important role of the arms is to help move the center of gravity of the body forward before the takeoff.[6] The contribution of the arms in performing this task is apparent from the outset of the jump. When the arms swing backward and upward, the forward shift of body weight begins (Fig. 4–8). The forward movement of the body weight continues as the arms change direction and move vigorously downward and forward. During the forward swing the arms remain nearly straight and form a long lever which is useful initially in the development of momentum and later in reaction to leg movement.[32] Flexion at the shoulder continues until the arms are fully extended and in line with the trunk (Fig. 4–9). This position is reached just before takeoff, and when arm movement decelerates the last phase of leg extension can be accomplished against less resistance. The arms remain essentially in line with the trunk, forming a long lever to react against the forward movement of the legs during the flight phase. When the knees are well under the body on the forward swing, the spine flexes slightly, and the arms extend somewhat at the shoulder joint in reaction to the rapid movement of the tucked legs. A continued forward reach of the arms after landing assists in moving the center of gravity forward over the feet for the retention of balance.

Arm action after takeoff is basically compensatory, and an alternate form is used by some skilled jumpers. Immediately after the body is airborne, the arms are moved backward to a hyperextended position as the legs are brought forward. Arms are then swung vigorously forward at landing to conserve momentum and carry the center of gravity forward ahead of the two points of support. The double-reversal arm action in this form must be performed swiftly. A pseudo-winging motion through the high-guard arm position sometimes is used to get the arms into the hyperextended position quickly enough to be effective at landing, and this should not be regarded as an immature form.

ACTIONS AT THE HIP, KNEE, AND ANKLE JOINTS PRIOR TO TAKEOFF

The crouch cocks the hip, knee, and ankle joints by placing them in deeper flexion. There is a minor crouch when the arms swing backward, and the crouch deepens when they swing downward and forward. The heels are pulled off the floor, and the arms begin to move upward to mark the beginning of the sequence of propulsive extension. Extension begins in quick succession at the hip, the knee, and the ankle with an imperceptible time lag before each new action begins.[21] The joints reach full extension immediately after takeoff. Zimmerman's poor performers had simultaneous rather than successive initiation of movement at these joints, and the movements failed to produce complete extension.[44]

THE TAKEOFF ANGLE

A projectile angle of 45° theoretically is the most effective takeoff angle for producing maximum distance when the initial velocity remains constant. When the angle is too large, not enough horizontal velocity is produced. If the angle with the horizontal is too small, there is insufficient height and not enough time to swing the legs forward under the body into effective position for landing. Generally, the angle of takeoff is lowered as propulsive force is increased and the better jumpers in a group tend to have a lower angle. The good jumpers studied by Zimmerman[44] had an average takeoff angle approaching 45° and the college men studied by Henry[19] had an average takeoff angle of 41.3°. The takeoff angle in most reported studies has been measured directly from high speed film. In contrast, Roy et al. computed takeoff angle for his average jumpers from horizontal and vertical velocities at takeoff and found angles of 26 to 29° for the 4 groups.[38] The difference between his findings and other reported results is significant and seems to be related to method because the film in his study actually shows angles in the 45° range.

ACTIONS AT THE HIP, KNEE, AND ANKLE JOINTS DURING FLIGHT (Fig. 4–9)

Full body extension is reached at takeoff. Then the lower legs begin to flex, and as they approach an angle of approximately 90°, the thighs also begin to flex. While the knees swing forward, the heels continue to move toward the buttocks. The delay in starting hip flexion tightens the tuck of the legs on the forward swing. A shortened lever created in this way can be moved forward more swiftly and with less effort. Continued flexion at the hips brings the thigh close to the trunk and permits the lower leg to swing forward into position for landing. The leg is essentially straight at the knee at the moment the heel touches the ground.

THE LANDING

The effective position for landing is with legs well forward and as straight as possible at the knees and with the trunk close to the thighs (Fig. 4–8). The closeness of the trunk and thighs keeps the center of gravity high but forward and allows the legs to reach forward for maximum distance without increasing the danger of falling backward when landing. The angle of the legs with the ground is 45° or less in skilled jumpers and the angle generally coincides with the in-flight path of the center of gravity. The instant the foot has purchase with the ground, there is flexion at the knees and ankles that permits a continued and uninterrupted movement of the body weight down its line of flight. Arms continue reaching forward to help keep the center of gravity moving forward and downward.

DEVELOPMENTAL FORM IN THE RUNNING LONG JUMP

The running long jump, as its name implies, is a combination of two basic skills, running and jumping. Following a fast but moderately short approach run, the jumper takes off into flight from one foot, and then lands on both feet simultaneously. Effective coordination of the run and the jump is difficult when the takeoff spot is specified, and the coordination problem is made even more complex by the tendency of the body to rotate forward at takeoff.

Some children can perform the running long jump before the age of 3 years if they run at less than full speed and are not required to take off from a particular place. Cooper and Glassow described the rapid adjustment made by a 33-month-old boy when he was asked to clear an obstacle, a rolled mat, in his path while running.[6] On his first attempt he took off from one foot and landed on the obstacle with both feet. Next he stepped on and took off from the obstacle, and on his third try he successfully cleared the rolled mat and landed on both feet. These uninstructed attempts show one child's approach to solving the problem. A different child might have used a less effective approach similar to one Wilson observed in her study of the development of jumping form.[43] The preschool children who were unsuccessful in performing the running long jump took off from one foot and landed on the other, using a typical leap.

Wilson did not find much uniformity or consistency in the form used by 4½- to 12-year-old children when they performed the running long jump. Boys were superior to the girls in performance and probably achieved the better jumps because of their faster approach rates. The angle of takeoff and the angle of landing tended to decrease with age, but no other clear-cut trends emerged from the study. Arm action was extremely inconsistent, and in-flight leg action was either a pendular swing or a hurdling action with the trunk in a vertical position (Fig. 4–10).

Additional information on the developmental form used in the running long jump is important to the understanding of intraskill as well as interskill development. However, efforts to study the skill combination will probably be largely unsuccessful until the standard testing

Fig. 4–10. Running long jump form used by an 11-year-old boy. The angle with the horizontal is high at takeoff and at landing. Arm opposition helps his in-flight adjustments.

Fig. 4–11. Unsuccessful attempt at hopping by a 15-month-old child. Forward loss of balance results in a step and an attempt to hop on the opposite foot.

approach which requires a designated takeoff board is modified drastically or abandoned entirely.

DEVELOPMENTAL FORM IN HOPPING

Hopping has been given a special meaning in the parlance of fundamental movement and the meaning is rather precise. A hop is a particular type of jump in which the jumper takes off from and lands on the same foot. Thus any jump that involves more than one foot or an exchange of feet between takeoff and landing does not qualify as a hop (Fig. 4–11).

Hopping performance has been measured more frequently than hopping technique has been analyzed, and as a result there is a greater accumulation of information about *what* occurs than about *how* it occurs. The scarcity of research on technique is quite understandable considering the limited use of hopping as a separate form of locomotion. Ordinarily it is used in combination with other skills. For example, it is done in a small space with vertical emphasis in dance steps, rope jumping, and gymnastics stunts, and in a larger area with more horizontal emphasis as an element in the pattern for skipping.

Early attempts at hopping are done mostly in-place with significant forward movement added only as skill improves. This trend is apparent both in performance and in form. Jenkins made some general observations on hopping technique more than fifty years ago.[20] She saw that hop-like jumps were made from two feet before they could be made from one, that an irregular series of jumps across the floor preceded regular hopping, and that hopping was done more easily on the left foot than on the right. For the most part these observations can still be made by anyone watching young children as they attempt to acquire proficiency in hopping.

Halverson's longitudinal data on a few children has been analyzed systematically and the results are quite revealing. She initially reported on the progress made by 1 boy over a 10-year period, from the age of 37 months to the age of 13 years.[15] During early unsuccessful attempts his arms were in a middle-guard position with the arm opposite his support leg extended sideward. His support foot did not clear the ground and a forward loss of balance sometimes caused his opposite foot to land and produce an unintentional gallop. His first successful hop resulted from a quick lifting of the foot at the peak of the upward thrust rather than from clearance by a fully extended leg. Some of the major changes in the boy's form were prophetic in terms of the more complete results reported later. These changes were the following:

1. A decrease in the amount of forward body lean.
2. A change in arm function from stabilization to opposition.
3. A change from clearance by leg flexion to clearance produced by leg thrust.
4. A change in the nonsupporting leg from an inactive forward position to a forward-upward swing connected with takeoff.
5. An increase in range and speed of movement at the hip, knee, and ankle of the support leg.
6. A change during landing from immediate extension following knee and ankle flexion to a delay in extension while the body pivoted over the foot.

A second report based upon additional longitudinal data showed the development of hopping expressed in the more precise terms of stages for two motor pattern components, arm action and leg action.[36]

Arm Action

Stage I. *High guard.* Arms are high and to the side for balance.

Stage II. *Bilateral assist.* Arms move upward from middle to high guard to assist in lifting the body.

Stage III. *Opposing assist.* Opposite arm moves forward synchronously with the swing leg. Other arm does opposite movement.

Leg Action

Stage I. *Momentary retraction.* At the peak of support leg upward movement, the foot is quickly lifted by hip and knee flexion and returned.

Stage II. *Fall and catch—swing leg in front.* Body weight moves forward, support leg has momentary retraction, and a quick forward shift of the support foot. Swing leg is in front ready to step if balance is lost.

Stage III. *Projected takeoff—swing leg assists.* Swing leg moves forward prior to or with projection from hip and knee extension.

Stage IV. *Projection delay—swing leg leads.* Swing leg range is increased and forward swing precedes the support leg thrust.

According to the investigators at the Wisconsin Motor Development Laboratory, the most elementary stage in the arm component and in the leg component always appear together and the most advanced stages of arm and leg development also are usually combined. Other combinations of component stages are found as hopping skill progresses.

It is interesting to note the similarities between the early stages of hopping and the early stages of vertical jumping. Remnants of similar arm action and leg lifting technique are still present in the vertical jump pattern of the 4-year-old boy shown in Figure 4–4. When forward motion and increased speed appeared in the later stages, the similarities

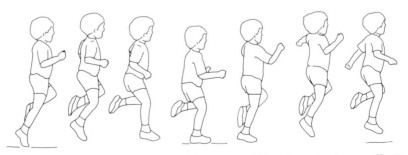

Fig. 4–12.   Forward hopping pattern used by a 5-year-old boy. Leg action is more effective than arm movement.

of the patterns with running also became apparent (Fig. 4–12). The final form with arm and leg opposition and support leg propulsion action is, for all practical purposes, a one-legged running pattern. There are some obvious exaggerations in the hopping pattern and some limitations because of the absence of the second support leg, but the similarities are undeniably present. Analysis of the hop in the hop-step-and-jump field event will add credence to the suggested similarities.

USE OF THE BASIC PATTERN OF JUMPING IN SPORT SKILLS

Advanced forms of jumping usually are found in combination with advanced forms of other basic skills. Jumping is combined with catching, running, or striking in the running high jump, the long jump, the volleyball spike, the basketball rebound, and the basketball jump ball. In some of these types of sport skills, jumping is the primary basic skill in the pattern; in others it is an important secondary skill. The specific role of the jump will be apparent as a few of these advanced skill patterns are examined.

JUMP BALL IN BASKETBALL

A basketball is tossed into the air between two opposing players who compete in an attempt to tap the ball to a teammate when it is in its downward flight. The height of the jump is important, but the timing of the jump with the flight of the ball is the critical aspect of the sport skill. The basic pattern of movements is almost identical to the pattern used in the jump and reach. Only the arm movement that controls the direction of the tap is variable. In Figure 4–5, the player crouches, lifts his arms to begin the jump, quickly extends at hips, knees, and ankles, and uses arm opposition to raise his tapping hand as high as possible. His basic jumping pattern must be effective, and his timing must permit him to reach the ball at the peak of his jump. These factors are essential in the successful use of the skill.

VOLLEYBALL SPIKE

The jump is but one of three basic skills that are combined in the volleyball spike. A short run precedes the jump, and a striking motion follows it. The function of the jump is to gain height so that the ball can be struck in such a way that it crosses the net at an acute downward angle. The movements in the pattern must be timed precisely in relation to the flight of the ball. Two or three running steps toward the net build up momentum for added height in the jump and move the spiker into the correct takeoff position slightly behind the downward trajectory of the ball. A two-footed takeoff is used by the spiker because with this form of vertical jump more upward thrust is possible and arm action can be coordinated more effectively after the takeoff. The pattern for

Fig. 4–13.   The volleyball spike. The total skill pattern includes a short run, a jump from a two-footed takeoff, and a hit. The arms initiate the jump and then quickly adjust for the spiking motion.

the jump that follows the preliminary forward steps is seen in Figure 4–13. The spiker's trunk remains upright during the crouch and pre-liminary arm swing. The jump begins with the upward lift of the arms and continues with extension at the hips, knees, and ankles prior to takeoff. The arms contribute to the propulsion and general coordination of the jump and then continue to move into position for the striking motion that is the climax of the complex pattern. As in the jump ball in basketball, the timing of the jump in relation to the flight of the ball is a critical factor in the performance of the skill.

Fig. 4–13 *continued.*

RUNNING HIGH JUMP

The basic pattern of the jump is present in this complex skill, but all aspects of it are not as readily apparent as they are in other sport skills involving jumping. Attention normally seems to focus on the technique for clearance of the bar and not on the upward thrust that contains the basic pattern. The movements producing the upward thrust are isolated for consideration in Figure 4–14. The sequence emphasizes the unique one-footed takeoff in the running high jump. The jumper leans backward as he plants his takeoff foot well ahead of his forward-moving center of gravity. The momentum he develops during the approach run is carried forward and his center of mass is forced upward over his

Fig. 4–14. Running high jump. A one-footed takeoff necessitates strong upward lift from the arms and the lead leg.

Fig. 4–15. Takeoff and bar clearance in the "Fosbury Flop" form of running high jump.

firmly planted and slightly bent takeoff leg. He swings the lead leg forward with a bent knee and then straightens the leg as it joins the arm in a vigorous lifting motion. Cooper stressed the need to keep the takeoff foot on the ground long enough for the arms and swinging leg to "contribute transference of momentum."[5] The lifting leg and arms act as one in the timing of this jump. Extension of the support leg continues the upward lift and provides the final force for the jump. Klissouras and Karpovich found little range of motion at the hip of the takeoff leg with most of the leg thrust coming from action at the knee and ankle.[27] Thus the aspects of the basic pattern that were present were arm and leg lift and knee/ankle thrust.

Despite the unique technique employed in bar clearance, the currently popular "Fosbury Flop" is an interesting example of the presence of basic jumping elements in the early part of the pattern. The selected positions in Figure 4–15 clearly indicate the basic arm/leg pattern and also illustrate the unusual flop clearance position at a later point in the jump.

ANALYSIS OF FORM IN JUMPING

Jumps are ballistic movements that occur rapidly. Direct visual analysis of a jumper's form in live performance must be based upon observations made during several jumps performed with maximum effort. Attention should be focused upon what seems to be the readily observable features of the jumping pattern.

Experience has shown that the following pattern elements can be seen and are extremely valuable in the general analysis of form in jumping.

Vertical Jump

1. Feet are nearly parallel and not more than shoulder width apart in the ready stance.
2. Knees are bent to about a right angle, and the trunk is only slightly forward in the preparatory crouch.
3. Body is in full extension from head to toes at takeoff.
4. Forward travel during the jump is minimal.

Arm action in the vertical jump is task-oriented, but the arms are not greatly hyperextended during the crouch regardless of their specific task after takeoff.

Standing Long Jump

1. Full body extension from toes through arms at takeoff.
2. Body angle near 45° with the horizontal at takeoff.
3. Legs out in front of the body with feet parallel at landing.
4. Body slides forward down the line of flight at landing.

Each of these observable items allows several aspects of the pattern of jumping to be evaluated in a single check. Problems in timing and movement coordination, for example, can be picked up in the failure of the body to be in full extension at takeoff. Study Figures 4–16, 4–17, and 4–18 for trends and stages in jumping.

Analysis according to developmental stage can also be done by using the stages proposed by McClenaghan-Gallahue or those in the Ohio State SIGMA for the standing long jump and by using the SIGMA or the Halverson-Roberton stages for hopping.

Fig. 4–16. Vertical jump by a 7-year-old boy. What are the mature aspects of his motor pattern?

Fig. 4–17.   Vertical jump by a 4-year-old boy. What are the developmental features of his form?

Fig. 4–18.   Standing long jump by a 10-year-old girl. How mature is her position at takeoff and how effective are her in-flight adjustments?

REFERENCES

1. Asmussen, E., and Bonde-Peterson, F.: Storage of elastic energy in skeletal muscles in man. Acta Physiol. Scand., 91:385, 1974.
2. Bangerter, B.L.: Contributive components in the vertical jump. Res. Q. Am. Assoc. Health Phys. Educ., 39:432, 1968.
3. Bayley, N.: The development of motor abilities during the first three years. Monogr. Soc. Res. Child Dev., 1:1, 1935.
4. Cavagna, G., Komarek, L., Citterio, G., and Margaria, R.: Power output of the previously stretched muscle. In Biomechanics II. Edited by J. Vredenbregt and J. Wartenweiler. Basel, Karger, 1971.
5. Cooper, J.M.: Kinesiology of high jumping. In Medicine and Sport. Vol. II. Biomechanics. Edited by J. Wartenweiler, E. Jokl, and M. Hebbelinck. Baltimore, University Park Press, 1968.
6. Cooper, J., and Glassow, R.: Kinesiology. St. Louis, C.V. Mosby, 1972.
7. Couper, M.: An analysis of the transfer of horizontal momentum to a vertical jump. Unpublished master's thesis. Northampton, MA, Smith College, 1965.
8. Dinucci, J.M., and Shows, D.A.: A comparison of the motor performance of black and Caucasian girls age 6–8. Res. Q. Am. Assoc. Health Phys. Educ., 48:4, 1977.
9. Felton, E.: A kinesiological comparison of good and poor jumpers in the standing broad jump. Unpublished master's thesis. Madison, University of Wisconsin, 1960.
10. Frederick, S.: Performance of selected motor tasks by three, four, and five year old children. Unpublished doctor of physical education dissertation. Bloomington, Indiana University, 1977.
11. Glassow, R.B., Halverson, L.E., and Rarick, G.L.: Improvement of motor development and physical fitness in elementary school children. Cooperative Research Project No. 696. Madison, University of Wisconsin, 1965.
12. Gutteridge, M.V.: A study of motor achievements of young children. Arch. Psychol., 244:1, 1939.
13. Haldeman, N.: A cinematographical analysis of the standing high jump as related to the basketball jump ball situation. Unpublished master's thesis. University Park, Pennsylvania State University, 1958.
14. Halverson, L.E.: A comparison of the performance of kindergarten children in the take-off phase of the standing broad jump. Unpublished doctoral dissertation. Madison, University of Wisconsin, 1958.
15. Halverson, L.E., Roberton, M.A., and Harper, C.J.: Current research in motor development. J. Res. Dev. Educ., 6(3): 56, 1973.
16. Hay, J.: Biomechanical aspects of jumping. In Exercise and Sport Sciences Reviews. Vol. III. Edited by J.H. Wilmore and J. Keogh. New York, Academic Press, 1975.
17. Heess, R.: Effects of arm position and knee flexion on vertical jumping performance. Unpublished master's problem. University Park, Pennsylvania State University, 1964.
18. Hellebrandt. F.A., Rarick, G.L., Glassow, R., and Carns, M.L.: Physiological analysis of basic motor skills: I. Growth and development of jumping. Am. J. Phys. Med., 40:14, 1961.
19. Henry, C.: Mechanical analysis of the initial velocity in the Sargent jump and in the standing broad jump. Unpublished master's thesis. Iowa City, University of Iowa, 1948.
20. Jenkins, L.M.: A comparative study of motor achievements of children five, six, and seven years of age. New York, Teachers College, Columbia University, 1930.
21. Johnson, B.: An analysis of the mechanics of the take-off in the standing broad jump. Unpublished master's thesis. Madison, University of Wisconsin, 1957.
22. Johnson, W.: A comparison of motor creativity and motor performance of young children. Unpublished doctor of education dissertation. Bloomington, Indiana University, 1977.
23. Keogh, J.: Motor performance of elementary school children. Department of Physical Education, University of California, Los Angeles, 1965.
24. Keogh, J.: Physical performance test data for English boys, ages 6–9. Phys. Educ., 58:65, 1966.
25. Keogh, J.: Developmental evaluation of limb movement tasks. Department of Physical Education, University of California, Los Angeles, 1968.

26. Keogh, J.: Analysis of limb and body control tasks. Department of Physical Education, University of California, Los Angeles, 1969.
27. Klissouras, V., and Karpovich, P.V.: Electrogoniometric study of jumping events. Res. Q. Am. Assoc. Health Phys. Educ., 38:41, 1967.
28. Lewis, B.: The relationship of selected factors to the vertical jump. Unpublished master's thesis. Iowa City, University of Iowa, 1959.
29. Martin, T.P., and Stull, G.A.: Effects of various knee angle and foot spacing combinations on performance in the vertical jump. Res. Q. Am. Assoc. Health Phys. Educ., 49:324, 1969.
30. McCaskill, C.L., and Wellman, B.L.: A study of common motor achievements at the pre-school ages. Child Dev., 9:141, 1938.
31. Milne, C., Seefeldt, V., and Reuschlein, S.: Relationship between grade, sex, race, and motor performance in young children. Res. Q. Am. Assoc. Health Phys. Educ., 47:4, 1976.
32. Payne, A.H., Slater, W.J., and Telford, T.: The use of a force platform in the study of athletic activities. Ergonomics, 11:123, 1968.
33. Poe, A.: Description of the movement characteristics of two-year-old children performing the jump and reach. Res. Q. Am. Assoc. Health Phys. Educ., 47:260, 1976.
34. Poe, A.: Development of vertical jump skill in children. Unpublished study. Madison, University of Wisconsin, 1970.
35. Rarick, G.L., and Dobbins, D.A.: Basic components in the motor performance of educable mentally retarded children: implications for curriculum development. Department of Physical Education, University of California, Berkeley, 1972.
36. Roberton, M., and Halverson, L.: The developing child—his changing movement. *In* Physical Education for Children: A Focus on the Teaching Process. Philadelphia, Lea & Febiger, 1977.
37. Roy, B.: Kinematics and kinetics of the standing long jump in 7-, 10-, 13-, and 16-year-old boys. Unpublished doctoral dissertation. Madison, University of Wisconsin, 1971.
38. Roy, B., Youm, Y., and Roberts, E.M.: Kinematics and kinetics of the standing long jump in 7-, 10-, 13-, and 16-year-old boys. *In* Medicine and Sport. Biomechanics III. Edited by S. Cerquiglini, A. Venerando, and J. Wartenweiler. Basel, Karger, 1973.
39. Ryan, T.: A comparison of selected basic gross motor skills of moderately retarded and normal children of middle childhood age utilizing the Ohio State University scale of intra gross motor assessment. Unpublished doctoral dissertation. Columbus, Ohio State University, 1977.
40. Tveit, P.: Variation in horizontal impulses and vertical jumps. *In* Biomechanics V-B. Edited by P.V. Komi. Baltimore, University Park Press, 1976.
41. Waterland, J.C.: Integration of movement. *In* Medicine and Sport. Vol. II: Biomechanics. Edited by J. Wartenweiler, E. Jokl, and M. Hebbelinck. Baltimore, University Park Press, 1968.
42. Willson, K.: The relative effects of various foot spacings on performance in the vertical jump. Unpublished master's thesis. University Park, Pennsylvania State University, 1965.
43. Wilson, M.: Development of jumping skill in children. Unpublished doctoral dissertation. Iowa City, University of Iowa, 1945.
44. Zimmerman, H.M.: Characteristic likenesses and differences between skilled and non-skilled performance of the standing broad jump. Res. Q. Am. Assoc. Health Phys. Educ., 27:352, 1956.

CHAPTER **5**

Throwing

Any movement sequence that involves thrusting an object into space by the use of one or two arms technically fits into the general category of throwing. The term has been applied by popular usage to so many different skills that an operational approach is necessary to arrive at a precise and formal meaning. In this presentation, a mature or skilled throw is considered to be a closely integrated movement sequence that is initiated by a forward step with the contralateral leg, followed by hip and trunk rotation, and concluded with a whipping arm action. Although this definition includes overarm, sidearm, and underarm motions, the unilateral overarm version is the one of major interest because it is the most commonly used form and because it has been studied extensively at both developmental and mature levels.

Many different patterns of throwing appear at the beginning of the developmental period. Consequently, it is necessary to adopt a broad definition of minimal form in order to include the variety of possibilities that mark progress toward the mature pattern. For the purposes of this chapter, any pattern in which an object is thrust into space cleanly with a unilateral or bilateral arm motion will be accepted as minimal throwing form.

THROWING PERFORMANCES OF CHILDREN

The development of throwing ability has been the subject of serious study for several decades. Form, accuracy, distance, and velocity at release have been used as criteria for evaluating the throwing ability of children. Because of the lack of objectivity involved in rating, form has been the least popular criterion used. Gutteridge devised a 10-point rating scale and used it to evaluate throwing ability in her study of the motor ability of young children.[14] No child at age 2 or 3 years was rated as being proficient, but there were indications of a progressive increase in the percentage of children at ages 4, 5, and 6 years who were given the high rating. The assigned ratings represented a wide range of ability at each age level. Although 85% of the children ages $5\frac{1}{2}$ to 6 years were considered to be proficient, the range of ratings for that age group extended from excellent to awkward. Ryan used the 4-level Ohio State SIGMA to evaluate the throwing form of 120 boys and girls ages 6 to 8 years.[35] He found the level of performance for the boys significantly more mature than that for the girls. Mahmoud observed a similar sex difference in throwing form at the preschool level.[27]

When accuracy is used as the standard for measuring throwing ability, investigators are troubled by not being able to use the same test for children of all ages. The recourse has been to modify the distance from which the ball is thrown, for different age levels at 2- or 3-year intervals. This procedure has the disadvantage of producing a break in the year-to-year data each time the testing procedure is changed. The result is a sketchy notion of the development of accuracy in throwing, but the evidence on accuracy is worthy of brief consideration. Frederick measured the throwing accuracy of $3\frac{1}{2}$- to $5\frac{1}{2}$-year-old black and Caucasian preschool children and found an increase in performance with age, a superiority of boys over girls, and no racial difference in performance.[12] In his comprehensive study of the motor achievements of children, Keogh limited the target throw for accuracy to children who had reached the ages of 7, 8, and 9.[23] He found an improvement in performance and a superiority of boys over girls at each of the three age levels. These general results were duplicated by Van Slooten with 960 boys and girls in essentially the same age range.[43] The children ages 6, 7, 8, and 9 showed annual improvement in a throwing-for-accuracy task, and the boys were significantly better than the girls at each age level. In an earlier but more comprehensive study, Wester compared the throwing accuracy of 232 boys in grades 3, 4, and 5.[44] The boys threw a baseball, a softball, and a volleyball at a target from distances of 20, 30, and 40 feet. Mean total scores increased from grade 3 to grade 5 and the subjects were more accurate from the shorter distances and with the two smaller balls.

The most frequently encountered criterion for determining throwing ability is the throw for distance. Despite differences in procedure and equipment, a strongly defined developmental trend has appeared in the literature. The trend starts at the preschool level where children show an increase in throw for distance at successive ages and boys show superior performance.[12,20,21] Studies using large numbers of children are consistently in agreement and firmly support the general trend of yearly improvement. Keogh studied 1171 children and found a linear year-to-year improvement, with the boys throwing significantly farther than the girls at each age level from 5 to 11 years.[23] A similarly comprehensive study was performed by Hanson who analyzed her data on 2840 children according to school grade rather than chronologic age.[17] Her findings of yearly improvement and male superiority parallel those of Keogh and have been supported by the additional studies of Nichols[28] and Van Slooten.[43]

Velocity at release, a technique used primarily in the Wisconsin studies on motor development, is yet another method of measuring throwing performance. It requires a special velocimeter that gives an automatic reading that can be converted quickly into a velocity score[34] or it involves calculations based upon measurements from film analysis or hand-timed performances. In several studies in which throwing velocity was measured, the results accurately repeated the performance picture presented in studies using the throw for distance.[13,28,30,33] Boys were superior to girls, and both boys and girls showed annual improvement.

The sex difference in throwing performance is extraordinarily large. The New York State Physical Fitness Test (1958) had an item requiring an overhand throw for accuracy. The 50th percentile scores for girls in grades 4, 5, and 6 were only 20%, 29%, and 37% as high as the scores for boys. The California Physical Performance Test norms for the softball throw for distance showed standards of performance for girls in grades 5 through 8 that were approximately 65% as high as the standards for boys at each grade level. Such enormous discrepancies are not observed in the performances of other basic skills.

The large sex differences in throwing and the relatively small differences in other power-type performances for children can be seen in the summary shown in Table 5–1, which includes data for 4000 children in grades 1 through 4.[19] Girls performed 96% as well as boys in the 50-yard dash and at least 90% as well as boys in the standing long jump, and yet they only performed between 54% and 57% as well in the throw for distance. This gap in level of performance appears at an early age and defies rational explanation. The only suggested reasons for the enormous sex differences in throwing performance that make much sense are related to experience and strength. However, both proposals lack the authority of evidence. An answer to the poser will be found eventually. Then, if enabling girls to throw as far and as accurately as boys is thought to be important, solutions can be sought to deal with the factors producing the discrepancy.

TABLE 5–1. SEX DIFFERENCES IN POWER PERFORMANCES*

Age	50-Yard Dash (seconds)			Standing Long Jump (inches)			Softball Throw (feet)		
	Boys	Girls	% G/B	Boys	Girls	% G/B	Boys	Girls	% G/B
6	9.9	10.3	96	44	42	95	44	25	57
7	9.7	10.1	96	45	42	93	50	28	56
8	9.2	9.6	96	50	45	90	63	35	56
9	9.0	9.3	97	53	49	92	74	40	54

*50th percentile scores. Adapted from Hardin and Garcia[19]

DEVELOPMENTAL FORM IN THROWING

Children use many types of throws as they begin to acquire skill in throwing, but the types do not seem to appear in a definite or precise order. A study by Jones provides some insight into the matter.[22] She analyzed the throwing patterns of 142 boys and girls ranging between $4^1/_2$ and $10^1/_2$ years of age. The children collectively used six different patterns when throwing a softball or a volleyball. Among the patterns were (1) bilateral overhand, (2) bilateral underarm from the front, (3) bilateral underarm from the side, (4) bilateral overarm, (5) unilateral underarm, and (6) unilateral overarm. The pattern a child chose to use depended upon his size and age and the size of the ball. Before the age of 8, only 2 boys and 2 girls used a unilateral pattern when throwing the volleyball, but after the age of 9, all boys used a unilateral overhand throw. Unilateral patterns were used exclusively when throwing the smaller ball, with the overhand unilateral pattern being used by 90.6% of the boys but only 68.1% of the girls. These might be regarded as *natural* throwing patterns because Jones had not instructed the children concerning which form to use.

The size of the ball was an important factor in Jones's study and presumably also had a significant bearing on the presence and the persistence of bilateral arm action in the patterns used by the children in a study by Deach.[7] She filmed the techniques a group of children 2 to 6 years old used to throw a volleyball. Of the four stages she found, bilateral arm action was used in the first three. Both arms were still involved at stage 3, but the preferred arm assumed more responsibility in the throw. It was not until the final stage of her developmental sequence that the one-arm overhand pattern with trunk rotation and arm-foot opposition was achieved. The children in Gutteridge's study did not abandon the two-arm method when a large ball was used but gradually were able to produce a clean throw with one hand when a small ball was available.[14]

UNILATERAL OVERARM PATTERNS

A definitive study of developmental form in unilateral overarm throwing was done many years ago by Wild.[46] She performed a cinematographic analysis of the throwing form of selected normal boys and girls at an age interval of 6 months from 2 to 7 years, and at a yearly interval from age 7 through 12 years. From a meticulous and comprehensive analysis of the data, 6 types of throws were identified, but the number was later reduced to 4 stages and each was associated with throwing development according to a particular age schedule. Subsequent observations have verified the presence of the general patterns but suggest that the patterns probably appear earlier than indicated in the schedule originally proposed.[15,31,34]

Fig. 5–1. Stage I. The ball is thrown primarily with forearm extension. The feet remain stationary and the body does not rotate, but there is a slight forward body sway. (Redrawn from Wild.[46])

Fig. 5–2. Stage II. Rotatory movement is added to the pattern. During the preparatory movement, the hand is cocked behind the head. Then the trunk rotates to the left, and the throwing arm swings around in an oblique-horizontal plane. (Redrawn from Wild.[46])

The impact of Wild's study on research relating to the development of throwing patterns has been so great that the four stages are presented here in detail and are accompanied by illustrations from the original data. The four stages continue to have a high degree of practical value because each is relatively easy to identify on the basis of a few major characteristics.

Stage I. This primal pattern was observed in children at ages 2 and

3 years. It consists almost exclusively of arm movement and occurs in the anteroposterior plane (Fig. 5–1). In preparation for the throw, the arm is brought either sideward and backward or upward and backward until the hand holding the ball is above the shoulder and the forearm of the throwing arm is flexed and extended backward. At the end of the backward motion of the arm, there is considerable retraction of the shoulders and a slight backward sway of the trunk. The throw consists of a forward and downward swing of the arm with extension of the forearm starting early. At the same time, the backward sway of the trunk is reduced. The feet do not change position during the throw, and the body does not rotate, except possibly after release.

Stage II. Children $3^1/_2$ to 5 years of age formed the group that demonstrated this basic pattern, which is characterized by a rotatory movement in the horizontal plane (Fig. 5–2). The preparatory motion involves a rotation of the trunk to the right with a sideward and backward swing of the arm until the throwing hand terminates in a position somewhat behind the head, with the elbow well flexed. The arm initiates the throwing motion with a forward swing in a high oblique or a more horizontal plane, and the trunk rotates to the left. The forearm extends anytime prior to the release of the ball, with the arm following through in a forward and downward movement. As in the first stage, the feet are together and do not move during the throw. The addition of the rotatory movement in this stage provides a greater distance over which to apply force in the throw. It represents an improvement over the first stage in terms of the leverage that can be applied by the trunk and shoulder girdle.

Stage III. Typical of the throwing pattern of children ages 5 and 6 was the addition of a same-side forward step during the throw, giving the pattern both anteroposterior and horizontal features (Fig. 5–3). Preliminary movements are similar to those employed in the previous stage. The feet are together and remain stationary while the trunk rotates to the right and the arm is swung sideward, upward, and backward to a position with the forearm flexed. A forward step with the right foot initiates the throwing motion and is followed by rotation of the trunk to the left and a forward swing of the arm in an oblique or in an essentially horizontal plane. The forearm extends later than in Stage II, and the arm follows through in a forward and downward motion. There is minor evidence of "opening" when the arm is drawn back farther as the step is taken. Forward force is added to the throw by the forward shifting of body weight during the step. However, using the foot on the same side of the body for the step limits the range of the backward preparatory movements of the throwing arm and continues to impose the awkward timing seen in the earlier patterns.

Stage IV. This pattern represents the mature or skilled form and was found commonly among boys $6^1/_2$ years of age and older and to a lesser

Fig. 5–3. Stage III. A forward step with the leg on the same side of the body as the throwing arm is added to the pattern. The step produces additional forward force for the throw. (Redrawn from Wild.[46])

extent among girls in the same age range. In the preparatory movements, the weight shifts to the right foot as the trunk rotates to the right and the throwing arm is swung backward and upward (Fig. 5–4). A forward step by the opposite foot is followed by counterclockwise rotation of the trunk, horizontal adduction of the arm, and extension at the elbow. The contralateral step allows more extensive "opening" and greater differentiation of the movements in the pattern.

Some of Wild's observations concerning the identification of the stages continue to have an impact on the understanding of motor pattern development. One important observation concerned the relationship between stages and trends. She recognized that "overlapping of features into chronologically adjacent types demonstrates emergence of one stage into the next."[47] Although different kinds of trends were noted, "the outstanding trend disclosed by the movement types is change from movements in the anteroposterior plane to movements largely in the

Fig. 5–4. Stage IV. In the mature pattern the arm and trunk rotate backward in preparation for the throw. A contralateral step moves the body weight forward, the hips, trunk, and shoulders rotate to the left, and the arm completes the throwing motion. (Redrawn from Wild.[46])

horizontal plane, and from an unchanging base of support to a left-foot-step forward."[47] This monumental work with all its implications served as a beginning in the study of stages and trends in throwing development. The research has continued in diverse directions and at increasingly more sophisticated levels. It has unraveled most of the secrets of sequential trunk rotation and whipping arm action.

A longitudinal study of improvements in the throwing form of a limited number of school girls was done by Singer.[40] Two good and 2 poor throwers were selected on the basis of initial ball velocity, and the 4 girls were filmed at ages 8, 9, 10, and 11 years. Figure 5–5 shows the year-to-year development of the form of one girl who was a good performer according to the velocity classification. It is significant to note that at age 8 she continued to manifest the same-side stepping action that Wild had identified with 5- and 6-year-old children. At age 10 the subject had abandoned the forward step with the same foot for the more effective opposite-foot-forward pattern. By age 11 she had increased the range of movement at most joints, and her only serious problem was a pushing arm motion in connection with release. The overall patterns of movement for both good and poor performers were considerably similar over the 4-year period, but greater range of joint

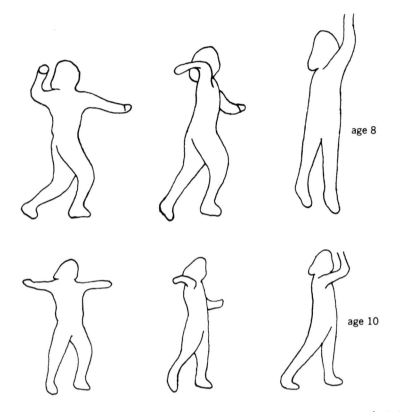

Fig. 5–5. Girl filmed while throwing for maximum velocity at ages 8, 9, 10, and 11. At age 8 she was classified as a good thrower based upon the criterion of initial velocity. (Redrawn from Singer.[40])

Age 8. Rotates trunk and cocks arm but restricts trunk rotation by stepping forward on right foot rather than on opposite foot.

Age 9. Little change in form over previous year.

Age 10. Shifts weight forward from right foot to left foot and acquires greater range of movement in shoulder-arm unit. (Evidence of opening.)

Age 11. Good range of motion at all joints but does not extend elbow effectively at the point of release. (Uses a pushing motion.)

movement and greater speed of torso and humeral rotation were pinpointed as the factors producing better performance.

Ekern analyzed the overarm throwing patterns of 2 boys and 2 girls from each of grades 2, 4, and 6 who were the best throwers based upon the measure of ball velocity.[10] The throwing patterns of the boys were more mature than the patterns of the girls in virtually every respect. In general, the boys in each age group had a greater range of movement, a longer and more effective stride, and a faster arm action. With an increase in age, there were increases in total range of movement and in forward and lateral trunk inclination at release for both boys and girls. The age increase for boys also brought about a change from a

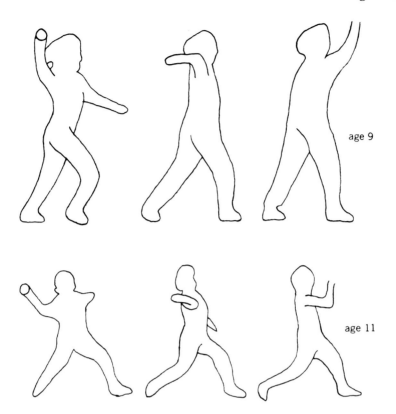

age 9

age 11

Fig. 5–5 *continued.*

circular to an elliptical path of the ball in the preparatory phase, and shoulder abduction near 90° and more elbow extension at release. These changes lead toward the acquisition of the whipping arm motion that is used in the mature pattern. Ekern detected two particularly important developmental characteristics in the throwing patterns used by the girls: their patterns tended to be arm-dominated and lacking in separation of pelvic and spinal rotation.

Changes in movement pattern that resulted from instruction in throwing at the kindergarten level were examined critically by Hanson.[18] The throwing patterns of 15 out of 18 boys and girls matured to some extent, and Hanson noted the following developmental trends: (1) in starting position, change from a narrow front-facing to a wider side-facing position; (2) in trunk rotation, change from "block" rotation to a pelvic-spinal sequence; (3) in arm action, less horizontal adduction of the humerus; and (4) in elbow extension, more delay in starting it. Hanson proposed that the development of trunk rotation might occur in three stages starting with pelvis and spine together, then a spine-pelvis sequence, and finally a pelvis-spine sequence. The order of the first and second stages has been reversed by subsequent investigation and it is now consistent with the top-dominated pattern that characterizes early overarm throwing development.

Other studies have involved expanding the number of stages in throwing development.[4,25,32] Leme added 4 patterns to Wild's original 6 in her study of the developmental aspects of throwing in a group of college women who were poor throwers.[25] Foot position, stride, body orientation, weight shift, trunk action, reverse arm movement, forward arm movement, and follow-through were the eight components examined in the analysis of each throw. The throwing patterns of almost all the 18 poor throwers fit into 1 of the categories, and only 2 of the other 10 types even appeared. The stage that most throwers had reached utilized block rotation of the pelvis and spine and a relatively short stride. There was a strong indication that arm movements provided more variability than other components of throwing form for the college women. This finding corroborates Hanson's observation of the large amount of variation in arm movements for the kindergarten girls in her study. Both groups of females were using immature form, so the variation in arm action could be a function of the developmental stage and it could also be one source of sex difference in the development of overarm throwing skill.

In a study of the throwing patterns of 110 educable mentally retarded (EMR) children between the ages of 7 and 12 years, Auxter detected 15 distinguishable patterns.[4] Each represented an improvement in development toward the objective of efficient throwing. He reported that progress in the 15 patterns was consistent with the progress in Wild's 4 basic stages, but the expanded group of patterns offered more discrimination in the identification of performance level. Auxter also observed that some of the elements of the throw, such as the number of integrated joint actions involved and the length of the stride, appeared to develop independently of one another. This feature of motor pattern development supports the need to consider component development both in terms of trends and in terms of an expanded number of stages.

The greater expansion of the number of stages in throwing occurred in the study of stage stability by Roberton.[31] She designated 5 categories of arm-trunk development as major stages and 8 categories of pelvic-spinal development as steps within the stages. Both stages and steps were ordered in terms of expected level of difficulty. The major stages and steps were then combined into a total of 25 possible minor stages. Each of 73 first-grade children in her study was filmed from 2 views while performing 10 maximum-velocity throws. Of the 25 minor stages that had been hypothesized, 18 appeared in the total of 727 throws and 2 that had not been hypothesized were identified and added. However, the distribution of throws among the minor stages was rather narrow. More than 80% of all throws appeared in 1 of 5 minor stages and 1%

or less of all throws appeared in each of 11 other minor stages. Thirty-eight percent of all the throws by the first-grade children fit into the minor stage "humerus oblique: simultaneous initiation of pelvis and spine (block rotation)," which was in the first major stage. Girls were represented only in the easiest two of the major stages, and boys were found in all five. If another feature such as the stride were to be added when hypothesizing stages of throwing development, the number of discrete stages would increase astronomically and the scattering of patterns would undoubtedly be more widespread than was found in the 25 minor-stage model. Roberton carefully placed her approach in perspective by referring to it as a "viable, developmental research paradigm for the overarm throw." It has been modified in terms of separate components and used as an evaluation check list in one study on the effects of instruction on overhand throwing development[16] and in another on the overarm throwing patterns of mentally retarded children.[8] The following is a compilation of the developmental categories within each of the components used in the two studies.

Preparatory Arm Action[24]

1. No backswing.
2. Elbow and humeral flexion.
3. Circular, upward backswing.
4. Circular, downward backswing.

Humeral Action

1. Oblique.
2. Aligned but independent.
3. Humerus lags.

Elbow Action

1. Elbow collapsed.
2. Elbow partially flexed.
3. Elbow held at right angle.

Forearm Action

1. No forearm lag.
2. Partial forearm lag.
3. Full (delayed) forearm lag.

Trunk Action

1. No trunk action.
2. Extension and/or flexion of the trunk.
3. Spinal rotation with the pelvis stationary or spinal-then-pelvic rotation.
4. Block rotation.

5s. Sidearm channel—differentiated rotation and no lateral flexion of the trunk.

5o. Overarm channel—block rotation and lateral flexion of the trunk.

6. Overarm channel—differentiated rotation and lateral flexion of the trunk.

Stepping Action

1. No step.
2. Same foot forward as throwing hand.
3. Opposite foot forward as throwing hand.

Anyone wishing to use these categories for evaluation of overhand throwing development should consult the references at the end of this chapter for complete descriptions of the actions. This system of analysis is not easy to use and it is time-consuming. The developers of the sequences recommend "observing one component at a time for each student for 5–10 trials." This means that 25 to 50 throws would be required for a complete categorization of the throwing form of one child. Under some circumstances the time expenditure would be worthwhile, but in most school situations less precise skill evaluation will suffice.

MATURE PATTERN FOR THE OVERARM THROW

Plagenhoef defined the throwing motion as "the properly timed co-ordination of accelerations and decelerations of all body segments in a sequence of action from the left foot to the right hand that produces maximum absolute velocity of the right hand."[29] His concept of the motion is based on a link system of movements starting from the planted left foot, moving upward to the left hip, diagonally across the pelvis and up the trunk to the right shoulder, through the right elbow, and out to the right hand. The proper coordination of movement in this system ultimately produces the whiplike arm action that typifies the mature overarm throw.

The coordination of accelerations and decelerations of body parts referred to by Plagenhoef was clarified by Atwater in a study of the throwing patterns of five skilled males, five skilled females, and five females of average ability.[2] She found that as a segment accelerates, the succeeding segment lags behind before acquiring the speed of the segment(s) moving it, and then quickly accelerates to reach an even greater angular speed as the preceding segment decelerates. In this way there is a buildup in velocity with the action of succeeding segments. Atwater concluded that "the ability to achieve initial ball velocities well above average appears to be directly associated with the thrower's ability to permit decelerating-accelerating motion of each segment to occur in sequence on top of the accelerating-decelerating speed of the preceding segment." Atwater's point explains in part why unitary patterns and unitary components such as block rotation are not effective in producing high ball velocity.

The importance of the various components of the throwing pattern to ball velocity was convincingly demonstrated by Toyoshima and associates who progressively eliminated components, which resulted in diminished ball speed.[42] Ball velocity in a normal overhand throw was 90.9 ft/sec. It was 76.8 ft/sec when the stride was eliminated, 57.7 ft/sec when the lower body was immobilized, 48.2 ft/sec when the upper body was also immobilized, and 38.7 ft/sec when only the elbow and wrist were free.

A capsule description of the sequence of movements in the basic pattern for the overhand throw is Step-Turn-Throw. This triad is a simplification of the movements in a complex skill, but it helps isolate key points for instructional emphasis and underlines the proper coordination and timing of movements. An outline of the full pattern for a right-handed thrower is as follows:

Preparatory Movement

1. The body pivots to the right with the weight on the right foot, and the throwing arm swings backward and upward.

Throwing Movements

2. The left foot strides forward in the intended direction of the throw.
3. The hips, then spine, and shoulders rotate counterclockwise as the throwing arm is retracted to the final point of its reversal.
4. The upper arm is rotated medially and the forearm is extended with a whipping action.
5. The ball is released at a point just forward of the head with the arm nearly extended at the elbow.

Follow-Through

6. The movement is continued until the momentum generated in the throwing action is dissipated.

This sequence is the general pattern of movements in a vigorous, forceful overhand throw. The order of the successive movements in the sequence is quite specific, but there is overlapping in conformance with the accelerating-decelerating principle of segment action. The precise manner in which each of the movements is performed may vary because of the starting position, the purpose of the throw, and individual differences in strength and flexibility, but the sequence remains constant. Collins found a remarkable similarity in the basic mechanics of the overarm and sidearm throws.[5] Diagrams of the movements used in the overhand throw by the adult male and the adult female in Collins's study are shown in Figure 5–6. Collins's findings were corroborated

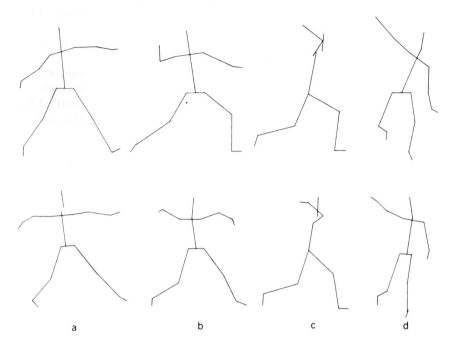

Fig. 5–6. Overhand throwing pattern of an adult female (lower) and an adult male (upper). (a) Beginning of pelvic rotation; (b) beginning of spinal rotation; (c) beginning of shoulder medial rotation; and (d) beginning of wrist flexion (front view). The similarities in the basic movements are evident. The conspicuous lack of lateral flexion in the female is the main difference (d), and it probably results from the restrictive position of her left leg. (Adapted from Collins.[5])

by Atwater who also studied the sidearm and overarm throwing patterns of skilled males and females.[1] Her conclusion was that the rate, sequence, and timing for pelvic rotation, spinal rotation, shoulder lateral rotation, shoulder medial rotation, and elbow extension were impressively similar for both throws.

PREPARATORY MOVEMENTS

The preparatory movements contribute to the throw only insofar as they put the body in a position for the application of effective leverage in the throwing motion. These movements can vary from the elaborate ritual used by baseball pitchers during their "windup," to the simple and ineffective backward twisting of the trunk employed by a child who stands in a forward stride position with his opposite foot forward. In mature form, preparation for the full overhand throw with maximum effort involves shifting of the body weight to the right leg and rotating the trunk approximately 90° to the right. The throwing arm is swung backward and somewhat upward, but ordinarily the cocking of the

Fig. 5–7. Mature overarm throwing form. Sequence is from bottom to top. (a) Lateral view; (b) top view; and (c) rear view. (Based on data from Atwater.[2])

throwing arm is not completed until well after the beginning of the throwing motion.

FORWARD STRIDE AND LEG ACTION

The series of forward movements in the throw begins with a vigorous stride. Body weight is driven forward from the right foot as the left foot strides well forward, reaching slightly to the left. Forward body movement initiated by the stride continues throughout the throwing motion and is terminated in the follow-through phase of the pattern.[26] Although body weight is shifted forward with the stride, the lower part of the body is blocked so that the link system can develop the whipping action of the arm. In high-velocity throws, the blocking leg often extends at the knee during the final action of the throwing arm and, by thrusting the left hip backward, it presumably contributes to the total body whip and to the linear velocity of the hand (Fig. 5–7).

The stride was found to be an important factor in a study that attempted to predict ball velocity from segmental analysis.[37] Vertical push-off leg force and stride length were key factors in ball velocity variance for 27 male members of a university varsity baseball squad. Length of stride seems to be related to level of skill and to throwing conditions. The average length of stride was 85.8% of standing height for 19 major league, 21 minor league, and 19 college pitchers who were filmed while pitching from a mound in competition.[38] By contrast, the average length of stride was 65% of standing height for the skilled males in Atwater's study,[2] 60% for the skilled females, and only 33% for average female throwers.

TRUNK ROTATION

Just before the left foot touches the ground, the pelvis starts to rotate to the left and it is followed in order by rotation of the spine and shoulders. Body mass continues to move forward during trunk rotation, and the throwing arm reaches its final cocked position in preparation for medial rotation. The acceleration produced by trunk rotation contributes significantly to the velocity of the throw. Toyoshima et al. calculated that stride and body rotation contribute 46.9% of the ball velocity at release.[42]

ARM MOTION

While the shoulders are rotating vigorously forward, the forearm is forced backward and downward until it is nearly horizontal and the elbow remains bent at about a right angle. This lateral rotation of the humerus is the final cocking of the arm before the whipping action begins. The humerus lags slightly behind a line through the shoulders until the trunk has rotated to the left and the shoulders are nearly perpendicular to the intended direction of the throw. Then forceful medial rotation at the shoulder starts to swing the forearm forward, and extension at the elbow begins shortly thereafter. Forearm extension causes the elbow to elevate and, along with lateral trunk flexion, raises the arm to an oblique angle above the horizontal. The forearm is still extending at the instant the ball is released, but the arm is nearly straight. Wrist action, which had been accepted as the final and greatest contributor to ball velocity in the overhand throw, is a controversial feature. Collins reported incredible angular velocity connected with prerelease wrist action, but her findings have since been discounted.[5] Dobbins used elgons to measure joint movement and a circuit breaker system to indicate ball release.[9] With his precise procedure, he found that 26° of flexion had occurred at the wrist during forearm extension and the wrist was still in a position of 20° of hyperextension at release. The adult throwers studied by Atwater[2] and Tarbell[41] seemed to show a change from wrist hyperextension to full extension before release, but the precise change was difficult to ascertain. Even Tarbell's analysis of a throw that had been filmed at a camera speed of 1500 frames per second failed to clarify either the matter of wrist action or the question of how the ball leaves the hand. In her recent assessment of the research on wrist action, Atwater suggested that radioulnar pronation probably is more responsible than wrist flexion for hand movement immediately before and after release.[3]

The point at which the ball is released varies but is approximately even with a lateral plane just in front of the head. The intended angle of release and other factors, such as the maturity of the arm action, determine the precise point. Those who throw with a whipping or flailing arm motion release the ball near the plane in front of the head; those who are "pushers" release the ball farther forward. The distinction between pushing and whiplike arm motions is critical to the understanding of the mature throwing pattern. The immature pushing motion is a result of adducting the arm horizontally until the elbow is nearly in front of the shoulder before extending the forearm. Those who use a pushing action have less total range of movement in their throwing patterns and depend more upon simultaneous component action and the speed of muscular contraction than upon other factors for ball velocity. By contrast, the early dynamic actions in the mature throw cause the arm to be swung like a whip. Rapid sequential movements including rotation of the pelvis, spine, and shoulder build up a velocity that causes the forearm to be flung into extension at a greater speed than could be produced by voluntary muscle contraction.[42]

THE FOLLOW-THROUGH

After the ball has been released, the throwing arm continues diagonally downward across the body toward the forward support foot. The follow-through is important because it permits deceleration of the throwing arm and assures a smooth and safe finish of the forceful movement.

SPORT SKILLS USING THE BASIC PATTERN OF OVERARM THROWING

The basic mature pattern of throwing is used in a wide variety of sport skills. Each sport skill in the category of throwing has unique aspects and different velocity requirements, but there is common adherence to the basic pattern.

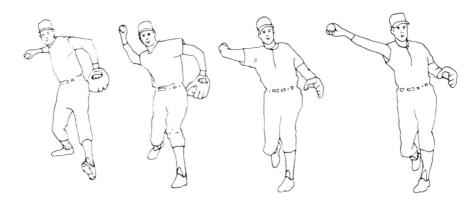

Fig. 5–8. Sidearm throw in baseball.

Fig. 5–9. Forward pass in football. Upper: skilled adult passer. Lower: 5-year-old passer.

THE SIDEARM THROW IN BASEBALL

Catching a rolling or bouncing ball and throwing it to first base quickly from an awkward position is a task that must be performed frequently by an infield baseball or softball player. The sidearm throw is used on this and on other similar occasions when a rapid arm action is needed. Finley demonstrated that the sidearm throwing action takes less time than the overhand motion because the arm is not cocked as far back.[11] He also pointed out that the sidearm throw imparts less initial velocity to the ball than the overhand throw. That is not a drawback in this situation because the reduced total amount of time for the throw is a more important factor than the initial velocity of the ball. If the sidearm motion is used in pitching, the situation is different because initial velocity is a more important factor. It is possible to provide the desired ball speed by using a full wind-up and expanded throwing motion. Sakaris found no difference in ball velocity when a fastball pitch was made using overhand and sidearm throws.[36]

The basic throwing pattern emerges clearly in the sidearm form of the player in Figure 5–8. He steps forward, rotates his trunk, cocks his arm, swings his elbow forward, and whips his forearm into extension. Movements in the sidearm throw generally are abbreviated in comparison to the exaggeration of the pitching motion or the throw to home plate from the outfield. Although the amount of body movement in the different forms of throwing used in baseball varies considerably, the same underlying fundamental movement pattern is present in each.

THE FOOTBALL FORWARD PASS

Stride, turn-cock, and throw. These steps in the fundamental throwing sequence are emphasized vividly in the series of actions in Figure 5–9. The movements are the same as in the baseball throw except that the arm motion of the passer is a bit lower than might be expected in the overhand throw. For this sequence of drawings, the football was thrown a distance of just 15 yards at a moderate rate of speed. The action at all joints would have been greater and the ball would have been released at a high point if the distance of the throw had been 40 or 50 yards.

A distinctive part of the passing pattern is the arm action, which is influenced by the size of the ball and by the method of release. The passer in Figure 5–9 carefully keeps his hand behind the ball when his arm is being cocked and then smoothly whips his hand forward so that the ball can be spun around its long axis and released without wobbling. The child is particularly aware of the problem of handling the football when learning to pass it. Even when using a junior-size ball, he limits his backswing and tends to push the ball ineffectively until he discovers the knack of imparting spin during release.

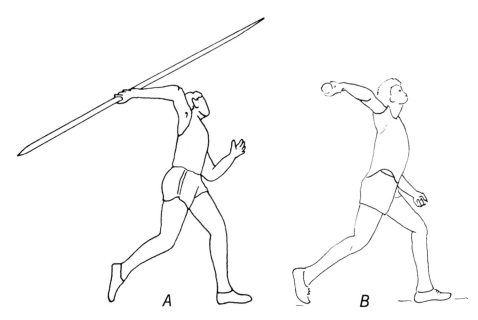

Fig. 5–10.   A, The javelin throw; and B, the baseball pitch. Note the similarities and the differences in the body positions in these two sport skills.

THE JAVELIN THROW

A grossly exaggerated version of the movements in the overhand throwing pattern is used in the javelin event in track and field athletics. The aim of the throw is to get maximum performance by throwing the javelin as far as possible. The goal of providing maximum effective velocity is apparent from the beginning of the movement. A run helps develop forward momentum, and a pivot or cross step turns the body in preparation for unleashing powerful angular forces. Once the throwing motion begins, it is an unraveling of the fundamental series of movements in the overhand throw, each vigorously delineated. The thrower in Figure 5–10a has been stopped after stepping forward, rotating his hips and trunk, and starting the forward movement of his throwing arm. This position compares favorably with the exaggerated position used in the overhand baseball pitch (Fig. 5–10b). The noticeable differences in position can be attributed to the greater forward momentum of the javelin thrower and his much higher angle of release.

OVERHAND BASKETBALL PASS

The overhand basketball pass is another specific sport skill in which much of the basic pattern of the overhand throw prevails even though maximum ball velocity at release is not the objective. It is demonstrated by the player in Figure 5–11 who takes a forward step, rotates his hips and trunk forward, swings his upper arm medialward, and extends his

Fig. 5–11. Overhand basketball pass. The forearm lags during trunk rotation, but the weight of the ball encourages pushing more than whipping arm action.

forearm just before the ball is released. The limitation of the backward swing of the throwing arm that was noted earlier in connection with the football pass is even more necessary in the overhand basketball pass. For most persons, the basketball is too large and too heavy to be controlled by grasping it with one hand, so a second hand helps raise the ball into the throwing position. Control of the ball at the end of the backswing is maintained by cradling it in the hand momentarily until forward motion of the arm begins, and then lateral rotation of the forearm is limited in the final stage of cocking. These adjustments limit the effective range of arm movement and interfere with the production of a whiplike motion.

The amount of backswing of the throwing arm in the overhand basketball pass varies according to the size, strength, and skill of the thrower. Children and unskilled players find the basketball truly an unwieldy object and tend to use more of a push than a throw in the final phase of arm action. Girls who are being tested on the basketball throw for distance tend to use a sidearm slinging motion because with this form they have improved leverage and a greater distance over which to develop velocity. However, when the throw must be accurate as well as far, the girls are inclined to return to the overhand throwing pattern.

DEVELOPMENTAL ASPECTS OF THE UNDERHAND THROW

The role of underhand patterns in the overall development of throwing is unclear. Underhand throws are used under certain circumstances, as was noted by Jones,[22] and sometimes one is even substituted for an overhand pattern by a child who is throwing for distance or for maximum velocity. There unquestionably is preferential development of overhand patterns, and this fact seems to be a reflection of the ultimate use to which throwing skills are put. Most of the throwing done in games and sports is overhand rather than underhand. Softball pitching is about the only high-velocity underhand throw used in popular games, and it is a specialized skill not widely practiced. Other underhand sports skills such as bowling and horseshoe pitching merely require rolling and tossing actions. Despite the lack of potential for a significant amount of future use, there is observable development of underhand patterns. Some of the changes that appear to be involved in the development were found in a recent study,[45] a discussion of which follows.

The unilateral and bilateral underhand throwing patterns of 76 kindergarten and first-grade children were examined in relation to developmental changes in foot and leg action, hip and trunk movement, and arm action.

Leg Action. Leg action closely resembled the simple patterns commonly associated with stage progress in overarm throwing. The progression included five phases, starting with feet together, followed by a forward stride position on the same side, a forward step with the same side foot, a forward stride position on the opposite side, and a forward step with the opposite foot. Ipsilateral leg involvement was minimal. Most of the throws were made with the feet together or with the contralateral foot forward. A lifting motion created by a slight dip followed by vigorous extension at the knee and ankle frequently was used by the less skilled throwers, sometimes in lieu of a forward step. The upward thrusting leg action shown in Figure 5–12 was observed less often as the amount of forward movement in the entire pattern increased. Gradual increases in the length of the forward foot position and in the length of the stride occurred as movement into the throw increased.

Trunk Action. In the underhand throw, trunk action involved flexion-extension, rotation, and a combination of the two types of movements. Flexion-extension was the exclusive trunk action in some simple patterns when the feet remained together. The trunk was flexed as the

Fig. 5–12. Lifting action with legs during an underhand throw.

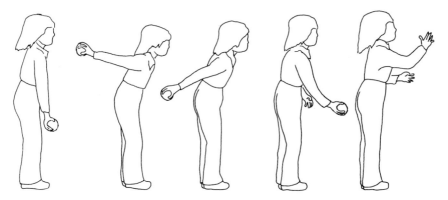

Fig. 5–13. Flexion/extension of the trunk as part of a developmental underhand throwing pattern.

Fig. 5–14. Trunk action in both anteroposterior and horizontal planes. Compare with figure 5–19.

Fig. 5–15. Throwing arm remains straight unless there is an exaggerated lift near the point of release.

throwing arm was drawn back and then extended as the throw was made (Fig. 5–13). Trunk rotation came into play and increased progressively with the length of the back swing and the length of the stride. Flexion and rotation were combined with increasing effectiveness as skill improved (Fig. 5–14). The trunk generally appeared to operate as a unit during rotation, but there was some evidence that the most skillful throwers in the group initiated rotation with the pelvis while delaying the shoulder turn. In some cases considerable sequential trunk rotation occurred because arm action was exaggerated, departing from the sagittal toward the horizontal plane in a low whipping discus-type throw.

Arm Action. Arm action was the most consistent part of the unilateral underarm throw. It occurred mostly in the anteroposterior plane. As the amount of backswing increased, the hand moved slightly toward the midline near the end and then swung lateralward to get back into the anteroposterior groove on the throw. The throwing arm was straight at the elbow from the beginning of the forward movement until close to release except when there was lifting action by the legs near the end of the throw (Fig. 5–15). Then the thrower tended to bend at the elbow and lift with the forearm at release or immediately afterward. The range of arm movement on the backswing increased especially as the forward

Fig. 5–16. A forward stride and forward trunk lean flatten the arc of the hand in the one-arm underhand throw.

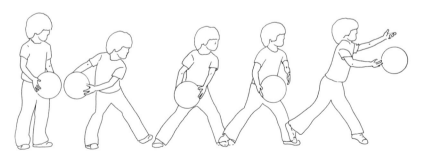

Fig. 5–17. Underhand throw of a large ball. A long stride with the opposite foot, use of two hands and bent elbows, and extensive shoulder rotation are common features of the throwing pattern.

step lengthened and the effort of the throw increased. These changes combined to produce an increasing amount of opening. An attempt to throw fast with a straight arm seemed to make the timing of release difficult for the young children. The point of release varied considerably even though the primary arm action did not. Late release, which was much more common than early release, occurred in many throws. It was especially common in the throws in which there was a lifting action by the legs just before release, and it was the least prevalent in the patterns that included a long stride by the opposite leg. The forward stride tended to flatten the arc of the hand and make it horizontal for a greater distance at the approximate point of release (Fig. 5–16).

When an 8-inch rubber playground ball was thrown, many of the children made adjustments in form because of the increase in size and weight. Most of the children used a two-handed throw and most had a *bent elbow* on the dominant throwing arm. Two hands were used to get the ball back into a position for throwing and to keep it under control during most of the forward arm movement (Fig. 5–17). The bending of the back arm served a dual purpose. It reduced the length of the throwing lever, effectively lessening the resistance to be overcome in the throw, and it offered natural protection against hyperextension stress at the elbow during the vigorous forward arm motion.

The bilateral arm action that was used with the larger and heavier

Fig. 5–18. Skilled underhand throw. Lateral view.

Fig. 5–19. Skilled underhand throw. Rear view.

ball influenced the underhand throwing patterns in additional ways. When both hands were used, more backward trunk rotation was needed to get the ball into the throwing position. Less backswing was possible with two hands on the ball, so the additional distance needed for applying force was gained either by taking a stride or by increasing the length of the stride. The longer stride and the shorter backswing combined to produce more of a pushing than a pendular arm motion. The children had less of a tendency to lift with the legs near release, but the upward thrust did not disappear from the patterns used when the larger ball was thrown. A child who lifted on a unilateral throw tended to lift somewhat when making a two-handed throw.

Some interrelationships were observed among components used in underhand throws, but distinct and frequently displayed whole patterns did not emerge from the study. Loosely structured whole patterns that can be used in the analysis of skill development might be assembled later when additional evidence becomes available or when the demand for an evaluation device increases.

MATURE FORM FOR THE UNDERHAND THROW

One distinctive feature of the mature overarm throw is the whipping arm motion with elbow extension. That same basic arm action can be executed in an underhand pattern if the trunk is sufficiently lowered and laterally flexed, but it is a difficult adjustment to make. The most commonly used underhand throw eliminates forearm extension, and the entire whipping action, such as it is, is performed with a straight arm. Thus, in the typical underhand pattern, the two-link arm action in the overarm pattern is replaced by a unitary flinging arm motion.

The fast pitch used in softball is a high-velocity underhand throw which, with slight modification, can serve as a model for skilled form. Both the windmill and the figure-eight styles of pitching have exaggerated motions in which the ball is moved through a maximum effec-

tive distance for acceleration. When these extreme wind-ups are eliminated, skilled underhand throwers demonstrate the following pattern
(Figs. 5–18 and 5–19):

1. A forward step with the opposite foot, slight forward trunk flexion,
   and a backward swing by the throwing arm. The pelvis and upper
   spine rotate backward in the process.
2. Forward rotation of the pelvis, followed in close sequence by
   upper spine rotation and arm flexion.
3. Ball release when the hand of the throwing arm is at a point just
   forward of a vertical line through the shoulder.

Two features in the basic underhand pattern are of special interest.
One is the relatively small amount of trunk rotation, and the other is
the sweeping arm movement. Trunk rotation in the single-arm underhand throw is relatively limited because arm action takes place predominantly in an anteroposterior plane around an axis perpendicular
to the vertical axis of the trunk. A small amount of lateral flexion toward
the side of the throwing arm allows the ball to be kept in an anteroposterior plane during the forward throwing motion. In the backswing,

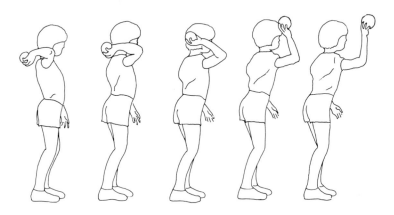

Fig. 5–20. Overarm throw by a 6-year-old girl.

Fig. 5–21. Overarm throw by a 6-year-old boy.

Fig. 5–22. Overarm throwing pattern of a 9-year-old girl.

the arm is brought to a hyperextended position above the horizontal. In order to reach that position, a small amount of outward rotation and abduction occurs at the shoulder joint. During forward arm movement, the elbow is virtually straight except when an extremely high-velocity throw is made. Then there is a tendency to keep the arm bent slightly at the elbow to protect against hyperextension strain. Wrist flexion is thought to contribute to high-speed underhand throws, but the nature of the contribution has not been clarified.[6,48]

ANALYSIS OF FORM IN OVERARM THROWING

Analysis of throwing patterns by direct observation is not difficult if it is kept at a simple level by dealing with features that are relatively easy to identify. The widely used stages suggested by Wild and adapted by others will suffice for most practical purposes. The stages illustrated in Figures 5–1, 5–2, 5–3, and 5–4 could be reviewed and then applied to the throwing patterns shown in Figures 5–20, 5–21, 5–22, and 5–23 as preparation for live evaluation of throwing. The same procedure can be followed using the Ohio State SIGMA, the five-stage Michigan State sequence, or the Roberton-Halverson check list, although the latter is more precise in some actions and not as easy to use as the systems that employ three to five stages.

Fig. 5–23. Overarm throwing pattern of a 7-year-old boy.

Fig. 5–24. Vigorous underhand throw by a 5-year-old boy.

Two features of high-velocity throwing that are quite difficult to analyze quickly by direct observation are the trunk rotation sequence and
the final throwing motion of the arm. Because both occur rapidly, direct
visual analysis can depend upon secondary as well as upon primary
information. The observer, for example, can be relatively confident that
a high degree of throwing skill has been reached if:

1. The trunk has been turned well away from the intended direction
   of the throw at the start.

Fig. 5–25. Underhand patterns used by a 6-year-old boy to throw a small ball (upper) and a large ball (lower). In what specific ways are the patterns different?

2. There is a long and vigorous forward stride with the opposite foot.
3. The throwing arm is swung downward and backward during the forward step.
4. The forward throwing sequence is explosively fast with a forearm lag and lateral trunk flexion near release.

That the important whipping action has occurred can only be inferred from these observable secondary features, but the probability that it has occurred is high. Careful, selective observation of three or four throws should allow a reasonably accurate stage or trend analysis for all but the most demanding circumstances.

ANALYSIS OF THE UNDERHAND THROW

Neither developmental patterns nor component steps have been formally established for all aspects of the underhand throw. Still it is possible to make some judgments regarding motor pattern development. Two critical features to be observed are leg action and arm/leg coordination. Each of the two features in an underhand throwing pattern can be analyzed easily for the presence of one of the following progressive steps.

Leg Action

1. Feet together.

2. Same side foot forward.
3. Opposite side foot forward.
4. Long forward stride with opposite side foot.

Arm/Leg Coordination

1. Arm backswing before leg action (unitary coordination).
2. Arm backswing during forward step (opening).

As progress is made in these two features of the underhand throwing pattern, there will be trends toward less upward and more forward body movement and toward a lower and more forward position during follow-through. These few points should serve as a tentative basis for a general evaluation of underhand throwing patterns. They can be applied in the analysis of the sequences in Figures 5–24 and 5–25.

REFERENCES

1. Atwater, A.E.: Cinematographic analysis of overarm and sidearm throwing patterns. AAHPER Research Paper, Washington, D.C., 1968.
2. Atwater, A.E.: Movement characteristics of the overarm throw: a kinematic analysis of men and women performers. Doctoral dissertation. Madison, University of Wisconsin, 1970.
3. Atwater, A.E.: Biomechanics of overarm throwing movements and of throwing injuries. In Exercise and Sport Sciences Reviews. Vol. 7. Edited by R.S. Hutton and D.I. Miller. Philadelphia, The Franklin Institute Press, 1979.
4. Auxter, D.: Throwing patterns of the mentally retarded. Research abstracts. AAHPER, Washington, D.C., 1973.
5. Collins, P.: Body mechanics of the overarm and sidearm throws. Unpublished master's thesis. University of Wisconsin, 1960.
6. Cooper, J., Adrian, M., and Glassow, R.: Kinesiology. St. Louis, C.V. Mosby, 1982.
7. Deach, D.: Genetic development of motor skills of children two through six years of age. Unpublished doctoral dissertation. Ann Arbor, University of Michigan, 1950.
8. DiRocco, P., and Roberton, M.: Implications of motor development research: the overarm throw in the mentally retarded. Phys. Educ., 38(1):1127, 1981.
9. Dobbins, D.A.: Loss of triceps on an overarm throw for speed. Unpublished master's thesis. Madison, University of Wisconsin, 1970.
10. Ekern, S.R.: An analysis of selected measures of the overarm throwing patterns of elementary school boys and girls. Unpublished doctoral dissertation. Madison, University of Wisconsin, 1969.
11. Finley, R.: Kinesiological analysis of human motion. Unpublished doctoral thesis. Springfield, MA, Springfield College, 1961.
12. Frederick, S.: Performance of selected motor tasks by three-, four- and five-year-old children. Unpublished doctor of physical education dissertation. Bloomington, Indiana University, 1977.
13. Glassow, R.B., Halverson, L.E., and Rarick, G.L.: Improvement of motor development and physical fitness in elementary school children. Cooperative Research Project No. 696. Madison, University of Wisconsin, 1965.
14. Gutteridge, M.V.: A study of motor achievements of young children. Arch. Psychol., 244:1, 1939.
15. Halverson, L.E., and Roberton, M.A.: A study of motor pattern development in young children. Report to National Convention of AAHPER. Chicago, 1966.
16. Halverson, L.E., and Roberton, M.A.: The effects of instruction on overhand throwing development in children. In Psychology of Motor Behavior and Sport: 1978. Edited by G.C. Roberts and K.M. Newell. Champaign, IL, Human Kinetics, 1979.
17. Hanson, M.: Motor performance testing of elementary school age children. Unpublished doctoral dissertation. Seattle, WA, University of Washington, 1965.

18. Hanson, S.: A comparison of the overhand throw performance of instructed and non-instructed kindergarten boys and girls. Unpublished master's thesis. Madison, University of Wisconsin, 1961.
19. Hardin, D., and Garcia, M.: Diagnostic performance tests for elementary children (grades 1–4). J. Phys. Educ. Rec. Dance, 53(2):48, 1982.
20. Hrkal, K.: An experimental study of the development of the mature form of the overarm throwing pattern in preschool children. Unpublished master's thesis. London, Canada, University of Western Ontario, 1977.
21. Johnson, W.: A comparison of motor creativity and motor performance of young children. Unpublished doctor of physical education dissertation. Bloomington, Indiana University, 1977.
22. Jones, F.: A descriptive and mechanical analysis of throwing skills of children. Unpublished master's thesis. Madison, University of Wisconsin, 1951.
23. Keogh, J.: Motor performance of elementary school children. Department of Physical Education, University of California, Los Angeles, March, 1965.
24. Langendorfer, S.: Longitudinal evidence for developmental changes in the preparatory phase of the overarm throw for force. Research Abstracts. AAHPERD, Washington, D.C., 1980.
25. Leme, S.A.: Developmental throwing patterns in adult female performers within a selected velocity range. Unpublished master's thesis. Madison, University of Wisconsin, 1973.
26. Lyon, W.: A cinematographical analysis of the overhand baseball throw. Unpublished master's thesis. Madison, University of Wisconsin, 1961.
27. Mahmoud, N.: The effects of instruction and practice on the overarm throwing patterns of preschool children. Unpublished doctoral dissertation. Eugene, OR, University of Oregon, 1979.
28. Nichols, B.: A comparison of two methods of developing the overhand throw for distance in four, five, six, and seven year old children. Unpublished doctoral dissertation. Iowa City, University of Iowa, 1971.
29. Plagenhoef, S.: Patterns of Human Motion: A Cinematographic Analysis. Englewood Cliffs, N.J., Prentice-Hall, 1971.
30. Rarick, G.L., and Dobbins, D.A.: Basic components in the motor performance of educable mentally retarded children: implications for curriculum development. Department of Physical Education, University of California, Berkeley, 1972.
31. Roberton, M.A.: Stability of stage categorizations across trials: implications for the 'stage theory' of overarm throw development. Unpublished doctoral dissertation. Madison, University of Wisconsin, 1975.
32. Roberton, M.A., and Halverson, L.E.: The developing child—his changing movement. In Physical Education for Children: A Focus on the Teaching Process. Edited by B.J. Logsdon et al. Philadelphia, Lea & Febiger, 1977.
33. Roberton, M.A., Halverson, L.E., and Langendorfer, S.: Longitudinal changes in children's overarm throw ball velocities. Res. Q. Am. Assoc. Health Phys. Educ., 50:2, 1979.
34. Roberts, T.W.: Incident light velocimetry. Percept. Mot. Skills, 34:263, 1972.
35. Ryan, T.: A comparison of selected basic gross motor skills of moderately retarded and normal children of middle childhood age utilizing the Ohio State University Scale of Intra Gross Motor Assessment. Unpublished doctoral dissertation. Columbus, Ohio State University, 1977.
36. Sakaris, J.: Biomechanical analysis of overhand and sidearm fastball pitching techniques in baseball. Unpublished master's thesis. Gainesville, University of Florida, 1978.
37. Sanders, J.: A practical application of the segmental method of analysis to determine throwing ability. Unpublished doctoral dissertation. Bloomington, Indiana University, 1977.
38. Schutzler, L.: A cinematographic analysis of stride length in highly skilled baseball pitchers. Unpublished master's thesis. Tucson, AZ, University of Arizona, 1980.
39. Seefeldt, V., Reuschlein, S., and Vogel, P.: Sequencing motor skills within the physical education curriculum. Paper presented at AAHPER meeting, Houston, 1972.
40. Singer, F.: Comparison of the development of the overarm throwing patterns of good

and poor performers (girls). Unpublished master's thesis. Madison, University of Wisconsin, 1961.

41. Tarbell, T.: Some biomechanical aspects of the overhand throw. *In* Proceedings of the C.I.C. Symposium on Biomechanics. Edited by J. Cooper. Athletic Institute, Chicago, 1971.

42. Toyoshima, S., Hoshikawa, T., Miyashita, M., and Oguri, T.: Contribution of the body parts to throwing performance. *In* Biomechanics IV. Edited by R. Nelson and C. Morehouse. Baltimore, University Park Press, 1974.

43. Van Slooten, P.: Performance of selected motor-coordination tasks by young boys and girls in six socio-economic groups. Unpublished doctoral dissertation. Bloomington, Indiana University, 1973.

44. Wester, B.: A comparison of the accuracy of throwing of third, fourth, and fifth grade boys. Unpublished master's thesis. Iowa City, University of Iowa, 1939.

45. Wickstrom, R.: Underhand throwing patterns of kindergarten and first grade children. Research abstracts. AAHPERD, Washington, D.C., 1982.

46. Wild, M.: The behavior pattern of throwing and some observations concerning its course of development in children. Doctoral dissertation. Madison, University of Wisconsin, 1937.

47. Wild, M.: The behavior pattern of throwing and some observations concerning its course of development in children. Res. Q. Am. Assoc. Health Phys. Educ., 9(3):20, 1938.

48. Wolter, C.: Comparison of measures of the elbow, radioulnar and wrist joints for fast, curve, and slow softball pitches. Unpublished master's thesis. Madison, University of Wisconsin, 1965.

49. Zollinger, R.: Mechanical analysis of windmill fast pitch in women's softball. Res. Q., 44(3):290, 1973.

CHAPTER **6**

Catching

Catching, as a fundamental skill, involves the use of the hand(s) and/ or other parts of the body to stop and control an aerial ball or object. This definition purposely is broad and inclusive. Its permissiveness regarding the use of multiple body parts makes it applicable to minimal form, and its reference to the use of the hands to deal with aerial objects ties it to mature form.

Although the general definition of catching is broad, the standard for skilled form is not. The model for mature form in this skill category is hand-catching. It has been the standard for evaluating effectiveness and efficiency in most research on catching technique, and it is the form used almost exclusively in sports in which ball-catching is a major skill. When other body segments are used in combination with the hands, the act becomes a form of trapping. Some forms of trapping are commonly seen early in the developmental hierarchy of catching but disappear as skill develops.

CATCHING PERFORMANCE

Proficiency in catching is developed at a comparatively slow rate. The evidence concerning its emergence is insufficient to provide a precise and convincing picture, particularly with respect to performance expectancy according to age. Observation of the catching behavior of children ages 18 months to 8 years led Seefeldt to conclude that success in catching a ball is possible for 2- and 3-year-old children.[17] The success to which he referred, presumably, is a form of trapping and is at the most primitive level of the 5-stage developmental sequence he helped identify (pages 150–151). Sinclair found evidence of success at an early age when trapping types of catches were used but saw little indication of active use of hands in the catching patterns of young children.[21]

Gutteridge reported that 56% of 78 five-year-old children and 63% of 67 six-year-old children were proficient catchers.[3] By contrast, 80%

of the five-year-old children in her study were rated as proficient throwers. These figures support the well-known fact that although throwing and catching have a close functional relationship, throwing is learned more quickly than catching.

Catching behavior is difficult to study because of the number of variables influencing the measurement of performance. Major variables are: (1) the size of the ball; (2) the distance the ball travels before it is caught; (3) the method of projecting the ball; (4) the direction of the ball in relation to the catcher; (5) the speed of the ball; (6) the precatch change of position required; and (7) the arm-hand action of the catcher. In addition, there are age-related sensory and perceptual factors. All of these variables are illustrated in the following presentation of details from investigations that have contributed bits and pieces to the current level of understanding of catching performance. Despite the evident difficulty of learning to catch, both boys and girls tend to show improvement in catching skill each year and at successive grade levels through the elementary school and beyond. The improvement trends are based upon success in catching increasingly smaller balls and upon greater effectiveness when using hand-catching technique.

Hoadley constructed a throwing machine capable of projecting a ball 16 feet and used balls of 3 different sizes in her study of the catching ability of 250 elementary school children in grades 1 through 4.[6] She found that boys and girls improved in the ability to catch large and small balls at successive grades, with the most significant increases coming between grades 2 and 3 for both sexes. At the first grade level Hoadley observed no sex difference in catching balls of any size, and at grades 2 and 3 she found no sex superiority in catching the large ball. Boys in this study were able to catch a small ball better than girls in grades 2, 3, and 4.

A hoop-controlled tennis ball catch was used by Seils to measure the catching ability of 510 primary school children.[19] The ball traveled 10 linear feet or less and through a controlling hoop before being caught. On the basis of this relatively simple test, Seils found improvement at successive grade levels, with boys showing better average performances at grades 1 and 2, and girls presenting a higher average score at grade 3.

The distance the ball traveled before being caught was increased in Warner's study of the motor ability of 841 third-, fourth-, and fifth-grade boys.[25] A ball was tossed to the catcher at chest height from a distance of 20 feet. Five trials were given with a volleyball and 5 with a tennis ball. Five catches out of 5 attempts with the volleyball were scored by 70.1% of the third-grade boys, 84.6% of the fourth-grade boys, and 92.5% of the fifth-grade boys. No one failed to make at least 1 catch with the larger ball. A perfect score on 5 attempts with a tennis ball was made respectively by 57.5%, 78.5%, and 87.2% of the third, fourth, and fifth graders. Less than 1% of the third-grade boys failed to make at least 1 successful catch of a tennis ball.

A different approach to the study of catching performance was used by Bruce.[1] He varied the trajectory and velocity of the ball and in several experimental conditions required the catcher to move in preparation for catching. A ball-throwing machine controlled the projection of the tennis balls that were used, and each catching attempt was rated on a carefully devised 5-point scale. The subjects were 480 children equally divided between boys and girls and among grades 2, 4, and 6. His findings verified both the expected improvement of performance with advancing grade level and the anticipated superiority of the catching ability of boys. The results showing the effects of precatch change of position and increased ball velocity on performance are of special interest. Performance was not adversely affected when lateral movement was required prior to catching. The children encountered substantial difficulty, however, when it was necessary to adjust by moving forward or backward. The performance of children in the second and fourth grades also deteriorated when the velocity of the ball was increased. Because the sixth-grade children were not bothered by the increase in the speed of the ball, Bruce suggested the possibility of a critical value for velocity beyond which catching performance is impaired. This study was particularly significant because it reached into the relatively unopened bag of problems connected with advanced catching skill. Adjustive movement, height of ball trajectory, and ball velocity are factors most certainly related to comprehensive catching skill.

Adjustive movement was a major feature in Pederson's investigation of the catching behavior of 600 first, third, and fifth graders.[14] Eleven relatively simple catching tasks were devised, including a variety of situations requiring the child to catch an aerial ball before or after it bounced and with or without precatch adjustive movement. An 8½-inch playground ball was rolled off a special piece of apparatus from a height of 12 feet either directly toward the floor or toward a rebound board located on a low platform. Each attempt was scored on a 5-point scale, which ranged from a noncontact miss (0) to an unbobbled catch (4). Catching ability, as measured by Pederson, improved significantly for the children in each of the successive grades included in the study. Boys were more successful than girls in grades 1 and 3, but there was no difference in performance at grade 5. The generally high level of success in the catching tasks could be attributed to the simplicity of the tasks and/or tester control of the start of precatch movement, which minimized the inevitable problems associated with timing.

Catching performance depends partly upon the effectiveness with which visual cues are used. Torres studied the relationship between figure-ground perceptual ability and ball catching ability in 10- and 13-year-old boys and girls.[23] She found no sex differences in ground-figure perceptual ability at either age level, but both sexes in the older group were better in this visual perceptual ability. The test of ball catching ability consisted of making the spatial adjustments necessary for catching when the ball approached at different angles. Boys in both age groups were superior to girls in making the necessary spatial adjustments, and the older group was significantly better than the younger group. However, figure-ground perceptual ability had only a slight positive relationship to catching ability as measured in the study. Other visual abilities apparently are more important in catching performance.

Stereoacuity, simple reaction time (RT), and ball sport experience were studied in relation to catching performance by Starkes.[22] In her first study, she used 8 males at each age from 8 through 13 plus 1 group of young adult males. Catching performance was measured by the ability to catch a 2¼-inch sponge rubber ball projected at 22.7 mph from a distance of 20 feet and by the ability to match where a ball would be caught by simultaneously touching a spot on the opposite side of a Plexiglas shield from where the ball struck. Ball-catching improved at each age and all subjects above the age of 12 made perfect scores. The ball-catching test was too simple for the two older groups but they continued to improve in the matching test. Analysis of the data indicated that age, ball sport experience, depth perception, and simple RT all contributed to catching performance and in that order of relative importance. In her second experiment, Starkes used the same procedure on boys and girls ages 6, 9, and 12. The ball test was too difficult for the 6-year-olds, so it was changed to an underhand toss from half the distance. With the modified test, boys were 82% and girls were 50% successful in ball-catching. In the regular catching and matching tests, boys surpassed the girls at both 9 and 12 year age levels. Starkes found no sex differences in simple RT or stereoacuity at any of the three age levels and no sex difference in ball sport experience at ages 6 and 9. As with the first study, age was the factor most closely related to catching performance.

Hellweg analyzed the perceptual and performance characteristics of the catching skill of the best and the poorest of a group of 6- to 7-year-old children.[5] The 10 best and 10 poorest catchers were selected on the basis of ratings by three judges who used a 5-point scale. The two groups were tested and found to have equally mature visual systems. They were also tested on the ability to judge the path of an approaching ball and indicate when it arrived at a predetermined point, and again there was no significant difference between the groups. The test of catching performance utilized a soft, fleece-covered ball 4 inches in diameter that was projected a distance of 15 feet before arriving at the catcher. The major visual difference between the groups was that the successful catchers appeared to track the ball until it was contacted, whereas the nonsuccessful catchers closed their eyes prior to contact. The nonvisual factors differentiating the groups were that the successful catchers initiated movement toward the ball earlier, and they were starting to give with the ball at contact rather than continuing to reach for it as the nonsuccessful group did.

Hellweg's finding on the importance of watching the ball is consistent with the results of a study by Whiting et al.[26,27] Whiting's group varied the amount of time during the early part of flight that a ball could be seen before it had to be caught. As the opportunity for watching the flight of the ball increased, the catching success of the 36 adult male subjects also increased. Subsequently Whiting concluded that a skilled catcher who has learned the flight characteristics of a ball does not need to keep his eyes on the ball during its entire flight. However, the less skilled the catcher is, the more important it is to watch the entire trajectory.

The importance of sufficient viewing time to catching performance has been verified under differing conditions with adult females and with adolescent males. Nessler,[13] who studied adults, investigated the effect of limiting room light so that the ball could be seen only the last 0.2 to 0.5 seconds of flight. A Ball-Boy projected a tennis ball a distance of 27 feet to a point on a wall 11 feet from the floor. Subjects stood 21 feet from the rebound wall and attempted to catch the ball as soon as light allowed its flight to be seen. For the 65 skilled college women who attempted to catch 20 balls under each of 5 restricted viewing conditions, the drop in performance with decreased viewing time was dramatic. It declined from an average of 16.49 catches at 0.5 seconds of viewing time to 6.43 at 0.3 seconds, to a low of 1.48 at 0.2 seconds. An important feature of the procedure was the lighting of the whole room, which required the catcher to pick the ball out of the entire display in order to make a catch. The emphasis in the task was on quick perception, fast reaction time, and rapid movement. The importance of perceptual speed in time-stressed situations like the one created in Nessler's study was supported by Hutt[7] who found a significant relationship between it and catching performance for 9- to 10-year-old boys.[7]

Viewing time and perceptual style were combined in MacGillivary's study of the catching behavior of 90 male high school students from grades 10 and 11.[9] Half the group were field independent and half were field dependent. The catching task for them was a one-handed catch of a tennis ball projected from 20 feet at a velocity of 40 ft/sec with an interception point 54 inches from the floor. After practicing the task for eight days, they were tested using varying amounts of viewing time. With performance judged on a 3-point scale, catching was increasingly more effective as viewing time progressed from 150 to 250 to 350 milliseconds. Subjects who were field independent performed better at the

2 shorter viewing times, but perceptual style made no difference at the 350-millisecond level.

Ball color has been investigated as another possible factor influencing catching performance. Different procedures have been used, and the research has yielded a variety of interesting findings. Riordan studied 32 preschool children who practiced catching an 8-inch ball that had been propelled by a two-hand chest pass from a distance of 15 feet and had bounced on a line 3 feet in front of them.[15] After 4½ weeks of practice, the 3-, 4-, and 5-year-old children were given 10 trials with red, yellow, and white balls. Neither the age nor the sex of the children affected their catching efficiency, but they were able to catch red and white balls significantly better than yellow ones. Color preference did not have a significant influence on the catching ability of the group.

Children from grades 2, 4, and 6 were the subjects in a similar study by Morris.[11] Fifteen boys and 15 girls from each grade were asked to catch yellow, white, and blue balls hurled at a speed of 45.8 ft/sec from a distance of 32 feet. Boys were better catchers than girls, and skill increased with age when a 5-point scoring system was employed. Yellow balls produced better performances at grades 2 and 6, while blue balls were more effective at grade 4. A blue ball against a white background was the best visual display, and a white ball against a white background was the worst.

Isaacs studied the effect of both ball size and ball color on the catching ability of 90 boys and girls whose average age was 89 months.[8] Colored balls 6 and 10 inches in diameter were propelled a distance of 10 feet at a speed of 8.5 mph, and a 5-point scale was employed for scoring. Males scored higher than females, color had no significant effect but preferred ball color did, and 6-inch balls were caught better than 10-inch ones. Unfortunately, the catching task was simple for the age group, and the scoring system valued hand catches which favored the smaller ball task.

The factor of direction of ball flight was added to the ball color variable by Shoney.[20] She studied 48 boys and girls between the ages of 8.5 and 11.5 years, varying the direction of red, green, and blue tennis balls which were propelled by a Ball-Boy. The direction of ball flight did affect catching ability, as might be expected. Shoney also concluded that the sex and skill level of the child had more influence on the ability to catch small balls than did color preference or object color.

As a whole, this group of investigations suggests the probability that ball color and color preference influence catching performance under certain conditions and not under others. The age of the catcher and the relative difficulty of the catching task seem to be the important variables. Because color preferences change with increasing age and preference is for colors that are easily and quickly seen, much more research taking these factors into consideration is needed before the precise effects of color on catching can be known.

Catching performance as measured by the ability to make a judgment concerning the flight of the ball and then move into effective catching position was the subject of a study by Williams.[28] She was more concerned about the preparatory judgments and adjustive movements than with the mechanics of stopping and controlling the ball. In her study, a Ball-Boy projected a tennis ball in a 34° or a 44° trajectory, at a fast or a slow velocity, to 1 of 6 predetermined positions. The positions were directly forward or backward or diagonally forward or backward to the left or to the right. Williams's 54 subjects included 9 skilled and 9 unskilled male players from the junior high school, the senior high school, and the college levels. She found the skilled players more than twice as accurate as the unskilled in judging the flight of the ball. When the ball moved directly toward the performer, he judged it more accurately than when it was to his right or to his left. For the group as a whole, the 44° trajectory was easier to judge, but for the unskilled, judgments were more accurate for balls projected at a 34° angle. The latter finding is an extension of the common observation that unskilled catchers of elementary school age have more difficulty judging a ball with a high angle of trajectory than one with a low angle. Apparently the velocity of the ball movement in this study was not critical enough to be a distinguishing factor, nor was the variability of the ages of the subjects. If the subjects had been younger and less experienced, Williams undoubtedly would have learned much more about precatch judgments and movements.

The *quality* of catching performance was studied by Ryan who used the four-level catching scale in the Ohio State University SIGMA.[16] One hundred twenty normal and an equal number of TMR children between the ages of 6 and 8 years were rated on the maturity of their catching form. Normal boys used more mature form than normal girls, and both groups of normal children were superior to those in the TMR group. Catching is known to be a complex skill for normal children, and its difficulty is greatly compounded for those who are mentally retarded.

It is apparent from the conglomeration of research just reviewed that relatively little is actually known about many of the factors involved in catching behavior. In fact, the more difficult aspects of catching performance have scarcely been illuminated and some may yet be identified. Much careful research remains to be done.

DEVELOPMENT OF SKILL IN CATCHING

The child's first important precatching experience requires him to deal with a rolling ball. He may sit with his legs spread and, when a ball is rolled slowly toward his central axis, attempt to grasp it or try to trap it against one of his legs. Controlling a ball rolled directly at him at a slow rate of speed is his easiest and earliest catching-related experience. Virtually no adjustment is required because the ball moves only in the horizontal plane. The child merely has to time a grasping or trapping movement with the speed of the rolling ball. From this rudimentary beginning, his perception of time-space relationships improves, and he becomes able to attempt more challenging tasks. As he rises from the sitting position, he learns to chase, stop, and control a rolling or a bouncing ball. The change from the stationary sitting position to more active involvement is an important step in the progression leading to comprehensive catching skill.

The transition from the stage of chasing the ball to the stage of responding to an aerial ball with actual catching movements is neither smooth nor rapid. When a child is introduced to this new form of catching, the initial response is rigid and somewhat reminiscent of the delayed reaction of the trapping technique used to capture a rolling ball while in a sitting position. If the aerial ball is presented too early, the child demonstrates no effective catching response. For example, if a light ball were tossed chest high at a 2-year-old, he probably would have no response, even though his arms were extended prior to the toss. Typically he would let the ball bump against his chest and would chase it after it had dropped to the floor. Before the age of 3 years, a child often needs to be told how to position his arms effectively in readiness for receiving an aerial ball. A child's first active catching response is an event that marks the beginning of a series of common developmental changes leading to mature form for catching an aerial ball.

Deach observed a first stage in catching characterized by a negative reaction and fear of the ball.[2] What appears to be a fear response can be detected in the form demonstrated by the 4-year-old children in Figure 6–1. There are companion reactions in their form that could be attributed to apprehension. One of these is the turning of the head to the side to avert the eyes and head from the line of the ball, and the other is the slight backward bending of the trunk away from the oncoming ball. Closing the eyes is an equally common indication of apprehension. Seefeldt found no evidence of the fear reaction in his subjects at ages 1½ to 3 years, but saw it in some who were 4, 5, and 6 years of age.[17] His explanation that fear of an aerial ball is behavior conditioned by unsuccessful catching attempts seems plausible, as does the suggestion that it is a natural defense maneuver. Whatever the reason, the fear response is commonplace in the catching behavior of children, and it is found often in their striking as well. Hellweg reported that 6- to 7-year-old unsuccessful catchers as a group closed their eyes prior to contact,[5] and Harper and Struna observed similar behavior in striking.[4]

In anticipation of catching a large light ball, the young catcher stands

Fig. 6–1. Unsuccessful attempts to catch a large ball by 4-year-old children. Each shows apprehension by turning the head to the side and by leaning backward slightly. The girl's catching effort involves limited movement, and the coordination of the boy's arm action is amiss. His arm action, which is quite common, frequently causes the hands to strike the ball and knock it upward.

facing the tosser and provides a scoop for the ball with extended arms and the front of the trunk. This is little more than preparation for a form of trapping in the upright position. The ball is tossed gently and accurately into the waiting receptacle from a very close distance (Fig. 6–2), and at this point little or no response is required or received from the child. With additional experience, the child participates increasingly by spreading both arms in readiness, by grasping at the ball with a clapping motion, and by clutching it against the body to complete

Fig. 6–2. A 33-month-old boy extends his arms before the ball is tossed. He waits for the ball without moving, responds after the ball has touched his hands, and then he gently traps it against his chest. It is essentially a robotlike performance.

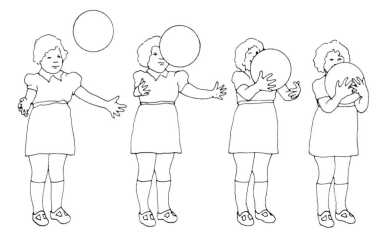

Fig. 6–3. A 4-year-old girl waits for the ball with arms straight and hands spread. Her initial response to the ball is a clapping motion. When one hand contacts the ball, she grasps at it and gains control by clutching it against her chest.

the catch (Fig. 6–3). Gradually the front of the body is eliminated from use in catching, and the ball is cradled in the arms. As progress continues through the developmental phases toward mature form, hands are brought into play to a greater extent and the child depends less upon his arms and body, although he might use his body to help secure the ball. Finally, the mature technique of catching a ball using the hands exclusively is achieved (Fig. 6–4). Development toward the mature form is encouraged by the use of balls of an increasingly smaller size.

During the transition to the form in which only the hands are used, development is marked by characteristic changes in arm position. The ball is addressed first with the arms straight and forward at shoulder

Fig. 6–4. The form used by a 5-year-old boy to make an effective hand catch of a ball thrown softly from a short distance.

level, then with the arms bent slightly and held lower in front of the body, and finally with the arms lower and forward and the semiflexed elbows pointing distinctly downward. The final position seems to be achieved earlier if the child practices with a small ball rather than mostly with a large one. Apparently the child thinks of using only hands when catching a small ball. No one thus far has reported a sequence of catching behavior based upon longitudinal data in which children are exposed exclusively to small balls. It is quite possible that

Fig. 6–5. Immature starting arm position—arms are straight and too high, and hands are poorly positioned for simultaneous contact. The four-and-one-half-year-old girl improves her hand position as the ball approaches, but the timing and coordination of her catching action are inadequate.

Fig. 6–6. The viselike hand position often used by children when catching a small ball.

the sequence and rate of skill development would be profoundly affected if only a small ball were used.

Arm and hand positions prior to and immediately following contact were analyzed in a cinematic study by Victors.[24] She subjectively evaluated the catching behavior of large groups of 7- and 9-year-old boys, and selected 5 good and 5 poor performers at each age level. Her subjects were filmed while attempting to catch balls 3 inches and 10 inches in diameter, tossed from a distance of 20 feet, and aimed at chest level. The performances of the boys varied considerably and individual catching behavior lacked consistency. It was apparent from the results of the study that the components of catching could be combined successfully in a variety of ways. Several initial arm-hand positions were effective. The only notably unsuccessful initial position was with the arms straight at the elbows and the hands waist high or higher (Fig. 6–5). This position is typical of the immature catching pattern and was used in the study only by unsuccessful 7-year-olds.

Victors also studied the grasping patterns used in the act of catching and found that successful catchers contact the ball simultaneously with both hands and effect closure in the same manner.[24] Hand position varied among successful catchers, but some patterns were used more frequently than others. The one most frequently used was a fingers-forward and palms-up pattern (Fig. 6–1). A viselike position formed by a bottom hand with the palm up and the fingers pointing forward and a top hand with the palm forward and the fingers pointing upward was also used often and successfully (Fig. 6–6). It is interesting to note the discrepancy between the form used by the children in this study and the form for handling a ball arriving at chest height suggested by some textbooks.

A closely integrated 3-phase catching procedure emerged from a film study of the techniques used by a group of 9-year-old English boys to

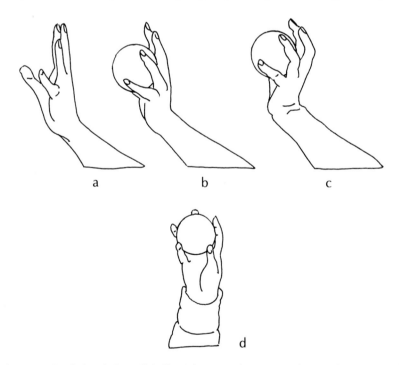

Fig. 6–7. Single-handed small ball catch. a, Ready position; b, initial contact at the metacarpal/basal segment joints of the first three fingers; c, impact reaction showing flexion at the wrist and retraction of the fingers; and d, hand closure with equal separation of the fingers. (Redrawn from Morris[12] with permission.)

make successful one-handed catches.[12] Each of 10 boys was given 3 attempts at catching a small ball projected a distance of 20 feet at a velocity of 33.6 ft/sec. Fifteen of the 30 attempted catches were successful, and the common elements of those catches became the basis for the 3-phase procedure. In the first phase, the arm was moved forward and upward to the estimated intercept position between the top of the shoulder and the top of the head. The wrist was extended placing the palm forward, the middle 3 fingers were spread slightly and pointed upward, and the thumb and little finger were abducted forming an inverted angle (Fig. 6–7a). In the second phase, the ball contacted the hand in the area of the metacarpophalangeal joints of the middle 3 fingers (Fig. 6–7b). The impact forced the wrist into hyperextension, extended the 3 fingers at the base, and caused them to curl forward at the tips. An instant before the ball was stopped, the 3 fingers momentarily lost contact but the palm surface adjacent to the base of the fingers did not (Fig. 6–7c). Also at impact, the thumb and little finger moved horizontally toward each other and supported the underside of the ball. In the third phase, the 3 middle fingers spread as they rebounded forward to work with the thumb and little finger to perform the grasp. The 5 digits did not begin the grasping motion until after the impact reaction, and they were equally separated at closure (Fig. 6–7d). Nearly three fourths of the errors were connected with the first phase—faulty hand position at initial contact. High contact did not stop the ball and low contact produced a forward rebound. It was observed that the boys did not make final adjustments in hand position, but apparently made early perceptual judgments regarding ball speed and direction and did not deviate from them. Morris finally suggested that the 3 components of successful catching (position location, grasp reaction time, and speed of hand closure) could be used effectively in slightly different ways by different individuals. A small error in hand positioning, for instance, might be compensated for by faster hand closure. This sort of latitude in technique without loss of success was in agreement with Victors's findings. A better understanding of possible adjustments in the act of catching requires a continuation of the research by Victors and Morris using lower intercept points and different size balls traveling at various velocities.

Thus far, this chapter has presented the development of skill in catching as a *trend* toward hand-catching, which is a reflection of the proximal-distal refinement of nervous control. The development can also be expressed in terms of *stages* that show the same refinement. For example, the development of catching skill was delineated into 5 stages by Seefeldt, Reuschlein, and Vogel.[18] They suggested the following:

Stage 1. The child presents his arms directly in front of him with the elbows extended and the palm facing upward or inward toward the midsagittal plane. As the ball contacts the hands or arms, the elbows are flexed and the arms and hands attempt to secure the ball by holding it against the chest.

Stage 2. The child prepares to receive the object with the arms in front of the body, the elbows extended or slightly flexed. Upon presentation of the ball the arms begin an encircling motion that culminates by securing the ball against the chest. The receiver initiates the arm action prior to ball-arm contact.

Stage 3. The child prepares to receive the ball with arms that are slightly flexed and extended forward at the shoulder. Many children also receive the ball with arms that are flexed at the elbow, with the elbow ahead of a frontal plane.

Substage a. The child uses his chest as the first contact point of the ball and attempts to secure the ball by holding it to his chest with the hands and arms.

Substage b. The child attempts to catch the ball with his hands. Upon his failure to hold it securely, he maneuvers it to his chest, where it is controlled by hands and arms.

Stage 4. The child prepares to receive the ball by flexing the elbows and presenting the arms ahead of the frontal plane. Skillful performers may keep the elbows at the sides and flex the arms simultaneously as they bring them forward to meet the ball. The ball is caught with the hands, without making contact with other body parts.

Stage 5. The upper segmental action is identical to that for Stage 4. In addition, the child is required to change his stationary base in order to receive the ball.

These stages do not appear to be easily distinguishable and probably require analysis of filmed performances in order to be useful. A simpler and more practical set of stages has been proposed by McClenaghan and Gallahue.[10] Their set includes only three stages: the initial stage, the elementary stage, and the mature stage. Head action, arm action, and hand action are the components emphasized at each stage. The material is too extensive to be included here, but anyone interested is referred to the source, where the descriptions are accompanied by illustrations.

MATURE PATTERN OF MOVEMENTS IN THE ACT OF CATCHING

Many aspects of a catch are quite specific and are related to particular catching situations. Yet after all movements and techniques peculiar to special forms of catching are stripped away, a bare pattern of arm and hand actions remains. That basic pattern consists of two phases: (1) moving the hands into an effective position for receiving the ball and (2) grasping and controlling the ball. To clarify the description of the catching pattern, it is assumed here that the ball to be caught is moving directly at the catcher.

The first phase is preparatory but crucial to the effectiveness of the second phase, the act of catching. The hands are moved forward to a position in line with the expected trajectory of the ball, and the position is reached prior to or no later than the instant of contact. In the second phase of the pattern, the hands perform in unison to contact and control the ball. After initial contact, the hands and arms give way with the ball in the continued direction of its trajectory. The process allows time for successful closure by the hands and distance over which to exert force to stop the ball. These are the essential aspects of all straightforward catching patterns. Both phases need to be amplified to establish their basic identity more completely.

PREPARATION FOR CATCHING

The function of the arms in the preliminary phase is to move the hands into position for the act of catching. To perform this task, the arms are raised in front of the body, moving the elbows forward of the

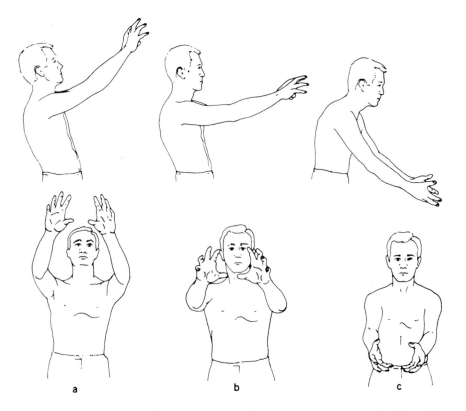

Fig. 6–8. Preparatory hand positions for a ball arriving: (a) Above the shoulders; (b) between the waist and shoulders; and (c) below the waist. Fingers point toward the ball and palms face obliquely rather than perpendicularly toward the ball.

trunk while allowing them to continue pointing in a downward direction. The precise position in which the hands must be placed is determined by the size of the ball, its trajectory, and the height of the point of contact. If the expected point of contact is almost chest high or above, the hands are raised to that level, the forearms are pronated slightly, and the fingers are pointed forward and upward (Fig. 6–8). The palms face obliquely forward, inward, and downward. If the ball is expected to arrive at waist level or below, the forearms are supinated, positioning the hands with the fingers pointing forward and the palms facing forward, inward, and upward. These two positions automatically juxtapose the thumbs or little fingers in a general way and form a cupped receiving unit with the fingers oriented toward the oncoming ball. Between the waist and lower part of the chest is an awkward area for which neither hand position is fully satisfactory. However, the ball usually is moving in a downward trajectory when it arrives in that area so that the commonly used hand position is with fingers forward and palms up. The flight of the ball finally determines the most effective hand position when the ball arrives slightly above the waist.

A conspicuous feature of the hand position is the manner in which the fingers are extended and point sharply in the direction of the ball immediately before contact. It appears that the fingers are more effective in closure and in controlling the ball when they point forward rather than more directly upward or downward. The illustrations throughout this chapter emphasize the prevalence of the extended finger position.

THE ACT OF CATCHING

Catching is a force absorption skill. It has been described as the act of reducing the momentum of an object in flight to the point at which it has zero or near zero velocity. This description is used frequently and places heavy emphasis on stopping rather than on controlling the ball. In the act of catching, control is gained by grasping the ball and by stopping its motion. These two requirements are satisfied in a continuous, if not simultaneous, process involving the arms and hands. The catcher contacts the ball with both hands at the same time and instantly begins to grasp and give way with it. Many skilled catchers begin the giving way motion just prior to the instant of contact, especially when the ball has considerable momentum. Most of the giving way occurs at the shoulder and elbow joints when the ball is large and is caught in the bare hands. Wrist action is detected in specific catching situations, notably in baseball, but it seems to be a minor movement in the basic catching pattern. The act of catching has been completed when the ball is fully under the catcher's control. If the catcher bobbles the ball during the process of gaining control of it, his performance is successful but less than skillful.

Fig. 6–9. Catching a basketball pass. The player steps toward the ball, partially extends his arms, spreads his fingers, and points them at the ball. Simultaneous contact is followed by giving at the elbow and shoulder joints.

VARIATIONS INVOLVING THE BASIC PATTERN OF CATCHING

Catching is an important skill in many of the games played in elementary schools. In the simple games played at the primary grade level, a medium-sized playground ball is used, and boys and girls play together. The tendency to present organized sports to boys at increasingly lower grade levels and to splinter girls off to less demanding games and activities is changing. The opportunity for early exposure to specialized catching skills involving a variety of balls is opening up for girls but on a less extensive basis than for boys. Unfortunately, a gap in catching skill exists between boys and girls and generally remains unbridged. Eventually children of both sexes use special catching skills in basketball and softball, and boys add the catching skills in football to their repertoire. These sports require the basic pattern of catching to be used in a way that is determined by the physical characteristics of different types of balls and the specialized uses of the balls in games.

CATCHING THE BASKETBALL PASS

The strong element of keep-away in the game of basketball requires careful execution of passing and catching skills. The passer must direct the ball at the receiver briskly and accurately; the catcher often must step toward the oncoming ball and reach out to shorten the distance it travels. Stepping toward the ball is strategically effective, but at the same time it increases the potential force of the ball at contact and complicates the timing of the catching movements. These difficulties are minor and do nothing to mask the presence of the basic pattern, which stands out vividly. In Figure 6–9, the player steps toward the ball, bends his trunk so that his arms can stretch forward, and keeps his elbows bent slightly and pointing downward. The fingers of his hands are well spread and pointing toward the ball to provide a large contact surface for satisfactory control. There is simultaneous contact and closure by both hands, and the arms give with the ball by bending at the elbows and the shoulders.

CATCHING THE FOOTBALL

Football is a game offering a wide variety of situations in which the ball must be caught. Ordinarily the player who catches the ball has the immediate secondary responsibility of kicking it or running with it. A basic pattern of catching movements is used, and the details of technique vary to accommodate the total situation.

Catching a Centered Football. When the ball is centered, it spins

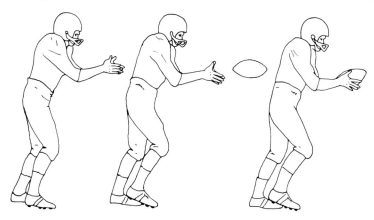

Fig. 6–10. Catching a centered football in preparation for a punt. Player begins to "give" with arms before ball is contacted.

Fig. 6–11. Catching a football pass: (a) From a stationary position; (b) while running at a diagonal to the thrown ball; (c) while running perpendicular to the flight of the ball; and (d) while running in the same direction as the flight of the ball.

around its long axis, travels at a brisk rate of speed, and must be caught in the hands only. The punter in Figure 6–10 steps toward the ball and demonstrates the same basic pattern of catching that was used by the basketball player in Figure 6–9. His arms are extended, his fingers point toward the ball, and his hands are in position for simultaneous contact. The punter necessarily limits the distance he uses for stopping the ball.

Immediately after he catches it, he must realign the ball in his hands while moving forward and then drop it in preparation for the kick.

Catching a Passed Football. The passed football is difficult to catch because it spins rapidly and moves with substantial velocity. The player assigned to be the receiver may be in a stationary position awaiting the ball and imminent tackle, he may be running at a right angle to the expected trajectory of the ball, or he may be moving away from the passer and in the same direction as the passed ball. In each instance the designated receiver's primary responsibility is to concentrate on catching the ball. His catching technique, which often includes a degree of "trapping," reflects the circumstances of his immediate position and anticipates the secondary tasks of protecting the ball and running with it.

The player in Figure 6–11a is in position and waiting for the ball to arrive. Since the ball will be in a downward flight when it is caught, his fingers are well spread and pointing forward, and his palms face upward. As the ball is received, it will be grasped and brought to a secure position trapped against the front of his body. The ball will be held in that snug position against the trunk until the receiver can turn and reorient himself from the task of catching to the new job of running.

If the catcher runs a path that is perpendicular or oblique to the flight of the ball (Fig. 6–11b and 6–11c), he adjusts the length of his arms so that his hands can make simultaneous contact. He frequently allows the ball to touch his trunk while stopping and controlling it during the catch. Later the ball is moved to a position that is secure and yet does not interfere with effective arm movement while running.

A player who runs in the same direction as the flight of the ball may have to reach back to catch it or may have to catch the ball over his shoulder. In either case, the catcher benefits slightly from the fact that the relative velocity of the ball at contact has been reduced by an amount equal to his running speed. Effective eye-hand coordination is a more significant problem than stopping the ball in this variation of catching. During the time the receiver is preparing to catch the ball, his eyes are between his hands and the ball. This is a reversal of the normal relationship and is the source of difficult eye-hand coordination. The receiver must raise his arms, position his hands for simultaneous contact, and adjust for the downward flight of the ball (Fig. 6–11d). After the problem of eye-hand coordination is surmounted at initial contact, the ball can be brought under control with a minimum of difficulty because the body and the ball move in the same direction.

CATCHING WITH A GLOVED HAND

In baseball and softball when a special glove is used to assist in catching, the basic pattern is modified slightly. Simultaneous closure by both hands is neither necessary nor strictly possible. The gloved

Fig. 6–12. Catching with a gloved hand. (a) The player anticipates the need to throw quickly and steps toward the ball. His gloved hand is positioned to stop the ball and his bare hand is ready to cover and grasp it; and (b) the player positions her gloved hand to stop the ball. Her bare hand is ready to help control the ball and grasp it for a fast throw.

hand, which is the non-dominant hand, assumes the primary responsibility for stopping and controlling the ball. In Figure 6–12, the ball is moving directly at the pocket of the glove, and the fingers of the bare hand point toward the ball in readiness to close over it after it has struck the glove. The bare hand helps control the ball after contact, but more importantly, it grasps the ball from the pocket of the glove in preparation for a quick throw.

The size of the baseball glove and its special properties for stopping and controlling the ball give an enormous boost to the catching skill of young boys. If a 7- or 8-year-old boy can position his glove in the path of the moving ball, he has a reasonable chance of making a successful catch because the large padded glove tends to envelop the ball when contact is made. Encouraged by early success in catching with a glove, the boy tends to develop a one-handed catching technique. The glove gives him a relatively wide margin for error, and he confidently puts it in the path of the ball with high hope and little concern for the lack of cooperation from his bare hand.

Wrist action gains importance when the glove is used in catching. A ball caught with the glove at some heights is contacted farther from the wrist, higher on the hand, and more toward the thumb than one caught using a bare-handed form. The large pocket encases the ball at contact, and controlled wrist extension becomes more important in the giving action used to stop the ball. The tethered pocket of the glove minimizes the danger of the ball rolling backward off the fingers if the wrist gives a carefully controlled amount during the act of catching.

Aside from the modified hand action caused by the use of the glove, the basic pattern of catching is used in baseball and in softball. The player reaches out for the ball with elbows remaining bent and pointing downward, the hand is positioned to stop and grasp the ball, and the force of the ball is diminished by use of the glove and a giving action by the wrist, elbow, and shoulder. The more skilled the catcher, the less the observed amount of giving at contact.

ANALYSIS OF FORM IN CATCHING

Unlike several other fundamental skills, the act of catching is not performed so quickly that many of its features are lost to direct visual observation. Simultaneous contact and closure are the most difficult aspects of the pattern to perceive. With this in mind, other phases of the pattern can be concentrated upon in direct analysis of catching. The attention of the analyzer might be directed primarily to the preparatory and the final actions. Items that could be looked for are the following:

1. Promptness and accuracy of precatch movement to a position in line with the trajectory of the ball.

Fig. 6–13. Movement prior to making a successful catch of a large ball.

Fig. 6–14. Arm and hand adjustments in preparation for the successful catch of a small ball.

Fig. 6–15. A 5-year-old boy catching a foam rubber football.

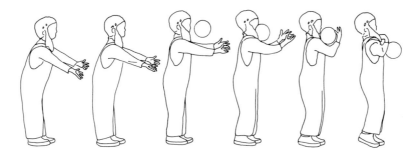

Fig. 6–16. A 3-year-old girl attempting to catch a softly tossed foam rubber ball.

2. Outreaching arm position with elbows bent somewhat and pointing downward.
3. Hands being in position to intercept the ball in its trajectory prior to contact.
4. Hand(s) contact only.
5. Retention of the ball.

The degree to which the above simple criteria are met gives a broad indication of progress toward or the existence of mature form. The sequences in Figures 6–1, 6–2, 6–3, 6–4, 6–5, 6–13, 6–14, 6–15, and 6–16 offer an opportunity to use some of the suggested checks.

Another approach is to use the stage characteristics suggested by: (1) Seefeldt, Reuschlein, and Vogel,[18] (2) McClenaghan and Gallahue,[10] or (3) the Ohio State University SIGMA. Each translates form into stages or levels of skill development. A final suggestion is to use a performance scale that is based on certain aspects of form. Those devised by Bruce[1] and Hellweg[5] are useful. Hellweg's scale, which is presented below for the purpose of illustration, is both objective and reliable. A 4-inch diameter ball was used when objectivity and reliability were determined.

Score	Characteristics
5	Hand contact, clean catch: the ball is contacted and retained by the hands only. The ball may be brought into the body on the follow-through after control is gained by the hands.
4	Hand contact, assisted catch: initial contact is made by the hands. The ball is juggled but retained using arms and/or body for assistance.
3	Hand contact, miss: initial contact is made by the hands, but the ball is dropped immediately or dropped following arm or body contact.
2	Arm and/or body contact, save: initial contact is on the arms and/or body and the ball is retained.
1	Arm and/or body contact, miss: initial attempt to contact is made on the arms and/or body above the waist and the ball is missed.
0	No contact or initial body contact below the waist. The subject may or may not attempt to contact.

REFERENCES

1. Bruce, R.: The effects of variations in ball trajectory upon the catching performance of elementary school children. Unpublished doctoral dissertation. Madison, University of Wisconsin, 1966.
2. Deach, D.: Genetic development of motor skills in children two through six years of age. Unpublished doctoral dissertation. Ann Arbor, University of Michigan, 1950.
3. Gutteridge, M.: A study of motor achievements of young children. Arch. Psychol., 244:1, 1939.
4. Harper, C.J., and Struna, N.L.: Case Studies in the Development of One-Handed Striking. Research paper presented at AAHPER meeting, Minneapolis, 1973.
5. Hellweg, D.A.: An analysis of perceptual and performance characteristics of the catching skill in 6–7-year-old children. Unpublished doctoral dissertation. Madison, University of Wisconsin, 1972.
6. Hoadley, D.: A study of the catching ability of children in grades one to four. Unpublished master's thesis. Iowa City, University of Iowa, 1941.
7. Hutt, J.W.R.: The relationship of some visual, perceptual, and cognitive factors with ball-catching performance of 9–10-year-old boys. Res. Papers Phys. Educ., 2:4, 1973.
8. Isaacs, L.D.: Effects of ball size, ball color, and preferred color on catching by young children. Percept. Mot. Skills, 51:583, 1980.
9. MacGillivary, W.W.: Perceptual style and ball skill acquisition. Res. Q. Am. Assoc. Health Phys. Educ., 50:222, 1979.
10. McClenaghan, B., and Gallahue, D.: Fundamental Movement: A Developmental and Remedial Approach. Philadelphia, W.B. Saunders, 1978.
11. Morris, G.S.D.: Effects ball and background color have upon the catching performance of elementary school children. Res. Q. Am. Assoc. Health Phys. Educ., 47:3, 1976.
12. Morris, P.R.: An operational analysis of ball-catching. Res. Papers Phys. Educ., 3:2, 1976.
13. Nessler, J.: Length of time necessary to view a ball while catching it. J. Mot. Behav., 5:3, 1973.
14. Pederson, E.J.: A study of ball catching abilities of first-, third-, and fifth-grade children on twelve selected ball catching tasks. Unpublished doctoral dissertation. Bloomington, Indiana University, 1973.
15. Riordan, K.D.: A study of the effects of ball color on the catching skills of three-, four-, and five-year-old children. Unpublished master's thesis. Lawrence, University of Kansas, 1979.

16. Ryan, T.M.: A comparison of selected basic gross motor skills of moderately retarded and normal children of middle childhood age utilizing the Ohio State University Scale in Intra Gross Motor Assessment. Unpublished doctoral dissertation. Columbus, Ohio State University, 1977.
17. Seefeldt, V.: Develpmental sequence of catching skill. Paper presented at AAHPER meeting, Houston, 1972.
18. Seefeldt, V., Reuschlein, S., and Vogel, P.: Sequencing motor skills within the physical education curriculum. Paper presented at AAHPER meeting, Houston, 1972.
19. Seils, L.: The relationship between measures of physical growth and gross motor performance of primary grade children. Res. Q. Am. Assoc. Health Phys. Educ., 22:244, 1951.
20. Shoney, M.H.: The effects of varying color and direction of projection on the catching performance of 8.5 to 11.5 year-old boys and girls. Unpublished master's thesis. Lafayette, IN, Purdue University, 1973.
21. Sinclair, C.: Movement and movement patterns of early childhood. Division of Educational Research and Statistics, State Department of Education, Richmond, VA, 1971.
22. Starkes, J.: Components of skill in catching. Unpublished doctoral dissertation. Waterloo, Canada, University of Waterloo, 1980.
23. Torres, J.A.: Relationship between figure-ground perceptual ability and ball catching ability in 10- and 13-year-old boys and girls. Research paper, AAHPER meeting, St. Louis, 1968.
24. Victors, E.: A cinematical analysis of catching behavior of a selected group of 7- and 9-year-old boys. Unpublished doctoral dissertation. Madison, University of Wisconsin, 1961.
25. Warner, A.P.: The motor ability of third, fourth, and fifth grade boys in the elementary school. Unpublished doctoral dissertation. Ann Arbor, University of Michigan, 1952.
26. Whiting, H.T.A.: Acquiring Ball Skill. London, G. Bell and Sons, Ltd., 1969.
27. Whiting, H.T.A., Gill, E.B., and Stephenson, J.M.: Critical time intervals for taking in-flight information in a ball catching task. Ergonomics, *13*:265, 1970.
28. Williams, H.: The effects of systematic variation of speed and direction of object flight and of skill and age classifications upon visuo-perceptual judgments of moving objects in three-dimensional space. Unpublished doctoral dissertation. Madison, University of Wisconsin, 1968.

CHAPTER **7**

Striking

In the realm of motor activity, striking is the act of swinging at and hitting an object. Striking skills are performed in a variety of planes and under widely varying circumstances. Overhand, sidearm, and underhand patterns are common, with many different implements being used for striking in each pattern. Body parts including the hand, the head, and the foot are among the implements used, as are special pieces of equipment such as the bat, the racket, the paddle, and the club.

Kicking is one of the major types of striking, but because of its relative importance as a basic skill it has been selected for separate, detailed treatment in the following chapter. Of the remaining striking skills, the skills most commonly used are those that are performed mainly with a sidearm pattern. Hence, the development of striking in that pattern receives major emphasis in this chapter, with some attention given to patterns performed in other planes.

PERFORMANCES OF CHILDREN USING STRIKING SKILLS

Little information is available concerning the performances of children using striking skills. The dearth of information appears to be related to the slow rate at which measurable skill develops and to the difficulty of measuring striking skill performance. A young child frequently can swing a bat or a paddle with reasonably effective form before being able to hit an object in such a way that a quantitative score can be obtained for the performance. Swinging and striking are part of the same act, but obviously they are not the same. Each must be evaluated in a different way. The form used in swinging at an object can be analyzed to determine the quality of the movement pattern, but the ability to make contact with the object is the real measure of striking performance. Of the two aspects of striking skill, performance is by far the more difficult to evaluate.

Efforts to use precise measures of performance in striking have been confined largely to the testing of school age children. Even at this level,

165

the results provide little more than a sketchy picture of the ability of children to use striking skills. Seils studied the motor performances of 510 primary grade children ranging in age from 71 to 106 months.[25] In his battery of gross motor performance tests, striking was measured by the use of a pendulum-controlled ball that was to be struck by a bat. The average performances on the test showed a constant increase for both boys and girls at successive grade levels. However, when all of the children were classified according to 3-month age intervals rather than grade, the evidence did not show the same constant improvement. Johnson used a procedure for testing striking skill similar to the one used by Seils.[15] The 624 elementary school children in grades 1 through 6 who were tested were asked to strike a ball that was swung over the plate. The average scores on the batting test were increasingly better at successive grade levels. Boys were considerably better performers on the batting test at grades 1 and 2, but thereafter retained only a slight advantage over the girls.

Sheehan investigated the actual batting performance of boys at the elementary school level.[27] The boys batted in a situation that was realistic but rather loosely controlled. Each was given 10 hits during a baseball batting practice in which the ball was thrown the regulation pitching distance by another player. One group in his study corresponded to the primary grade level (ages 7, 8, and 9), and another to the intermediate grade level (ages 10, 11, and 12). The respective average scores of 21.6 and 27.1 for the two groups suggest that the batting ability of boys improves at the elementary school level.

The volleyball serve for distance was used in one study to measure striking performance in an underarm pattern. According to the scores registered by the 2840 elementary school children tested by Hanson, boys and girls improve regularly in this form of striking.[12] The average distance that the volleyball was served was significantly greater at successive grade levels, and boys served farther than girls in each grade.

The batting form of 120 normal and 120 TMR boys and girls between the ages of 6 and 8 years was assessed by Ryan.[24] He used the Ohio State University SIGMA, which entails evaluating the form that a child uses to strike a suspended ball with a plastic bat. Boys used more mature form than girls in each I.Q. group and the children of normal intelligence performed at a higher level than the moderately retarded children.

Some of the visual and perceptual factors presumably related to striking performance have received attention in a few studies. Moran looked into the factors of ball color and background color as they affected the striking performance of second, fourth, and sixth graders.[19] Fifteen boys and 15 girls at each grade level used a paddle racquet when attempting to strike various colored plastic balls projected from 32 feet at a speed of 45.8 ft/sec. Performance was best with yellow balls at grades 2 and

6, and with blue balls at grade 4. White balls were the least effective, and there was no difference in performance when the background was white or black. Striking skill improved at each grade level and boys were superior to girls, although the advantage decreased as age increased.

Field independence, as measured by the Children's Embedded Figures Test, was not significantly related to the performance on a striking test for 34 children in the 77- to 96-month age range.[17] The children were asked to swing a wooden paddle in a sidearm pattern and strike a tennis ball after it had bounced from a 10-foot drop. Boys were significantly better than girls in performance but apparently the task was so simple that field independence was not an important factor in performance.

A special piece of apparatus was devised by Ridenour to test the striking ability of 80 boys and girls between the ages of $6^1/_2$ and $7^1/_2$ years, under a variety of conditions.[22] The movement of a 6- or an 8.2-inch diameter ball was controlled completely as it travelled 8 or 16 feet, at a speed of 2.6 or 4.7 ft/sec to an intercept point at or 15 inches above or below shoulder level. The task was to strike the moving object with a paddle as soon and as hard as possible. The highest frequency of object interception occurred when the object moved for a short distance at a slow speed, to a high point at the side. Males had a higher frequency of hits than females and object size alone was not a factor in performance.

McGrath added movement and timing factors to a striking task for sixty 7-, 9-, and 11-year-old boys and girls.[18] A tennis ball was projected in a long or short trajectory by a Prince Ball machine and the task was to move into position and strike it with a sidearm pattern after it had bounced. The children in the 7-year-old group had many complete misses because of the difficulty of the task. More full and partial contacts were found in the performance of the older two groups, and the 9-year-old group performed better than the 11-year-old group. Boys' performances were better than the girls' but the disparity decreased with age.

The paucity of evidence is a signal to be cautious about making statements concerning the ability of children to use striking skills. Although there appears to be a general trend toward improvement during the elementary school period, the rate and the nature of the improvement are quite vague and need to be studied much more extensively.

DEVELOPMENTAL FORM IN STRIKING

The earliest form used in striking seems to be derived from an overarm motion that occurs in the anteroposterior plane. The child naturally uses this action whenever he hits something with his hand, and he makes little effort to modify his movement if given an implement with

Fig. 7–1

which to strike (Fig. 7–1). The simplicity of the pattern is consistent with the abilities of the young child, whose reaction time, movement time, strength, balance, and perception are limited. When the overarm pattern is used, the child can face the object to be struck and gain the advantage of being able to look almost directly at it throughout the striking movement. The pattern permits him to limit the total range of motion and the number of levers to be applied while striking, thereby reducing the amount of strength, balance, time, and coordination required. The overarm pattern offers the greatest assurance of success in most tasks involving striking, and the child tends to revert to it whenever the need for success is high.[11] There is a constant threat of intrusion by the overarm striking pattern when the child tries to learn to strike in the horizontal plane. He finds it difficult to abandon the natural but

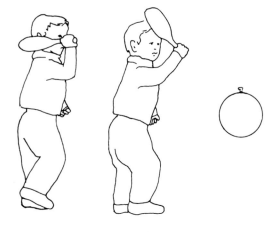

Fig. 7–1. Immature overarm striking pattern. The striking action by the 22-month-old child is primarily an extension of his forearm. After preliminary steps and a brief pause, he steps forward using a unitary same arm-same leg pattern and confines his movements to the anteroposterior plane.

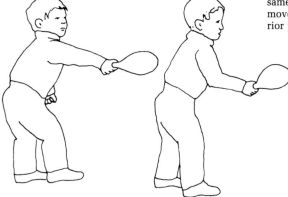

ineffective overarm motion for the more complicated but useful sidearm pattern. The deep-rooted nature of the immature overarm swing is evidenced by the manner in which it lingers or reappears, especially in sport skills that require a one-handed swing.

The emergence of the overarm pattern was observed by Deach in connection with her investigation of the development of striking skill in the underhand pattern.[6] Her 2- to 6-year-old subjects were given the task of using an underhand volleyball serving motion to strike a ball held in the opposite hand. In the most rudimentary performance, the ball was given impetus by an overarm throwing motion without any indication of a hit. This initial technique was superseded by a push and by an overhand hit before the underhand striking pattern was achieved. Halverson and Roberton observed the same overhand pattern

Fig. 7–2. Swing in a vertical plane. The child (age 33 months) turns to face the object squarely and then swings the bat, extending her forearms and uncocking her wrists. Her forward trunk bend is the counterpart of rotation that develops around a vertical axis in more mature form.

when children were first asked to hit a ball from their own toss.[9] During the phases in which the overarm pattern was used by Deach's subjects, accompanying changes in the movements of the legs took place. From a stationary position, progress was made to a forward step with an ipsilateral arm-leg pattern, and finally to the mature contralateral arm-leg pattern. Corresponding enlargement of the rotatory movements of the hips and trunk accompanied the changes in leg position and action. In general, the early development of the underhand striking pattern

Fig. 7–2 *continued.*

seemed to follow a sequence quite similar to the early developmental sequence for the skill of throwing. However, one should not interpret this observation to mean that the overhand throwing motion emerges before the overhand striking motion. Infants seem to strike and throw equally well when using an overarm pattern, but there is no evidence for assuming that either occurs prior to and is the basis for the appearance of the other.

SIDEARM PATTERN

If a child is allowed to develop striking skills without special assistance he seems to progress slowly from striking in a vertical plane (Fig. 7–2), downward through a series of planes that are increasingly flatter to one that is predominantly horizontal (Figs. 7–3 and 7–4). He tends to progress to the pattern in the latter plane earlier if provided

Fig. 7–3. A 4-year-old boy attempts to strike a ball using a sidearm pattern. His swing in the upper series is "top-dominated" and rigidly performed. Immediately after the unsuccessful swing, he drew back the bat and reswung. The swing in the lower series obviously is more forceful, and the form is improved in nearly every respect.

with encouraging opportunities to practice striking skills done in the sidearm pattern. Especially helpful are those that are basically task oriented and sport skill related.

Information on the development of the sidearm striking pattern is scarce. One of the important sources has been the longitudinal motor development study conducted at the University of Wisconsin.[9] The

Fig. 7–3 *continued.*

researchers increased task difficulty by carefully manipulating and subtly changing the circumstances under which children were asked to perform.[8,10] Special attention was focused on equipment, ball presentation, and performance cues. In the early attempts to strike in the sidearm pattern, the movement was initiated by arm action and was followed by limited rotation in the upper spine. The trunk rotation appeared to be a result of the swing rather than a contributing force. Progressively, the children abandoned the arm-dominated and unitary

Fig. 7–4. A 4-year-old child demonstrates the general movement pattern used in an effective swing in a horizontal plane. He rotates around his long axis and lowers his bat to meet the downward-arching trajectory of the ball. There is clear evidence of "opening" in the pattern.

patterns and replaced them with one in which there was a forward weight shift, a greater range of joint actions, and more separation of the rotatory elements in the striking pattern.

A report on the development of one-handed striking in two children from the Wisconsin longitudinal study detailed changes observed in the patterns used by a 3-year-old boy and a 3-year-old girl who had

Fig. 7–4 *continued.*

been filmed several times over a period of a year.[13] The girl began with an arm-dominated pattern and no weight shift or trunk rotation. She progressed during the year to a swing initiated by a forward step and followed by simultaneous block rotation and arm swing. Because the boy had demonstrated this pattern at each of the four film sessions, his progress was noted primarily in terms of subtle changes, including an increase in the length of the initial stride. The stride was found to be particularly significant at this level. The investigators suggested that "opening up" appears in the sidearm striking pattern as soon as the child begins to use a forward step to initiate the swing. As the forward step is taken, the striking implement is drawn back farther in preparation for the forward swing. This gives a greater distance over which to apply force and build up velocity for hitting. It also tends to cause rotation around the long axis of the body.

Progress in trunk rotation around the vertical axis in sidearm striking is similar, in the less complicated aspects, to progress in trunk rotation in overarm throwing. Roberton and Halverson have reported three stages that are common to both.[11,23]

Stage I. Top-dominated rotation. Upper spine rotates after arm movement has begun.

Stage II. Block rotation. Entire spine rotates at the same time during either backward or forward rotation.

Stage III. Differentiated rotation. Pelvic rotation initiates the action and is followed by rotation of the upper spine.

Ordinarily, when the final stage is reached, differentiation exists in other aspects of the swing as well, and the sequential aspects of the pattern are well established.

In a different study, 33 children between the ages of 21 and 60 months were filmed while attempting to perform striking movements in a sidearm pattern with a bat and with a paddle under various conditions.[29] These preschool children used striking patterns similar to the ones observed by Halverson, with the exception that those who were less than 30 months old invariably used the overarm pattern when striking at a suspended object with either of the implements. They adjusted to the height of the ball by bending forward at the waist before starting to strike. The amount of forward trunk bend was increased as the height of the ball was lowered. Some turned to face the ball in a preliminary adjustment, and others occasionally accompanied the turn with a forward step by the leg on the same side as the striking motion. Although the overarm pattern tended to persist, children beyond the age of 30 months responded favorably when encouraged to strike a suspended ball using a one-arm or a two-arm pattern in a horizontal plane. Progress in the development of an effective sidearm striking pattern was indicated by the changes observed in the patterns used by the older children in the group. Some of these changes were the following:

1. More use of a forward step or a forward weight shift to initiate the pattern (delaying arm action, causing "opening"). This was the most critical change. Without it there was little evidence of change in other aspects of pattern maturity.
2. More freedom in the swing with increased range of motion at the various joints (unfreezing of the overall unitary pattern).
3. More definite hip and trunk rotation preceding the action of the arms in the swing.
4. More distinct uncocking of the wrists during the swing.

When using a two-arm swing, several of the 4-year-old children demonstrated a pattern of striking that was amazingly similar to the mature pattern (Fig. 7–4). They initiated the movement with a forward weight shift, then rotated their hips and trunks, and followed smoothly with an arm swing, uncocking their wrists just prior to contact.

Most of the children seemed to be slightly more effective with the two-arm than with the one-arm swing. Effective patterns in either version were demonstrated *only* when the child used a full and forceful swing. The forceful swing resulted in opening with greater range of motion and helped differentiate the movements in the pattern. Even when younger children used rather wild striking motions, the forceful swings were consistently *more mature in form*, although rarely were they more successful in terms of actual hitting.

OBLIQUE PATTERN

The 33 preschool children in the Wickstrom study had a task that required a ball to be struck with an oblique downward swing.[29] A ball was placed on the mat in front of the child who was given a bat and asked to hit the ball in a particular direction. The responses varied considerably but contained enough common elements to suggest broad developmental directions.

The youngest children used an overhand chopping movement exclusively, striking the top of the ball whenever contact was made (Fig. 7–5). They bent at the knees and waist to start the movement and followed the upper body adjustment with a downward arm-dominated swing. This swing closely resembled the primitive type of overhand motion that had been used by some of the younger children to strike at the ball when it was suspended at waist height. The older children in the group used swings that showed progression and increasing effectiveness. In one of these, the child moved his bat out to the side, took a lateral stride while bending at the knees or waist to lower his trunk, and used the equivalent of a sidearm batting swing (Fig. 7–6). A more advanced pattern was characterized by an initial weight shift accompanied by a sideward and downward swing of the bat and a slight forward bend of the trunk (Fig. 7–7). It was concluded with the uncocking of the wrists and block rotation in the follow-through. The children who showed the most effectiveness did so by swinging in a more upright position, by swinging through a larger arc and in a single plane, and by swinging with a more sequential pattern.

Responses to the task of hitting a ball on the ground indicated that a few of the children already possessed some of the rudiments of the type of swing that is used in golf (Fig. 7–15). It is quite possible that preschool children are ready for exposure to the striking skills that require limited perceptual judgments at a much earlier age than is currently expected. Further study of striking tasks of this sort are needed

Fig. 7–5. Typical use of the immature overhand striking pattern in an attempt to strike a ball that is on the ground. In the lower sequence, the 33-month-old child bent at the knees and waist as she performed the chopping swing. The 49-month-old girl in the upper sequence released a hand and used the bat as a hammer.

Fig. 7–5 *continued.*

before the above findings can be evaluated and before realistic expectations for skill development in this category can be set.

MATURE PATTERN USED IN STRIKING

The mature pattern for all the common striking skills contains a basic sequence consisting of three swiftly merging movements. The sequence can be described briefly as Step-Turn-Swing and occurs as follows:

1. Body weight is shifted in the direction of the intended hit while shoulders and arms are coiled in the opposite direction.
2. Hips and spine are rotated in rapid succession in the same direction as the weight shift.

Fig. 7–6.   Beginning of a golf-type swing in an oblique plane. A step is taken, and the bat is swung downward and then pushed forward in a sidearm pattern. The 4-year-old boy lowers his body early in the swing so that the sidearm batting motion can be executed from a more favorable position.

3. Arm(s) swing around and forward in close succession with the other rotatory movements.

Each type of striking skill has its own body of detailed movements that fit around the basic three-point pattern. The timing of the movements is task specific with some individual variation within each task.

SPORT SKILLS USING THE BASIC PATTERN FOR STRIKING

BASEBALL BATTING

Many variables contribute to successful hitting in baseball, including judgments, adjustments, and the swing. The swing is probably the most

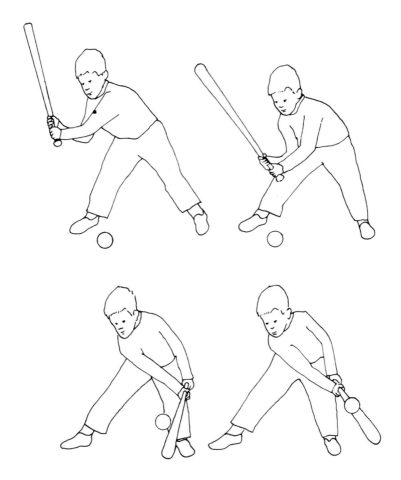

Fig. 7–6 *continued.*

stable of all the factors. In the swing, the batter attempts to develop as much velocity with his bat as he can without sacrificing control over its movement. The design of the basic pattern of his swing helps him produce the desired bat velocity.

In the course of the baseball swing, the body rotates approximately 90°, and the bat moves through an arc of more than 180° before contact (Fig. 7–8). When the forces producing these movements are applied correctly, there is a continuous acceleration of the bat that causes velocity to increase until contact is made with the ball.[21] The batter readies himself for the swing by assuming a position in which his side is turned

Fig. 7–7. Golf-swing pattern of a 4-year-old girl showing an improvement over the form used in Figure 7–6. The bat starts sideward and downward, accompanied by weight shift and little if any rotation. Wrists uncock and the follow-through keeps the bat primarily in one plane of movement. Typically, the form for the striking task is more effective than the performance.

toward the pitcher, his weight is toward his back foot, and his bat is cocked around his back shoulder (Fig. 7–9). The swing starts with a step in the direction of the ball, which is accompanied by additional backward rotation of the shoulders and bat. It is followed sequentially by forward rotation of the hips and the spine, and by the uncocking of the wrists. The final wrist snap results mostly from forceful extension at the elbow of the back arm.[26]

The precise timing for the addition of each new force in the pattern is determined by individual abilities. Kitzman found that all the batters

Fig. 7–7 *continued.*

in his electromyographic study used the same basic movement pattern, but the experienced batters had earlier involvement of primary muscles, a fact implying an earlier application of certain forces.[16] Another factor in the timing of the movements is the cessation of forward movement onto the front leg. The forward leg acts to stabilize the trunk for final rotatory movements in the latter phase of the pattern (Fig. 7–9) and contributes to the link action or whipping motion of the swing. The batter actually blocks further forward movement with a locked, almost straight front leg before the bat is swung fully around for contact. Children quickly develop this refinement after they learn to use the forward shift of weight to initiate the striking motion (Fig. 7–4).

The final speed of the bat is determined, in part, by the length of the batter's forward arm during the swing. To produce a longer lever for greater bat velocity, the forward arm becomes nearly straight at the elbow early in the arm swing. The front arm stabilizes at an angle of

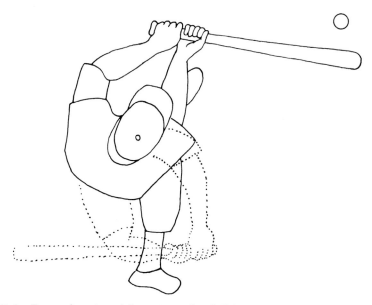

Fig. 7–8. Range of motion of the swing in baseball batting. The bat swings around as well as forward due to the forward step of the batter. He rotates his trunk approximately 90 degrees and swings his bat through an elongated arc of about 180 degrees before the bat contacts the ball.

168 to 177° at the elbow,[7] and the back elbow remains flexed. After a timely delay, the back arm extends vigorously at the elbow to couple with the forward arm for the so-called wrist snap at contact (Fig. 7–9). This is but one of the many elements of the swing that are combined to satisfy the specific objective of high bat velocity at impact.

A form of batting that does not emphasize bat velocity is used in cricket, a sport that is popular in England and in some of the countries formerly in the British Empire. An example of the swing is shown in Figure 7–13.

FOREHAND STROKE IN TENNIS

In the game of tennis it frequently is necessary for a player to scurry about on the court and hurriedly adapt strokes merely to keep the ball in play. Under these circumstances, the player tries to be as effective as possible and attempts to retain most of the essential elements of the basic strokes. When there is ample time for the execution of a full stroke, the basic step-turn-swing pattern with appropriate specifics is utilized.

In the standard forehand ground stroke, the player pivots smoothly into position for the swing. Weight is moved to the back foot as the body is rotated 45 to 90° away from the net and the racket is drawn back. Then in an almost simultaneous succession of movements, the weight is shifted toward the net and is followed by forward rotation of

Fig. 7–9. Mature pattern of batting form. The sequence starts with the forward step, followed quickly by hip, trunk, and arm rotation. Forward movement of the trunk stops before contact, but a whipping rotation from the shoulders and arms continues. The pushing motion of the right arm and an uncocking of the wrists at impact are the final significant forces that produce bat velocity.

the hips, trunk, and racket arm.[8] During the forward swing the racket arm remains slightly bent at the elbow and at the wrist (Fig. 7–10).

Accuracy takes precedence over sheer velocity as a point of emphasis in tennis ground strokes. In a study of the factors involved in the accuracy of the forehand stroke, Blievernicht concluded that skilled players do not change any particular part of the basic swing to control direction.[1] They simply adjust all segments from the beginning of the stroke to achieve the desired racket position at contact. The problem of accuracy is not so easily solved by beginning players. They usually neglect to step forward and tend to overemphasize rotation, thus failing to achieve the elongated arc that emphasizes forward racket movement and contributes to accuracy. Beginners tend to revert to the overhand pushing motion characteristic of the immature striking pattern if they are unsuccessful in controlling the lateral direction of the ball. Unfortunately, it is possible to get a temporary improvement in accuracy with

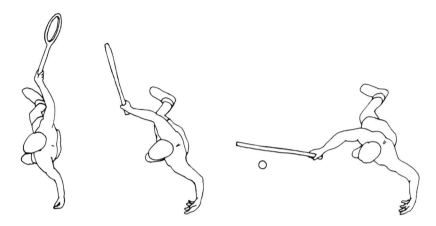

Fig. 7–10. Top view of the forehand stroke in tennis. The weight shifts forward, the hips and trunk rotate, and the arm swings the racket forward in an elongated arc. (Drawn from film loaned by Jean Blievernicht.)

the immature stroke, but it is not possible to make progress in achieving an effective pattern of striking. When given the advantage of appropriate practice with manageable equipment,[28] young children can develop a creditable tennis swing without having to be mired in the pushing stage.

GOLF STROKE

Striking is performed under unique circumstances in the game of golf. A stationary ball is struck by a player who has an unhurried opportunity to adjust his position and prepare for the swing. The seeming advantage of hitting a nonmoving ball does not significantly reduce the inherent difficulty of the task. The golfer's complex problem is to coordinate all the movements in his full swing so that the head at the end of the golf club is moving with high velocity and is precisely positioned at impact. He has virtually no margin for error.

The complicated golf stroke is built around the basic striking pattern. The joints are cocked by rotating the hips and trunk away from the ball, and by bringing the club up and around to a position behind the back shoulder (Fig. 7–11). Acceleration of the club head on the downswing is extremely rapid, with the forces producing it being applied in swift succession. The downward swing to impact is completed in a fraction of a second. The sequence of joint movements consists of forward action of the left knee, hip rotation, spinal rotation, shoulder action, and finally, wrist and hand action. The delayed wrist action is an important distinguishing factor in effective swings.[5,14] If the downswing is performed correctly, the club head moves in a single plane and describes a long forward arc as a result of rotation and a shifting of body weight. Carlsöö's preliminary comparison of the golf swings of

Fig. 7–11. Mature golf swing. Club head develops velocity through approximately a 270-degree arc prior to impact. The basic shift-turn-swing pattern for striking skills appears in close sequence in this particular sport skill.

Fig. 7–12. Underhand volleyball serve. The server cocks his arm backward and upward as he steps forward, he rotates his shoulders to the left as the striking arm swings forward, and he drops his support hand away from the ball just before contact. A high-floating trajectory results.

Fig. 7–13. Batting in cricket. The batter must protect the wicket behind him and at the same time score runs. In the upper sequence it was possible to step, rotate, and swing smoothly. The three contact positions shown below are a result of different swings.

championship and average players revealed an arm-dominated pattern in the latter group.[2] He suggested that average players do not use the momentum of the trunk, swing mostly with the arms, and often fail to apply wrist movement at the end of the downswing. In children, these features would be associated with developmental patterns.

UNDERHAND VOLLEYBALL SERVE

The underhand volleyball serve is used by comparatively few competitive players because other serves have greater offensive value. However, it is a familiar sport skill, and it can be used to illustrate striking in an underhand pattern. The pattern combines forward and rotatory movements to produce a controlled hit with submaximal velocity. The step-turn-swing pattern is present but there is relatively little trunk and shoulder rotation in connection with the turn because the arm swings in a sagittal rather than a horizontal plane. The server steps forward while cocking his arm backward and upward, rotates his shoulders to the left, and swings his striking arm forward, dropping his support hand from under the ball just before contact (Fig. 7–12). The high trajectory of the ball is consistent with the type of serve.

ANALYSIS OF FORM IN STRIKING

For young children, progress in striking can be noted more easily in terms of improvement in the swing than in terms of changes in hitting performance. However, the two aspects of striking are closely tied together. Neither can be evaluated properly unless the circumstances under which the child is asked to perform are carefully controlled. When trying to analyze two-arm striking form, for example, one should provide a task that encourages a forceful swing at an object that is reasonably easy to hit (such as a ball suspended from a cord or one resting on a batting tee). Several swings should be observed so that one has ample opportunity to search for the presence of discriminating factors. It usually is helpful in the overall analysis to start looking for evidence of "opening up" in the swing and then to continue checking for other key elements in the pattern. Two elements that are quite difficult to detect are sequential trunk rotation and wrist action. Other items relating to form that can be seen more readily are: (1) preparatory rotation of the entire body; (2) forward stride or weight shift and "opening;" (3) blocking action by the forward leg; (4) whipping arm action; and (5) horizontal plane of swing (not an oblique or a chopping motion). Increasing familiarity with these items makes it easier to pick out top-dominated, unitary, and sequential swings. Careful analysis of the sequences in Figures 7–14, 7–15, and 7–16 will help develop the familiarity with key features that is necessary in live-action evaluation.

Fig. 7–14. Prior to being filmed, the $4^{1}/_{2}$-year-old girl shown in this figure had never had a bat in her hands. Which aspects of the basic pattern does she use naturally?

Fig. 7–14 *continued.*

Fig. 7–15.   A downward striking pattern of a 4¹/₂-year-old boy.

Fig. 7–15 *continued.*

Fig. 7–16. Striking patterns of the same boy at age five years, three months. Upper: one-arm swing. Lower: two-arm swing. How are the two swings similar?

REFERENCES

1. Blievernicht, J.: Accuracy in the tennis forehand drive: cinematographic analysis. Res. Q. Am. Assoc. Health Phys. Educ., *33*:776, 1968.
2. Carlsöö, S.: Kinematic analysis of the golf swing. *In* Medicine and Sport. Vol. II: Biomechanics. Edited by J. Wartenweiler, E. Jokl, and M. Hebbelinck. Baltimore, University Park Press, 1968.
3. Cooper, J., Adrian, M., and Glassow, R.: Kinesiology. St. Louis, C.V. Mosby, 1982.
4. Cooper, J., Bates, B., Bedi, J., and Scheuchenzuber, J.: Kinematic and kinetic analysis of the golf swing. *In* Biomechanics IV. Edited by R. Nelson and C. Morehouse. Baltimore, University Park Press, 1974.
5. Cochran, A., and Stobbs, J.: The Search For the Perfect Swing. London, Heinemann Educational Books, 1968.
6. Deach, D.: Genetic development of motor skills in children two through six years of age. Unpublished doctoral dissertation. Ann Arbor, University of Michigan, 1950.
7. Finley, R.: Kinesiological Analysis of Human Motion. Unpublished D. P. E. Thesis. Springfield, MA, Springfield College, 1961.
8. Gelner, J.: Analysis of some of the body levers contributing to the force in a tennis forehand drive. Unpublished cinematographic analysis. Madison, University of Wisconsin, 1963.
9. Halverson, L.E., and Roberton, M.A.: A study of motor pattern development in young children. Report to the National Convention of AAHPER, Chicago, 1966.
10. Halverson, L.: Development of motor patterns in young children. Quest, Vol. VI, May, 1966.
11. Halverson, L., Roberton, M.A., and Harper, C.J.: Current research in motor development. J. Res. Dev. Educ., 6:56, 1973.

12. Hanson, M.: Motor performance testing of elementary school age children. Unpublished doctoral dissertation. Seattle, University of Washington, 1965.
13. Harper, C.J., and Struna, N.L.: Case studies in the development of one-handed striking. Research paper, AAHPER meeting, Minneapolis, 1973.
14. Hunter, C.: The sequence of hip and selected upper-extremity joint movements during the golf drive. Unpublished D. P. E. dissertation. Springfield, MA, Springfield College, 1971.
15. Johnson, R.: Measurements of achievement in fundamental skills of elementary school children. Res. Q. Am. Assoc. Health Phys. Educ., 33:94, 1962.
16. Kitzman, E.: Baseball: electromyographic study of batting swing. Res. Q. Am. Assoc. Health Phys. Educ., 35:166, 1964.
17. Lee, A., et al.: Field independence and performance on ball-handling tasks. Percept. Mot. Skills, 46:439, 1978.
18. McGrath, S.: Developmental changes in elementary school children's movement to intercept a moving object when ball trajectory is varied. Unpublished doctoral dissertation. Toledo, OH, University of Toledo, 1979.
19. Moran, G.: The effect of ball color and background color on the striking performance of second, fourth, and sixth grade children. Unpublished doctoral dissertation. Eugene, University of Oregon, 1975.
20. Nieman, R.: A cinematographical analysis of baseball batting. Unpublished master's thesis. Madison, University of Wisconsin, 1960.
21. Puck, E.: Mechanical analysis of batting in baseball. Unpublished master's thesis. Iowa City, University of Iowa, 1948.
22. Ridenour, M.: Influence of object size, speed, direction, height, and distance on interception of a moving object. Res. Q. Am. Assoc. Health Phys. Educ., 48:1, 1977.
23. Roberton, M., and Halverson, L.: The developing child—his changing movement. In Physical Education for Children: A Focus on the Teaching Process. Edited by B.J. Logsdon, et al. Philadelphia, Lea & Febiger, 1977.
24. Ryan, T.: A comparison of selected basic gross motor skills of moderately retarded and normal children of middle childhood age utilizing the Ohio State University Scale of Intra Gross Motor Assessment. Unpublished doctoral dissertation. Columbus, Ohio State University, 1977.
25. Seils, L.: The relationship between measures of physical growth and gross motor performance of primary-grade children. Res. Q. Am. Assoc. Health Phys. Educ., 22:244, 1951.
26. Shapiro, R.: Three-dimensional kinetic analysis of the baseball swing. Unpublished doctoral dissertation. Urbana, University of Illinois, 1979.
27. Sheehan, F.: Baseball achievement scales for elementary and junior high school boys. Unpublished master's thesis. Madison, University of Wisconsin, 1954.
28. Ward, T., and Groppel, J.: Sport implement selection: can it be based upon anthropometric indicators? Mot. Skills: Theory into Practice, 4:103, 1980.
29. Wickstrom, R.: Developmental motor patterns in young children. Unpublished film study, 1968.

CHAPTER 8

Kicking

Kicking is a unique form of striking in which the foot is used to impart force to a ball. The kick is singled out for special discussion primarily because its highly specialized form makes it the only common form of striking in which the arms do not play a direct role. The types of kicks used most frequently by children in spontaneous play and in organized games are the punt and the place kick. In the punt, the ball is dropped and then kicked before it touches the ground; in the place kick, the ball is stationary when it is kicked. Both types of kicks and some variations are included in the following discussion of kicking patterns.

KICKING PERFORMANCE OF CHILDREN

Gesell reported that a child can kick a ball at age 24 months, and although he mentioned the form that might be used, he did not supply details concerning the procedure for measuring the performance of the 2-year-old.[8] In his discussion of the kicking ability of older children, he described performance in terms of the distance a soccer ball could be kicked through the air. According to Gesell, the 5-year-old can kick the soccer ball a distance of 8 to $11^{1}/_{2}$ feet and the 6-year-old can kick it a distance of 10 to 18 feet. Gesell's report suggests that observable kicking behavior takes place at an early age but that kicking performances of children are difficult to measure in quantitative terms before the age of 4 or 5 years. His data also suggest an annual measurable improvement in performance starting approximately at the age of 5 years.

The 5-, 6-, and 7-year-old children tested by Jenkins recorded successively better mean scores on the soccer kick for distance.[12] At the respective ages, the mean scores for the girls were 8.0, 10.1, and 15.0 feet and for the boys were 11.5, 18.4, and 25.4 feet. The scores exhibit an increasing superiority for the boys at each of the 3 age levels. Dohrman also used the soccer kick for distance and found that 8-year-old boys and girls improved significantly in performance between test periods in the fall and spring of the same school year.[6] The boys in Dohrman's study followed the trend of being able to kick farther than girls.

Hanson tested 2840 boys and girls in grades 1 through 6 on the soccer punt for distance, which is a departure from the type of kick used in the previously mentioned studies.[11] Boys' performances exceeded those of girls, and both sexes improved at successive grade levels. Still another type of kicking test was used by Johnson,[13] who measured the kicking accuracy of 624 boys and girls in grades 1 through 6. The children improved in kicking accuracy at each grade level, and the boys were significantly more accurate than the girls at grades 3, 4, and 5. Similarly, Van Slooten's study of performances on motor coordination tasks showed that the boys in the group of 960 six-, seven-, eight-, and nine-year-old children were superior to the girls both in kicking for distance and in kicking for accuracy at each age level.[24] The mean performances of boys and girls improved in each skill at each successive age level.

Kicking for accuracy was also the type of test used by Frederick in his study of a select group of 3- to 5-year-old children who attended day-care centers.[7] He found an improvement in performance with an increase in age, but detected no sex or racial differences in kicking accuracy among the preschool children.

Place kicking performance was determined by analysis of form in Ryan's study.[22] Normal and TMR children between the ages of 6 and 8 years were evaluated on the four-level Ohio State SIGMA. The normal and TMR boys used more mature form than the girls in the respective groups, and the children with normal intelligence performed at a higher level than those who were mentally retarded.

The question of sex differences in kicking performance was answered in a different way in a study by Williams.[26] He taught the drop kick to elementary school boys and girls in a seven-lesson unit. The ball was to be kicked immediately after it bounced—on the half volley. At the initial testing, he observed no sex differences in accuracy of kick, percentage of successful kicks, or combined distance and accuracy, but the boys in grades 3 and 5 kicked farther than the girls in their respective grade levels. After seven sessions of instruction and practice, the girls caught up on the kick for distance and no significant sex differences were found on any of the tests used to measure drop kicking performance. The initial power disparity apparently was eliminated by experience.

Although the accumulation of evidence concerning the performances of children in kicking skills is not as massive as it is for some other fundamental skills, it is diverse nevertheless and shows a general trend toward annual improvement.

Fig. 8–1. Upper: Primal kicking form by a 21-month-old girl. From a short run, she nudges the ball with her left leg and makes a pushing-kicking movement with her right foot. Lower: A 24-month-old boy demonstrates a definite kick with arm opposition and exceptional height on his follow-through.

DEVELOPMENTAL FORM IN KICKING

THE PLACE KICK

Gesell indicated that children are ready to kick shortly after they are able to run.[8] His suggestion places the possible starting time at 18 months or at any time after the skill of running has been achieved. In support of this suggestion of early readiness, Roberts and Metcalfe have found that participation of pelvic rotation in the kick over and above that used in running appears to develop as early as at 2 years of age.[20] Despite the early capability, kicking behavior before the age of 2 years is extremely unpredictable and perhaps unworthy of serious classification. If a ball is placed in front of a child and he is encouraged to kick it, his response could vary from running against it or nudging it with a leg, to squatting and hitting it with a hand. The very young child moves against the ball and pushes at it with either leg, making contact at some point on the front part of the lower leg (Fig. 8–1, upper). The movements are haphazard and barely recognizable as a pattern. A child at this age is limited to a pushing action with a leg because lack of balance restricts the leverage of leg movements. Hence, enough force to cause the ball to become airborne cannot be developed unless a featherlight ball of some sort is used. From this very elementary re-

sponse, the child begins to show steady progress in kicking behavior
(Fig. 8–1, lower).

In her study of the development of motor skill by children, Deach
defined kicking as "consisting essentially of a striking movement in
which the leg swings through an arc and meets the ball at a more or
less advantageous point on the arc."[5] Her observations of the kicking
behavior of children ages 2 through 6 years were based upon kicking
a stationary ball from a starting position immediately behind it. These
conditions for testing kicking behavior encouraged a pendular leg swing
and undoubtedly had a significant influence on the four developmental
stages she identified from the filmed performances (Figs. 8–2 and 8–3).

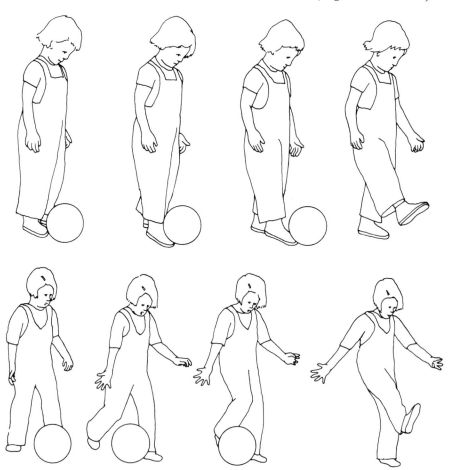

Fig. 8–2. Upper: Stage I in Deach's sequence. The girl keeps her kicking leg nearly
straight and scarcely involves the rest of her body in the movement. Lower: Stage II.
Additional leverage for the kick is gained by lifting the lower leg backward and upward
in preparation for the kick. There is a small amount of opposition from the arms and
slight backward trunk lean. (Drawn from film loaned by Deach.)

Fig. 8–3.   Upper: Stage III in Deach's kicking sequence showing increased preliminary extension at the hip, greater arc in the leg swing, and additional body adjustments. The lower leg is slightly overcocked. Lower: Stage IV. Effective cocking at the hip and the knee, forceful kicking action requiring backward trunk lean, and extensive arm adjustments during follow-through. (Drawn from film loaned by Deach.)

In the first stage, there was minimal forward movement by the lower leg and little accompanying movement by the arms and trunk. The kicking movement was essentially a forward and upward action with the kicking leg remaining relatively straight at the knee during the entire movement. Characteristic of the second stage was a preparatory backward lift of the kicking foot caused by flexion of the lower leg. The third stage produced a significant increase in the total arc of the leg swing and required a definite compensating movement from the opposite arm. Preliminary extension of the kicking leg at the hip was responsible for the clearly visible increase in leg action. In the final stage of development, greater range of motion by the kicking leg occurred in the preparatory as well as in the contributory actions. Additional preparatory hip extension made a more forceful kick possible, which in turn required more extensive compensatory movements from the arms and the trunk. Earlier extension of the lower leg coordinated with the movement of the thigh to help effect the more forceful kick.

If the changes in Deach's four stages in kicking were stated in terms of trends, they would include the following:

1. An increase in the range of preparatory movement at the hip and the knee of the kicking leg.
2. An increase in the total range of motion for the kicking leg.
3. A tendency to start farther behind the ball and move the total body forward into the kick.
4. An increase in compensatory trunk lean and arm opposition.

Overall, the stages show gradual change from a relatively straight pendular leg action with little body movement to a sweeping, whiplike leg action with gross body movement.

It is interesting to note that the children in Deach's study almost invariably tended to retract the kicking leg after completing the kick. They did not allow leg momentum to carry the rest of the body forward in a follow-through motion. This tendency to withdraw the kicking leg is a clearly identifiable aspect of developmental form in kicking. It can be observed in the early developmental stages of both the place kick and the punt, though more prominently in the former than the latter. As the child increases the scope and force of the kicking action, he switches from the practice of *kicking at* the ball to the more effective habit of *kicking through* it. The developmental trend of gradually increasing forward body momentum before the kick helps generate a forceful kicking motion and encourages a forward follow-through. The faster the preliminary steps, the greater is the encouragement for the child to kick through the ball. In Figure 8–4, the 38-month-old girl walked toward the ball, kicked it, and then briskly withdrew her kicking foot, thus stopping her forward motion. By contrast, the 34-month-old child in the same illustration ran forward and continued her forward movement after the kick. The difference between the two performances highlights the contribution of quick forward steps to the kick-through technique that is part of the mature pattern. It also is a reminder of the similarity of the movements involved in running and in kicking and the naturalness of combining the two skills. An additional benefit of the forward prekick movement is the potential for more pelvic rotation and a greater distance over which to apply force for the development of velocity of the kicking leg.[4]

During the time kicking skills are being developed, the child learns that forward movement prior to the kick is the rule rather than the exception. Another principle that is learned is that kicking through the ball is the way to achieve greater distance.

In the developmental stages of kicking identified by Deach, the kicking leg is cocked increasingly more, first at the knee then at the hip.[5]

When the child learns he can kick the ball harder and farther by cocking his leg, he frequently exaggerates by overcocking and thereby loses the advantage he intended to gain. Evidence that the lower leg has been overcocked is the closeness of the heel to the back of the thigh as the leg swings forward in the kicking motion. The kicking action of the boy in the lower sequence in Figure 8–3 is an example of this developmental phenomenon. The boy leans forward, hyperextends his thigh, and overcocks his lower leg as his thigh swings forward. At the point where his lower leg should be nearly extended, it is still flexed at almost a right angle. The contribution that his thigh makes to the kicking motion is diminished greatly by the delay in the extension of his lower leg. This negative influence of overcocking is overcome gradually as the child realizes that there is a point beyond which further cocking is a hindrance rather than an advantage. Then the full advantage of preliminary cocking at the hip and knee can be regained. As skill improves, the lower leg begins to uncock earlier, and the leg becomes increasingly straighter at the knee when the ball is contacted. These important changes in the timing of the kicking movements lead toward the whipping leg movement of the mature pattern.

As kicking skill continues to develop, the child uses a preferred leg more consistently and becomes more adept in adjusting the placement of the support foot as the ball is approached. Boys seem to begin making successful adjustments in positioning the support foot at an earlier age than girls, according to Deach.[5] The lingering problem of ineffective placement of the support foot is shown in Figure 8–13. Children, ages 5 through 10, are shown at the instant they make contact with the ball. Each has made slightly different body segment adjustments because of the position of the support foot relative to the ball, but the common elements of a basic kicking pattern are still evident.

The part of the foot that contacts the ball in the early developmental stages of kicking is determined more by chance than by design. Where the child happens to place the support foot in relation to the ball determines how the kicking foot contacts the ball and how the ball responds to the kick. The child keeps the ankle locked at a right angle during the kick and typically delays lower leg extension, causing the knee to lead the kicking motion. Because these aspects of the kicking pattern vary only slightly, the ball is contacted with the instep if the support foot is close to the ball and with the toes if the support foot is far behind the ball. Both extreme positions of the support foot tend to produce a low trajectory or a rolling ball. The ball should be contacted below its center with the foot swinging in an upward arc to put the ball into flight. If the support foot is planted reasonably close to the ball, it is possible to get an aerial ball by kicking either with the instep or toes, especially when a large, light ball is kicked. The plasticity of this type of ball allows it to compress extensively and stay in contact

Fig. 8–4. Upper: A 38-month-old girl demonstrates the typical kick-retract leg motion. She kicks *at* the ball rather than *through* it. Lower: The 34-month-old child runs at the ball, kicks it, and moves forward onto the kicking leg. The kicking-through action is more mature and is encouraged by brisk forward movement prior to the kick.

with the forward-moving foot. In the instant before the ball recoils from the foot, upward as well as forward force can be applied to the ball to give it an upward trajectory. An additional advantage of using the light ball is that the child is encouraged to kick forcefully because there is no need to be afraid of hurting the foot at contact.

THE PUNT

The punt is a difficult form of kicking for the child because it entails a complex coordination of body movements. The body must be moved forward, and the ball must be dropped accurately and kicked before it

Fig. 8–4 *continued.*

touches the ground. The child commonly develops the movement pattern used in kicking the stationary ball well before the actions of the arms and legs can be effectively coordinated in the punt. In the first attempts at punting, the child characteristically tosses the ball upward in preparation for the kick rather than holding it forward and dropping it (Fig. 8–6). This ineffectual contribution from the arms causes the ball to be contacted too far above the ground and kicked upward or even backward over the head. The child's punting performance does not begin to improve rapidly as long as the ball is tossed rather than dropped. Many children respond quickly with more coordinated effort when it

Fig. 8–5. Upper: The 4½-year-old girl drops the ball without taking a preliminary step. Failure to move forward when dropping the ball caused her to contact it near her knee. Lower: She placekicks from a run.

is suggested that they "hold the ball low and just drop it." Some of the typical coordinations of the actions of the arms and the legs in the punt are illustrated in Figures 8–5, 8–6, and 8–7.

Because of the difficulty of the timing involved in the punt, the skill ordinarily is not expected to be present in an effective pattern until a child is 5- or 6-years-old. Nevertheless, Halverson and Roberton reported that one of the boys in their longitudinal study unexpectedly

Fig. 8–5 *continued.*

demonstrated the ability to punt at age 2 years and 9 months.[10] The child undoubtedly possessed unusual ability and, in addition, probably had an unusually early exposure to the skill. A subsequent study of the punting skill of preschool children furnished further evidence to support the proposal that early development of skill in punting results from early opportunities to observe and to practice it.[25] An excellent example of the role of experience can be found in Great Britain. The 3- to 5-year-old boys who attend the nursery schools in England readily

Fig. 8–6. A 4½-year-old boy tosses the ball into the air and waits for it to descend before stepping forward to begin his kicking pattern. The ball eventually drops beyond the toe of his kicking leg despite his reaching effort. His upward toss obscured the basic effectiveness of his kicking pattern.

show the influence of an intense national interest in soccer by the relative maturity of their kicking skills.

Although the amount of data on the changes in kicking behavior of children is limited, it comes from different sources and is reasonably consistent. Observations from a longitudinal approach are in general agreement with observations from a cross-sectional approach.[10,18,25] Based on the findings of these studies, the most prominent developmental changes in the kicking pattern are as follows:

Fig. 8–6 continued.

1. More forward movement from steps taken prior to the kick.
2. An increased tendency to drop the ball forward (rather than to toss it upward) in preparation for the kick and to drop it before the support foot is planted.
3. More forceful and extensive action at the hip and knee of the kicking leg.
4. More backward trunk lean to accommodate the forceful forward movement of the kicking leg.
5. Increasingly straighter angles at the knee and ankle of the kicking leg at contact.

Fig. 8–7. A partially effective developmental punting pattern. The ball is dropped before the support foot touches the ground and the basic pattern is used. However, the kicking leg is not completely extended at the knee at contact.

6. More movement of the kicking leg toward the midline of the trunk in the follow-through.
7. Increasing tendency for the body to continue forward and upward after the kick.

Many of these developmental changes apply to the place kick as well as to the punt. In each case they signify positive development toward a mature pattern of kicking.

Fig. 8–7 *continued.*

BASIC PATTERN OF MOVEMENTS IN MATURE KICKING FORM

There seems to be a general pattern consisting of a few movements common to all the basic kicks.[2,9,17,20] According to Roberts and Metcalfe, "The motions of the leg and thigh in a football punt and place kick follow a pattern very similar to that of a soccer kick. The segments are inclined more forward particularly in the punt since the ball is contacted in the air but the sequence and the rate of motion are very similar in all three kicks."[20]

From the evidence currently available, the movements in the basic mature kicking pattern are as follows:

1. Preparatory forward step on the support leg to rotate the pelvis backward on the opposite side and to extend the thigh of the kicking leg.
2. Forward pelvic rotation and swing of the kicking leg with simultaneous flexion at the hip and at the knee.
3. Vigorous extension of the lower part of the kicking leg.
4. Momentary slow-down or cessation of thigh flexion as the lower leg whips into extension just before the foot makes contact with the ball.
5. Forward swing of the opposite arm in reaction to the vigorous action of the kicking leg.

This pattern is merely a framework and is only suggestive of precise coordination and timing. The pattern gains body as it is filled in with details used in various types of kicks. Precise action of the kicking leg and adjustments by the arms and trunk are determined mostly by two major factors: (1) the intended trajectory of the ball; and (2) the height of the ball from the ground when it is contacted. These factors account for most of the special adjustments made by the kicker in particular sports.

USE OF THE BASIC PATTERN OF KICKING IN SPORT SKILLS

The punt and versions of the place kick are prominent skills used in football and in soccer. Skillful kickers in these two sports use a form that is marked by the presence of a basic pattern with additional movements that are task specific.[20]

THE INSTEP KICK IN SOCCER

The place kick in soccer is often a goal attempt, and a low trajectory is desired with an emphasis on speed and accuracy. These objectives are achieved by contacting the ball with the instep rather than with the toe. Several important adjustments are made to assure effective instep contact (Fig. 8–8). Starting at an angle that is slightly oblique to the

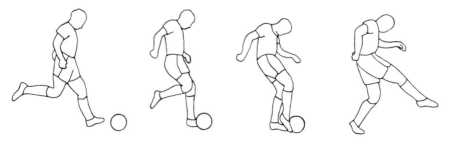

Fig. 8–8. Mature form in the instep kick in soccer. Placement of the support foot and corresponding body adjustments position the instep for contact.

intended direction of the flight of the ball, the kicker takes a short step and then a jump step. Approaching the ball from an angle allows the kicker to shift his weight after the jump step by leaning toward his support leg. With his body leaning in this direction as he kicks the ball, the kicker can swing his leg through a longer arc and still have his instep in correct position for contact.

The support foot is placed in an effective position relative to the ball as the kicker lands from the jump step. Placement is to the side of the ball away from the kicking foot and varies from slightly in front of to slightly behind the ball. Adjustments in body movements accommodate small deviations in the placement of the support foot without apparent loss of effectiveness.[2] Before the support foot has touched the ground, the kicking leg begins to flex at the hip and at the knee (Fig. 8–8). At the point in the swing at which the knee forms a right angle and the thigh is past the perpendicular, the lower leg begins its forceful extension. The thigh continues to move forward well ahead of the lower leg, but its forward movement decelerates and finally ceases or nearly does so an instant before the ball is contacted. At contact, the lower leg is approximately perpendicular to the ground and still extending, the ankle is in extension, the trunk is leaning slightly sideward and forward, and the opposite arm is swinging forward in reaction to the movement of the kicking leg. The kicking foot appears to be dragging because it does not lead the kicking leg as in other place kicks in which the toe contacts the ball (Fig. 8–9). The position of the kicking foot at the instant

Fig. 8–9. Instep soccer kick by female college soccer player. Compare the features in her movement pattern with those shown in Figure 8–8.

of contact is of vital importance because it dictates the pattern of early adjustments characteristic of the instep kick in soccer.

THE PLACE KICK IN FOOTBALL

The place kick is used in football in an attempt to score either a point after a touchdown or a field goal, and to kick off. The traditional forward-facing toe-contact style of place kicking has been supplanted at the college and professional levels largely by the "sidewinder" soccer style, which is a variation of the previously described instep kick. Reasons for the change to the soccer type of kick vary, but mainly it seems to be a simple choice of increased distance over slightly better accuracy. Despite what has happened to kicking style in high-level football, the toe-contact place kicking technique continues to be used in high school and the lower grades, so it is included in the brief discussion of special kicking patterns.

In the place kick used in scoring attempts, there is an urgent need for sharp elevation in the trajectory because of various defensive efforts to disrupt the flight of the ball. The kicker can produce the desired line of flight by contacting the ball well below its center with the kicking foot moving in a forward upward arc. This effective motion at the instant of contact is the result of adjustments in the kicking pattern.

The two preliminary steps the kicker usually takes help him develop forward momentum, rotate his pelvis, and cock his kicking leg. The

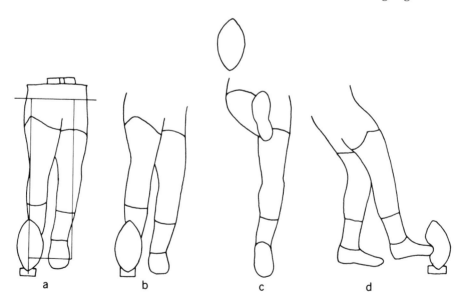

Fig. 8–10. Football place kick. Leverage from hip rotation (a); positions of the support and kicking legs at contact, frontal (b) and lateral (d); and medialward swing of the kicking leg during follow-through (c). (Redrawn from Becker.[1])

Fig. 8–11. The place kick and the kickoff in football. An extended and vigorous approach in the kickoff develops considerable forward momentum that is transferred to the ball (lower). The emphasis on quick elevation of the ball in the place kick requires less forward lean of the trunk and produces a high rather than forward follow-through (upper).

first step is the shorter of the two and is followed by a lunge or jump step. At the end of the second step, the support foot is placed 6 to 12 inches behind and to the side of the ball so that the kicking leg can swing forward freely (Fig. 8–10). The center of gravity of the body is lowered during the longer step, and then it moves forward and upward during the kicking motion. Before the support foot touches the ground, the thigh of the kicking leg begins to swing forward to develop momentum for the kick. As the thigh swings forward, the pelvis naturally rotates forward, and the lower leg flexes to reduce the resistance of the forward leg swing and to increase the distance it needs for powerful extension. After the lower leg has been cocked to about a right angle with the thigh, it reverses its action and begins to extend forcefully. The trunk is inclined forward slightly as the thigh is swung forward and upward into position. There is a brief slow-down or pause in the movement of the thigh immediately before contact, but the lower leg continues to swing forward and upward forcefully. The kicking leg is almost straight at the knee at contact (Fig. 8–10). The kicking foot tends to be moving in a slight lateral arc as it comes forward because of the rotation of the pelvis. The leg swings into a groove in the intended direction of the kick before the ball is contacted and continues in this direction until the ball is airborne. Natural pelvic rotation moves the kicking leg toward the midline again in the follow-through (Fig. 8–10). Hip rotation contributes significantly to the force developed during the kick, but it must be integrated correctly to avoid a misdirected flight.[1]

The kickoff in football is a minor variation of the place kick pattern. The ball is elevated on a tee prior to the kick, and the objective of the kick is distance coupled with a high, arching trajectory. These special requirements in the kickoff alter a few of the details in the total pattern of the kick. A longer run in preparation for the kickoff is desirable and is possible because the kicker is not hurried by onrushing defenders. The kicker builds up momentum with an increased run, but the additional forward velocity developed in the process carries him through the kicking position more quickly. He adjusts by placing his support foot farther behind the ball and by decreasing the amount of backward trunk lean prior to the action of the kicking leg. In effect, he kicks more through the ball, and his trunk tends to lean forward during the strong forward follow-through of his kicking leg. The basic but minor differences in the body positions in these two versions of the place kick are apparent in Figure 8–11. Soccer-style kickers also utilize the lengthened run and vigorous punch-through leg motion when kicking off.

THE PUNT

The task of contacting the moving ball above the ground requires adjustments in the kicking pattern that seem to be concentrated in the final phase before contact is made. Nevertheless, the timing and co-

Fig. 8–12. The punt in football. A two-step approach is used, the ball is dropped before the support foot touches the ground, the thigh swings forward, the trunk stays back, and the foreleg is extended at contact.

ordination of all the movements must be controlled precisely from the instant the movement pattern begins.

Several of the initial movements in the punt are identical to those used in the place kick. Ordinarily, two forward steps precede the kick. The kicker steps forward onto the kicking leg, holding the ball in front of that leg with extended arms. The ball is dropped before the support foot touches the ground and forward body motion causes the ball to continue in the same direction. The thigh and lower part of the kicking leg begin to flex before the support foot contacts the ground (Fig. 8–12). Ground contact with the support foot is well in front of the center of gravity, and in line with the middle of the body.[14] The support leg is nearly straight at the knee. This straight-leg position keeps the trunk well back and not only helps translate forward motion into angular motion but also allows the ball to be contacted well above the ground. Forward rotation of the hip helps to bring the kicking leg forward into position for a powerful kicking action. Forceful extension of the lower leg accompanies decelerating thigh flexion, and the foot is extended at the ankle. At the instant of contact (Fig. 8–12), the leg is approximately straight at the knee, the trunk is inclined backward, and the opposite arm is forward in reaction to the action of the kicking leg. The center of weight then continues to move forward and upward, and the kicking leg follows through moving toward the midline of the trunk.[3] If the follow-through is vigorous, the support foot might be lifted off the ground. When this happens, balance is maintained principally by a short hop on the support foot. This total pattern of movements applies equally to the punt in football and to the punt in soccer.

SPECIAL BIOMECHANICAL CONSIDERATIONS

Kicking, like throwing and striking, is a link pattern involving several segments that combine to produce a high final propulsive velocity. The sequence of segmental motion in kicking has been investigated repeatedly and is well established, but the precise manner in which energy is transferred from one body segment to another still is not understood.[15,16]

Putnam's recent study of hip/knee action in kicking has been helpful but has not supplied a final answer.[19] She found evidence that the "summation of speed" principle operated during the leg action of the kick. That is, each succeeding segment in the sequence began to rotate after the one immediately preceding it reached its maximum velocity. At the same time, the deceleration of the thigh after reaching its peak velocity that has been reported in other kinematic studies of kicking continued to occur. It is not clear that the deceleration is necessary, even though it most certainly occurs, nor that it truly contributes to final velocity. Putnam apparently does not regard the deceleration as a necessity and suggested that the level of the performance of the kick could be improved by starting the lower leg extension sooner and by decelerating the thigh less during lower leg extension. Considering the uniformity of the patterns shown by skilled kickers, the likelihood of effecting the suggested changes seems remote at this time.

ANALYSIS OF FORM IN KICKING

The basic kicking motion can be acquired relatively early, but children usually have difficulty using it successfully in simple games, even when they have control over prekick ball movement. When kicking a stationary ball, the child is troubled by effective placement of the support foot; when punting, the child has difficulty controlling the drop of the ball. Both problems detract from the effectiveness of the basic kicking pattern. Knowledge of the problems typically associated with the development of kicking skill can be used to advantage in the observational analysis of form. Those aspects of the kicking pattern involved in the problems can serve as focal points in the analysis. The observer might try to determine whether the kicker does the following:

Place Kick

1. Takes one or two steps prior to the kick.
2. Places support foot to the side and slightly behind the ball.
3. Uses whipping leg action and arm opposition.
4. Follows through with kicking leg (forward and toward the midline).

Punt

1. Takes one or two preliminary steps.
2. Holds the ball forward and drops it.
3. Uses whipping leg action and arm opposition.
4. Follows through high and toward the midline with kicking leg.

The timing of lower leg extension is a critical feature in mature form, but it occurs in such a swift sequence that it cannot be dissected by direct observation. Most of the other features are observable and useful in the evaluation of the relative maturity of the kicker's motor pattern. Observations are usually made from the side view but those made from a front or back view sometimes reveal problems that cannot be detected from the lateral perspective (Fig. 8–17). The kicking sequences in Figures 8–14, 8–15, and 8–16 should be analyzed carefully to get the basic features in mind before proceeding to the advanced level of analysis with live kickers. Those who prefer to use stages in the evaluation of kicking patterns can use the Ohio State SIGMA for the place kick or the stages presented by McClenaghan and Gallahue.

Fig. 8–13. Discuss the probable outcome of the flight of the ball for each of the kickers shown at the instant the ball is contacted. What adjustments in body positions might produce a more effective kick? Which aspects of the basic pattern of kicking obviously have been used by each?

Fig. 8–14. The kicking form used by a 4-year-old boy.

Fig. 8–15. The 9-year-old boy whose kicking form is shown here preferred to kick without shoes.

Fig. 8–15 *continued.*

Fig. 8–16. A 7-year-old boy punting.

Fig. 8–16 *continued*

Fig. 8–17. A common developmental problem. The kicker did not have his support foot sufficiently near the midline of his body, but it was not obvious until *after* the ball had been kicked.

REFERENCES

1. Becker, J.: The mechanical analysis of a football place kick. Unpublished master's thesis. Madison, University of Wisconsin, 1963.
2. Burdan, P.: A cinematographical analysis of three basic kicks used in soccer. Unpublished master's thesis. University Park, Pennsylvania State University, 1955.
3. Carlson, J., and Albright, R.: Illustrating kinesiological principles: a comparative analysis of two styles of punt kicking. In Proceedings, Kinesiology: A National Conference on Teaching. Edited by C. Dillman and R. Sears. Urbana-Champaign, University of Illinois, Department of Physical Education, 1977.
4. Cooper, J.M., Adrian, M., and Glassow, R.B.: Kinesiology. St. Louis, C.V. Mosby, 1982.
5. Deach, D.: Genetic development of motor skills in children two through six years of age. Unpublished doctoral dissertation. Ann Arbor, University of Michigan, 1950.
6. Dohrman, P.: Throwing and kicking ability of eight-year-old boys and girls. Res. Q. Am. Assoc. Health Phys. Educ., 35:464, 1964.
7. Frederick, S.D.: Performance of selected motor tasks by three, four and five year old children. Unpublished doctor of physical education dissertation. Bloomington, University of Indiana, 1977.
8. Gesell, A.: The First Five Years of Life. New York, Harper & Brothers, 1940.
9. Glassow, R., and Mortimer, E.: Analysis of kicking. DGWS Speedball-Soccer Guide, 1966–68, AAHPER, Washington, D.C.
10. Halverson, L., and Roberton, M.A.: A study of motor pattern development in young children. Report to the National Convention of the AAHPER, Chicago, 1966.
11. Hanson, M.: Motor performance testing of elementary school age children. Unpublished doctoral dissertation. Seattle, University of Washington, 1965.
12. Jenkins, L.: A comparative study of motor achievements of children five, six and seven years of age. Teachers College, Columbia University, Contributions to Education No. 414, 1930.
13. Johnson, R.: Measurements of achievement in fundamental skills of elementary school children. Res. Q. Am. Assoc. Health Phys. Educ., 33:94, 1962.
14. Kermond, J., and Konz, S.: Support leg loading in punt kicking. Res. Q. Am. Assoc. Health Phys. Educ., 49:1, 1978.
15. MacMillan, M.B.: Determinants of the flight of the kicked football. Res. Q. Am. Assoc. Health Phys. Educ., 46:1, 1975.

16. MacMillan, M.B.: Kinesiological determinants of the path of the foot during the football kick. Res. Q. Am. Assoc. Health Phys. Educ., 47:1, 1976.
17. Plagenhoef, S.: Patterns of Human Motion: A Cinematographic Analysis. Englewood Cliffs, NJ, Prentice-Hall, 1971.
18. Poe, A.: Developmental changes in the movement characteristics of the punt—a case study. Research Abstracts, AAHPER, Washington, D.C., 1973.
19. Putnam, C.A.: Segment interaction in selected two-segment motions. Unpublished doctoral dissertation. Iowa City, University of Iowa, 1980.
20. Roberts, E.M., and Metcalfe, A.: Mechanical analysis of kicking. *In* Medicine and Sport. Vol. II. Biomechanics. Edited by J. Wartenweiler, E. Jokl, and M. Hebbelinck. Baltimore, University Park Press, 1968.
21. Roberts, E., Zernicke, R., Youm, Y., and Huang, T.: Kinetic parameters of kicking. *In* Biomechanics IV. Edited by R. Nelson and C. Morehouse. Baltimore, University Park Press, 1974.
22. Ryan, T.M.: A comparison of selected basic gross motor skills of moderately retarded and normal children of middle childhood age utilizing the Ohio State University Scale of Intra Gross Motor Assessment. Unpublished doctoral dissertation. Columbus, Ohio State University, 1977.
23. Smith, W.H.: A cinematographic analysis of football punting. Unpublished master's thesis. Urbana, University of Illinois, 1949.
24. Van Slooten, P.H.: Performance of selected motor coordination tasks by young boys and girls in six socio-economic groups. Unpublished doctoral dissertation. Bloomington, University of Indiana, 1973.
25. Wickstrom, R.L.: Developmental motor patterns in young children. Unpublished study, 1968.
26. Williams, W.: Personal communication. Unpublished master's thesis. Charlottesville, University of Virginia, 1976.

CHAPTER 9

Developmental Patterns: Special Skills

Interest in the developmental aspects of skill acquisition has gone beyond the study of basic motor skills. Other activities have been the subject of recent research, and several are included in this chapter to supplement the material on the fundamental motor patterns already presented.

BALL BOUNCING: DRIBBLING

Dribbling is one ball handling skill that most children are exposed to during their preschool years and that virtually all children learn to perform with some degree of proficiency by the time they move into the intermediate grades in elementary school. It is a skill that is widely practiced and yet it has not been studied extensively.

Deach analyzed the bouncing patterns used by a group of 2- to 6-year-old children and identified four stages of development.[1] *Stage 1* was a two-handed downward or diagonally forward overhand throw with no attempt to follow the ball. *Stage 2* was an attempt to catch the ball after a single bounce. *Stage 3* was an attempt to hit the ball after a single bounce, using one or more overhand swings with an out-stretched arm. *Stage 4* was a series of successive hits using a bent arm and palm/finger contact. In the final stage the feet were together, the body was bent forward at the waist, and ball contact was at about chest height. One significant finding from the study was that children use simple throwing, catching, and striking techniques in various ways when learning to bounce a ball. This implies the existence of a relationship between stationary dribbling and some of the fundamental motor skills during the early development of bouncing skill.

Several continuous bounces are needed to demonstrate the attain-

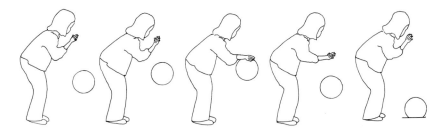

Fig. 9–1. Hitting motion that is characteristic of unskilled dribbling.

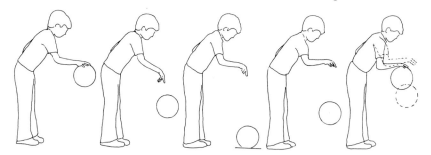

Fig. 9–2. Reduction in hitting action but continuation of exaggerated movement at the wrist.

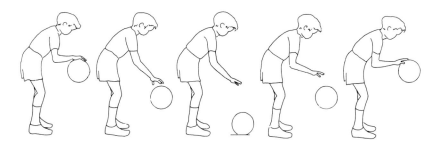

Fig. 9–3. Pushing action by the dribbling arm. Hand contact is not uniform.

ment of control, so a criterion of 3 or 4 consecutive bounces should be used to determine minimal form in stationary dribbling. A study of 115 children between the ages of 4 and 7 years who met the criterion of 4 continuous ball bounces suggested how progress toward skilled dribbling probably occurs.[6] The study noted an overall developmental trend in the movement pattern used in stationary dribbling from one that basically involved *hitting* to one that definitely involved *pushing*.

A distinct hitting motion, similar to the one mentioned by Deach, characterized the stationary dribbling pattern used by children with the lowest level of skill (Fig. 9–1). The patterns of children in this category contained most or all of the following elements:

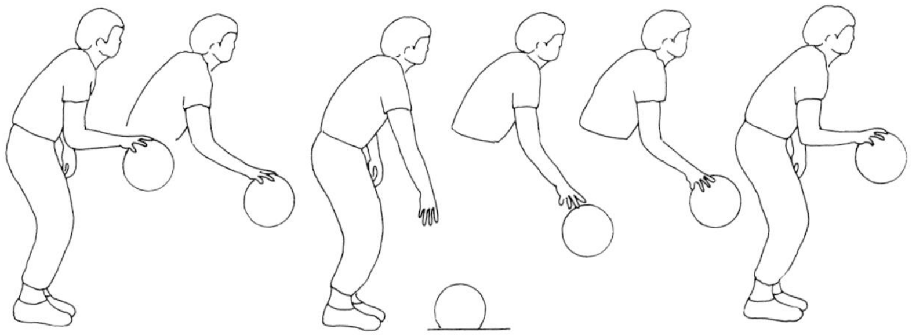

Fig. 9–4. Skilled form in stationary dribbling. The pushing action is clearly demonstrated.

1. Fingers of the hitting hand were together and often slightly hyperextended at contact.
2. Wrist action produced a slapping motion.
3. Limited elbow extension was followed by quick retraction of the hitting hand.
4. Eye-hand coordination was poor, resulting in variation in type of hand contact, direction of hit, and timing of contact.

These elements of form underwent progressive change as skill improved (Figs. 9–2 and 9–3). The transition from hitting to pushing was achieved by a gradual increase in the degree of extension at the elbow, an increased delay in the retraction of the dribbling hand, a greater consistency in hand position at contact, and more continuous contact from the upper part of the rebound through the downward push.

Mature form for stationary dribbling is a rhythmic, well-coordinated series of pushes containing the following elements (Fig. 9–4):

1. The ball is pushed toward the floor mostly by action at the elbow. Extension at the elbow is nearly complete, while the range of motion at the shoulder and wrist is limited.
2. The dribbling arm stays extended with fingers pointing toward the ball until it rebounds from the floor.
3. As the ball rebounds, the forearm flexes, bringing the dribbling hand toward the horizontal.
4. Recontact with the ball occurs about $2/_3$ of the way up on the rebound, and fingers spread just before contact.
5. The hand rides up with the ball and contact is unbroken until after the downward push for the next bounce. Fingers are curved to conform to the shape of the ball and the palm is in contact with the ball by the peak of the rebound.

Dribbling in a stationary position is much simpler than dribbling while moving forward or in a variable pattern at a fast pace. Dribbling while moving is really a sport skill that is used almost exclusively in basketball-type games. The difficulty of the skill is due partly to the fact that the ball loses forward speed after each rebound and a special push is necessary to maintain the desired forward speed. This requires a unique adjustment in the movement of the dribbling arm. Skilled dribblers maintain hand contact with the ball for a relatively long time and use an above-the-waist-level bounce.[4] After the ball is released on the downward push, the dribbling hand hyperextends and the forearm is supinated about 90°, causing the fingers to be pointing sideward. The ball is recontacted on the back side at about the center with the hand in this rotated position and with the fingers well spread. It is pushed forward with the forearm pronating and the hand moving to the upper back quadrant and is then pushed forward and downward in the next dribble. The unique rolling, pushing motion by the hand and forearm occurs prominently when dribbling is done at a fast forward speed and when there are sharp, rapid changes of direction while dribbling.

Movement and speed compound the problems children have when learning to dribble. Imprecise and brief hand contact and inconsistent force application are but two of the many problems that make controlled dribbling while moving difficult for beginners. If movement is added to dribbling only as skill is gained, the difficulty in controlling the ball is minimized.

ROPE JUMPING

Individual rope jumping is a moderately difficult, motor coordination skill involving action of arms and legs in a unique timing pattern. The vertical jump from one or two feet is quite natural but the rope turning action used in the skill is not. As with dribbling and a few other complex skills, some children at the preschool level are able to learn the skill and most children in the primary grades can demonstrate at least minimal form. Minimal performance for individual rope jumping involves two or more consecutive successful jumps over a rope that is turned continuously around the body in the anteroposterior plane.

In order to see the changes that mark progress in rope jumping form, it is necessary to inject the element of speed. This is the same approach used in analyzing mature form in running, jumping, throwing, kicking, and striking. The element of speed narrows the variety in form used by skilled performers and provides a common standard for judging developmental progress. The following description of mature form is based upon skilled jumping performed at or near maximum velocity.[8]

MATURE FORM

Rope Turning Movement

The rope is turned by means of wrist-forearm circumduction, with the elbow acting as the major pivotal point. The rope is held in a power

Fig. 9–5. Front and side views of the body position used in maximum-speed rope jumping. Feet are lifted slightly for rope clearance.

grip with the thumbs to the outside. The upper arms extend downward and obliquely sideward with the elbows near the sides of the trunk and the forearms bent sideward roughly at an angle of 135°. As the rope is turned, it describes a circular path and the hands remain near waist level in a position mostly in front of the forward plane of the trunk.

Jumping Movement

Rope clearance is more of a leg lifting movement than a typical upward jumping motion. With the body in a semi-crouched position (Fig. 9–5), the feet are quickly raised and then pushed back downward after the rope has passed under the body. There is little plantar flexion at push-off, the feet clear the floor one to three inches, and the legs are close together. There is slight flexion at the hips and knees, and the head is essentially stationary during the jumping movement.

Turn-Jump Coordination

The jump begins as the rope passes the vertical and starts downward. The rope touches the ground approximately even with the front of the

Fig. 9–6. Skilled form in moderate-speed rope jumping. The entire body is lifted for rope clearance.

feet, and the amount of clearance is greatest as the rope passes beneath the body.

Two key features of the pattern are the limited arm action which provides a nearly circular rope turn, and the lifting type of jump which minimizes the time needed for leg action. When rope jumping is done at less than maximum speed, arm action is approximately the same but the jump begins later, the trunk is more upright, and the body is thrust slightly upward during rope clearance (Fig. 9–6). This form is often regarded as the mature pattern even though it lacks the exaggeration needed to accommodate maximum-speed rope turning.

The relationship of height of jump to rope speed was investigated in a cinematographic study by Town, Sol, and Sinning.[6] They found that "when the cadence is slower, the subject must jump higher to remain in the air longer in order to coordinate with the rope swing." The average vertical displacement of the center of gravity was reduced for the jumpers as the rate of jumping was increased.

DEVELOPMENTAL FORM

A child who is trying to learn to jump rope seems to adopt the single-minded goal of turning the rope and jumping over it one time. Little thought is given to continuity and the effort to achieve the one-jump goal is usually exaggerated. One common result is a unitary pattern in which both the jump and the rope turn start at the same time (Fig. 9–7). Exaggerated upward leg action accompanied by deep forward trunk

Fig. 9–7.   The frustrating results of starting the jump and the rope turn at the same time.

bend is also quite typical and it, too, works against continuity. Another major problem is the awkward position of the arms when the hands move backward beyond the body plane as the rope is being turned. Hyperextension of the shoulder tends to block the turning motion and consequently part of the momentum of the rope is lost. Then when the rope is moved again it goes forward into the jumper rather than upward and over his head. After these critical problems of timing and arm action have been encountered and solved, it is possible for a child to progress to the point of satisfying the two-jump criterion for minimal form.

Developmental Changes in the Arm-Hand Turning Pattern

In the earliest successful pattern, the hands start at shoulder height and go upward, forward, and downward as the arms extend at the elbows.[8] The hands remain a little more than shoulder width apart until they start backward, at which point they begin to move sideward with the elbows bending to allow forearm rotation and wrist circumduction. The thumbs extend outward as the hands pass the backward plane of the body and then move upward and inward to the high starting position. This pattern of movement produces the narrow elongated loop at the front of the turn and a wide, fore-shortened loop at the back of the turn (Fig. 9–8).

Progressively, the arm-hand movement pattern in the rope turn

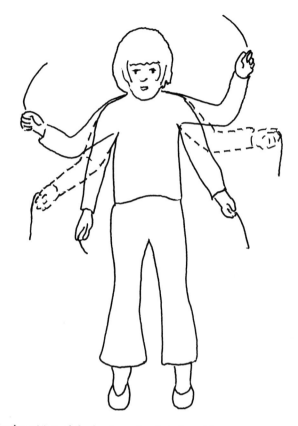

Fig. 9–8.   Hand position of the beginner tends to be wide on the back of the rope turn and narrow on the front.

undergoes change and the path of the rope becomes less elliptical and more circular. Some of the notable changes are the following:

a. The hands are better coordinated and move through less total range of motion each turn.
b. The center of the turning motion for the hands moves more forward.
c. The hands remain away from the sides during more of the turn.
d. The angle at the elbow becomes more constant throughout the turn.

These developmental changes seem to occur gradually and coincidentally. However, the rate of change in the pattern producing the rope turn definitely accelerates after the time-consuming intermediate hop has been eliminated from the jumping pattern. Progress toward mature form is much more rapid following that change in form.

Developmental Changes in Jumping Movements

In their early attempts at rope jumping, children often jump forward over the rope as they would in performing a standing long jump. The folly of this practice becomes apparent when it consistently interferes with continuity, and the child gradually changes to the more effective approach of jumping upward while passing the rope under his feet. The step-push jump and the two-footed jump are most commonly used by the beginner to clear the rope. Both styles usually involve an intermediate hop, and they are similar in at least one other important respect. Both involve extensive knee flexion after leaving the ground in order to get the feet well off the ground at the height of the jump. The effort seems directed at creating an abundance of space for the rope to pass through, and it helps provide a wide margin for error in the timing of the jump with the turn of the rope. By contrast, the intermediate hops are simply miniature jumps with the feet barely leaving the ground. These hops are mostly for rhythm or timing and they allow slow rope turning, which is helpful to the minimal-form jumper.

Specific changes are connected with improvement in each of the jumping styles, but the developmental trends they share are of greater importance:

a. There is increasingly less total height in the main jump for each rope turn.
b. There is progressively less flexion at the knees for clearance during the main jump.
c. There is a decrease in the distance the feet are apart during the jump.
d. The intermediate hop during each rope turn finally is eliminated.

Developmental Changes in Arm-Leg Coordination

Coordination of the turn and the jump is directed toward the goal of reaching the height of the jump at the instant the rope passes under the body. The urgency of this timing increases as the speed of the rope increases and as the height of foot clearance decreases. In the early phase of skill development when the rope is turned slowly to accommodate the rhythmic hop, precise timing is not as critical. The jump starts when the rope enters the lower forward quadrant of the swing. If a hop is not used, the rope turn is faster and the jump is begun slightly earlier.

The speed of the rope is not uniform throughout the turn when slow jumping is being done. It obviously is greatest in the lower front part of the turn when the rope is pulled backward and under the feet, and is slowest on the upward forward recovery.

There is a crucial point in the lower back arc of the rope turn when it seems especially difficult for the beginner to prevent the rope from losing its momentum. A slight hitch in the turning motion when the rope should begin its upward swing can quickly break the continuity of rope movement. Because facility of wrist and forearm movement depends upon proximal-distal development, developmental immaturity could be a source of the problem for young jumpers.

As the speed of jumping increases, the demand for precise timing of the movements likewise increases. With less time to complete the total pattern, the margin for error in the coordination of the turning and jumping movements is diminished. If the quest for increased speed is pursued patiently, improvement in the timing of the parts of the total pattern occurs gradually and automatically.

Rope Length and Skill Development

The rope is a piece of equipment and, as is the case in other basic skills, the characteristics of the equipment used do have an influence on skill development. Weight and length are two of the features of a jump rope that are especially important. The rope must be heavy enough to allow the jumper to get it going and build up sufficient angular momentum to produce continuity. Very light clothesline rope or nylon line does not have that property, and the use of either complicates the efforts of the beginner. The length of the rope is of greater consequence. If a rope that is long enough to go from one armpit to the other after looping under the jumper's feet is taken as standard, the greater the departure from that length in either direction, the more difficult it is to use. When a rope is too long, the beginner cannot even get it started. When a rope is too short, it tends to be pulled up into the feet on the upward/forward recovery or it requires forward bending and high foot lift for success. A *slightly* long rope seems to be an advantage to the relatively unskilled jumper if it can be set into motion. It has an elongated oval path which allows the rope to be pulled back along the ground and kept low for a longer period of time. The extra length also provides more time for adjustment in jumping rhythm at a point in skill development when a jump-hop technique is used. With the slightly longer rope, the jump begins when the rope is in the lower front quadrant of the turn. As skill develops and jumping speed increases, the length of the rope must be shortened or it becomes a hindrance (Fig. 9–5).

FORWARD ROLL

There are many complications connected with the study of the developmental aspects of the forward roll and other moderately complex skills. One of the problems is determining the form that distinguishes minimal performance and another is establishing skilled form. It usually is easier to arrive at a standard for minimal form than it is to determine the precise characteristics of skilled form. In a roll, according

Fig. 9–9. Skilled forward roll starting from a deep crouch (upper) and from a semi-squat position (lower). The higher starting position helps the tumbler build up momentum for returning to feet after the roll.

to tumbling terminology, the body turns over completely while in contact with a supporting surface. A forward roll occurs in the sagittal plane around a lateral axis, and minimal form requires a forward turn-over of at least 180°—over the head and onto the back. According to this definition, the typical beginning attempt that results in a sideward fall does not qualify as minimal or developmental form in the forward roll.

Skilled form, as the mature standard, is difficult to determine because it can vary depending upon starting position and other aspects of technique. For example, if a forward roll is started from a deep squat position with both hands on the floor (Fig. 9–9), a vigorous push is necessary to develop enough momentum to complete a turn and get the body up over a new base of support. Arms must push downward to help keep pressure off the head and neck, then hands either grasp legs to keep them in a tight tuck or reach forward during the effort to get up over the feet again. By contrast, if a roll is started from a semi-squat position, the knees bend as the hands reach for the mat, and then extend to push the hips over at the same time that the arms act to lower the body under control allowing the head to turn under. The back of the head contacts the mat, and this starts the forward turn over on the supporting surface. Hip flexion is extensive and knees flex tightly during the roll on the back. Arms either grasp ankles to develop a tight tuck and bring the head and chest forward or merely reach forward to help get the body weight over a new point of support. Clearly, the semi-squat start produces a more effective forward roll because angular momentum is built up from a combination of leg push and gravitational force, making it easier to complete the turn. Skilled form should recognize the more effective technique and at the same time allow some freedom for individual variation in details of the starting position and the amount of head contact. Skilled form in the standard forward roll then would be a continuous forward turnover in the sagittal plane starting from and returning to a two-footed support without using the hands to push into the final position.

Since children prefer to be close to terra firma when exploring the forward roll, the possibility of their developing enough turning speed for easy success is remote. Two complications that must be kept in mind when interpreting data on the development of the skill are the child's fear of losing balance and his disadvantageous body segment proportion. Children initially are apprehensive about rolling forward over their heads and, as a result, ease into the starting position and supply virtually no forward push. Moreover, they are definitely handicapped by a developmental anatomic factor. That anatomic feature is the size of the head, which is disproportionately large for young children, and it creates a problem both at the beginning and at the end of a forward roll. During the preschool years and while in the primary grades, a child has a relatively large head that gets in the way and makes the starting of a forward roll difficult. The sideward fall that characterizes many early attempts to roll is caused to a considerable extent by the large head segment which cannot get tucked out of the way conveniently. The head must be rolled over starting with surface contact at the upper forehead and continuing over the top and down the back to the shoulders. Then when the body does get over, the large head is at the end of a long lever (head, neck, and trunk) that resists being raised over the new base of support. The hand push at the end of the roll that is so common during the developmental phase is closely related to the problem of getting the heavy upper body going upward and onto the feet. These two factors are of major importance in understanding behavior that occurs during initial attempts to do a forward roll.

Much of the information on forward roll development is based upon observation, with little data available from controlled investigations. An effort to bridge that gap was made by Roberton and Halverson[5] and followed up in a recent study by Williams.[10] The component approach was used in an effort to determine the developmental characteristics of the forward roll. Actions were hypothesized for three components: head and neck, hands and arms, and hips and legs. The actions were then described in terms of steps which represented progressive difficulty and higher levels of skill. There were two to four steps in initial and late phases for the three components and an additional four steps in a middle phase for the arm/hand component. Forty-nine children

A

B

C

Fig. 9–10. Hand/arm component phases in the forward roll; initial phase on the left, late phase on the right, and steps A, B and C from top to bottom. (Redrawn from Williams[10] with permission.)

ages 5, 7, and 9 years were filmed while performing five forward rolls each and the performances were analyzed for the presence of the steps in the phases of the components. Williams found that five of the seven component phases appeared to be properly ordered. Brief descriptions of the steps in those five component phases are as follows:[11]

Hand/Arm—Initial Phase (Fig. 9–10)

Step A. *Hands used unequally,* uneven frontal alignment, elbows bent about 45°.

Step B. *Broad base of support,* elbows bent more than 90°.

Step C. *Narrow base of support,* hands in line and slightly ventral to the head, elbows bent about 90°.

Late Phase (Fig. 9–10)

Step A. *Humeral abduction as balance is lost,* elbows wide at 90°, hands contact surface lateral to hips.

Step B. *Hands contact surface next to hips with contact of hips,* hands push to help complete roll.

Step C. *Arm position remains ventral,* hands do not touch mat, elbows extend, arms reach forward.

Head/Neck—Initial Phase

Step A. *Vertex of head is initial point of contact,* head dorsiflexes as forward balance is lost.

Step B. *Vertex is initial point of contact*, head ventroflexes allowing body to curl.

Step C. *Crown of head is initial point of contact*, head is tucked before beginning the roll, carries little weight.

Late Phase

Step A. *Shoulders remain on surface*, until lower back contacts surface, hyperextension of neck through mat contact by lumbar area.

Step B. *Shoulders remain on surface*, until midback contacts surface.

Step C. *Sequential loss of contact with surface*, head remains flexed throughout movement.

Hip/Leg—Late Phase

Step A. *Hip/knee extension exceeds 120°*, with lower back contact.

Step B. *Hip extension greater than 90°*, knee flexion, with lower back contact.

Step C. *Hip extension less than/equals 90°*, knee extension to 120°, with lower back contact.

Step D. *Hip extension less than 90°*, knee flexion 20° or less, hips/knees remain flexed throughout.

Some of these steps can be seen in the forward roll attempt by the 38-month-old girl shown in Figure 9–11.

Although the number of children studied was small, the sequences

Fig. 9–11.   Forward roll by a 38-month-old girl. Which of Williams's component phases does she demonstrate?

Fig. 9–12. Dysrhythmic time-step pattern used in horizontal ladder travel. (Illustration courtesy of Gabbard and Patterson.)

of the hypothesized steps in the five component phases seemed to be accurate based upon more advanced performance by the children in the older age categories. Williams had some reservations about the component phases but concluded that the component approach works in describing the developmental actions in the forward roll. The steps in some phases hypothesized trends such as "a trend toward using the head for increasingly less support while inverted."[11] Other developmental trends can be suggested from the Williams study and from other unpublished data.[9] Some trends apply to the entire skill and can be broadly stated while others pertain to a skill component.

Overall trends are toward a more vigorous push and toward a tighter tuck throughout the roll. These trends involve changes in components and component interrelationships or linkages. One example is the trend toward more head flexion all through the roll. The body in tumbling tends to "follow the head." That is, head flexion or extension reflexly encourages the same kind of movement by many other segments of the body. Early head flexion in the forward roll starts the tuck sooner, making the back round and producing hip and knee flexion. If a fear reaction from falling forward at the start of the roll causes the head to extend, hip extension and arm extension/abduction also tend to occur. These and other apparent changes need to be studied systematically with a large group of children representing a wide age range including preschool children, to ascertain what can happen and to get some insight into why it does.

HORIZONTAL LADDER TRAVEL

A type of gymnastic skill that is commonly used on playgrounds was the subject of another developmental study. Gabbard and Patterson analyzed the hand movements used by 356 children between the ages of 4 and 9 years during their attempts to travel across an overhead horizontal ladder.[3] The children started with the preferred hand on the first rung and were instructed to move across the ladder as far as they could. Several children were unable to perform at a minimal level. Eighty percent of the 4-year-olds, 40% of the 5-year-olds, 13% of the 6-year-olds, and even 7% of the 7-year-olds could not support their body weight with one hand long enough to grasp a second rung. Those who could traverse one or more rungs demonstrated movement patterns that represented progressively higher levels of skill. There were four different basic patterns.

Dysrhythmic Time-Step. The rungs are traversed one by one. The same hand always reaches for the next rung and the opposite hand then joins it so that both hands are on the same rung. The child in Figure 9–12 is using a reach right, close left; reach right, close left sequence.

Rhythmic Time-Step. The rungs are traversed in order, and hand

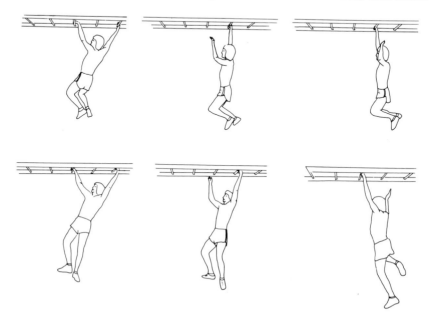

Fig. 9–13. Bilateral swing pattern—the most advanced of the four used in horizontal ladder travel. (Illustration courtesy of Gabbard and Patterson.)

movements are alternated to grasp successive rungs. Each hand moves to the next rung in a hand-ahead-of-hand pattern. No rung is skipped or occupied by two hands.

Unilateral Swinging. This pattern is similar to the dysrhythmic time-step. The same hand always leads and is joined by the other but one rung is skipped on each reach by the lead hand. The additional reach produces an increase in body swing.

Bilateral Swinging (Fig. 9–13). This combines some of the features of rhythmic time-step and unilateral swinging patterns. Hands alternate reaching forward for a new rung as is done in rhythmic time-step and each time one rung is skipped, as is the case in unilateral swinging. Body swing is increased significantly.

At each age level the use of more advanced patterns increased. Rhythmic time-step was the most frequently used pattern between the ages of 6 to 9. The investigators acknowledged that grip and upper body strength, experience, and individual preference were factors that might have influenced performance, but they did not comment on the possibility that increased length of upper limbs at successive age levels might encourage rung skipping.

The study actually covered only one major component of the patterns used in traveling across a horizontal ladder. There was reference to an increase in body swing when rungs were skipped but precise forward-backward and lateral swing patterns including timing and accompanying leg action were not analyzed. These important aspects of skill development as well as arm movements, particularly those that occur at the elbow, await clarification.

In a study prior to the one just described, Gabbard and Patterson determined the grip preferences of 223 children ages 2 to 8 years who were observed while attempting to travel across a horizontal ladder.[2] After age 2, a high majority of the children preferred the thumb-over-bar to the thumb-under-bar grip. Neither this study nor the subsequent one related grip preference to pattern of hand movement, so interrelationships between the two pattern components remain unknown. Despite the small amount of information available, the developmental aspects of this unique skill are being unraveled bit by bit, and eventually the full picture should be known.

REFERENCES

1. Deach, D.: Genetic development of motor skills in children two through six years of age. Unpublished doctoral dissertation. Ann Arbor, University of Michigan, 1950.
2. Gabbard, C., and Patterson, P.: Grip preferences of children on ladder apparatus. Percept. Mot. Skills, 50:1168, 1980.
3. Gabbard, C., and Patterson, P.: Movement pattern analysis on the horizontal ladder among children 4 to 9 years. Percept. Mot. Skills, 52:937, 1981.
4. Hay, J.: The Biomechanics of Sport Techniques. Englewood Cliffs, N.J., Prentice-Hall, 1978.
5. Roberton, M., and Halverson, L.: The developing child—his changing movement. *In*

Physical Education for Children; A Focus on the Teaching Process. Edited by B. Logsdon, et al. Philadelphia, Lea & Febiger, 1977.
6. Town, G., Sol, N., and Sinning, W.: Effect of rope skipping rate on energy expenditure of males and females. Med. Sci. Sports Exerc., 12(4):295, 1980.
7. Wickstrom, R.: Acquisition of a ball handling skill: dribbling. Research Abstracts, AAHPERD, Washington, D.C., 1980.
8. Wickstrom, R.: Rope jumping: a preliminary report on developmental form. Research Abstracts, AAHPER, Washington, D.C., 1974.
9. Wickstrom, R.: Unpublished study.
10. Williams, K.: Developmental characteristics of a forward roll. Unpublished master's thesis. Madison, University of Wisconsin, 1979.
11. Williams, K.: Developmental characteristics of a forward roll. Res. Q. Exerc. Sport, 51(4):703, 1980.

Index